W9-CEL-719

A Friendly Introduction to Software Testing

Bill Laboon

© **2017-02-24**
Compiled in PDFLaTeX
for AKS and CKN

Contents

Chapter 1

Introduction

Let me say that I rarely ever read introductions to technical books; I won't be offended if you don't read this one.

1.1 The Story So Far

A long time ago, in a company far, far away, I was a test lead. One of my responsibilities was to interview potential test engineers for our team, and I found that many candidates did not have a background in testing. Those who did well in their career often picked things up as they went. Even those who had degrees in computer science (or a related field) had often not learned about software testing. Developers had to learn how to properly test their own code, often following the old "apprentice" model by asking more senior developers what needed to be tested.

I figured that I could complain about it, or do something about it. I was able to convince the Computer Science department at the University of Pittsburgh to allow me to develop and teach a class on software testing. This small class has grown to cover many different aspects of software quality, and become a popular, ongoing course (CS 1632: Software Quality Assurance, if you're interested in taking it!). I developed my own curriculum, as I couldn't find a good book or syllabus on the subject that struck the right balance between theory and application. Finding a good book to use was even more difficult than finding a good Quality Assurance (QA) Engineer to interview! Once again, I figured I could either complain about it, or do something about it, and once again, I chose the latter.

1.2 Testing and Quality Assurance

Testing software is a big part of the software development process, and useful not just for those looking specifically for a career in QA. A developer who doesn't care about software quality is not a good developer. This book is targeted to those interested in software testing or writing tests as a developer.

1.3 What This Book Covers

This book is intended to provide a relatively comprehensive overview of software testing. By the end, my expectation is that the reader will have all the skills necessary to enter the workforce in the field of quality assurance, although I feel that managers, developers, and others involved in the software development process may also find it very useful.

To that end, the book starts with a generalized overview of the field—what is software testing, anyway? It's difficult to study something without understanding what it is! We'll then move on to some of the theory and terminology used by those in the software testing industry. I'll let you in on a little secret—this is probably the least interesting part of the book. However, we really should be speaking the same language when we talk about concepts. It would be difficult to explain concepts in plumbing if I were forced to avoid using the word "pipe" for fear of someone not understanding it.

After that, we'll move on to the basics of developing a manual test plan, and dealing with defects that are found in the process of executing it. Manual tests are rarer now than they used to be; automated tests have relieved much of the tedium of executing them. There are definite benefits to developing tests *qua* tests without worrying about a specific language syntax or tool chain, though. We'll also go over how to properly record our testing and report defects that are found from our testing.

Once writing manual tests is old hat, we can move on to automated tests—system-level and unit tests. Automated tests allow you to very quickly execute tests, from either a very low level (like making sure a sorting algorithm works correctly) to a very high level (ensuring that you can add something to your cart on an e-commerce website). If you've actually executed some manual test plans, you'll see why letting the computer execute all of the tests for you is such a time-saver. Perhaps more importantly, it's an excellent aggravation-saver, as repeatedly running manual tests is one of the fastest ways to drive a tester insane.

Finally, we get to the really interesting stuff! This section of the book is where we'll get to read about specialized kinds of testing, like combinatorial, performance, and security tests. The world of software testing is quite a large one—testing embedded software is very different from testing web applications, performance testing is very different from functional testing, and testing for a startup's first prototype product is very different from testing for a large company developing a medical device.

1.4 What This Book Does Not Cover

This book is an introductory text to the world of software testing; there's definitely lots of room to explore and go into more detail on all of the topics here. However, the purpose isn't to try to rival *War and Peace* in length, but to provide a general introduction to the field. Spending lots of time on the intricacies of each of them might be interesting to me or to a small subset of the people reading the book, but my goals are to provide a good foundation of practical software testing knowledge, and give a taste of some of the various specialties and subfields in the industry. Consider it a whirlwind tour of Europe instead of studying abroad for a year in Paris.

1.5 A Note on Language Choice

The examples I give are in Java and use much of the Java tool chain (e.g., JUnit). This is not due to some particular love of Java. There are certainly other languages which have a good claim on being easier to use or more helpful in avoiding defects. However, Java does serve as a *lingua franca* amongst developers nowadays. It is a standard, popular, ALGOL-derived programming language, so even if you're not familiar with it, you can probably reason out what's happening.

Chapter 2

What is Software Testing?

Let's start with a few things that it is not:

1. It's not finding every single defect.

2. It's not randomly pressing buttons, hoping that something will break.

3. It's not hoping that something will break, period.

4. It's not something you do after all the programming is complete.

5. It's really, REALLY not something you postpone until users start complaining.

2.1 A Definition of Software Testing

At a high level, software testing is a way of providing an estimate of software quality to stakeholders (that is, people who have a direct interest in the system, such as customers, users, and managers). While stakeholders may not directly care about the quality of software, they are interested in managing risk. This risk can take many forms. For customers, using software involves risks that they will lose data, risks that their operations will fail, risks that they will spend more money on the software than it will save them. For internal stakeholders, risks may include not releasing a software system on time (or at all), losing customers by releasing a substandard product, or even facing a lawsuit. By testing software, you can provide a better estimate of how much risk the stakeholders will have to take on.

Software testing provides an independent view of the software product. Developers are notorious for—consciously or unconsciously—taking it easy on the code that they write. I wish I could say that when I write code, I avoid this, what with my focus on software quality. However, oftentimes my conversations with someone testing my software go like this:

Me: "I got the square root routine working! It's twice as fast as it was before!"

Tester: "Hmm... when I pass in a letter instead of a number, the program crashes."

Me: "Oh, I'm sure nobody will type in a letter."

Tester: "When I give it a negative number, the program crashes."

Me: "Well, we don't really support imaginary numbers. So I didn't check for that."

Tester: "I type in 2.0, and it throws an error that it can't deal with decimals."

Me: "Yeah, it probably should, but right now it only works for integers for input. But the user probably knows that."

Tester: "Okay, when I give it 2, the screen just fills up with decimals..."

Me: "Well, obviously! The square root of two is irrational, it will keep calculating until the universe ends in heat death! Just put in the square of a positive integer."

Tester: "When I type in 25, it gives me the answer 3."

Me: "OK, that's probably wrong. I only ever tested it with an input of 9, so it passed all of my tests!"

(...and so on.)

Keep in mind that I am someone who teaches a class on software testing. Even I can't help being nice to the poor little functions that I write. The job of the tester is to be the drill sergeant to my helicopter parent. I can nurture the poor little function, but it's not going to know what it's capable of until it experiences some discipline.

2.2   Verification and Validation

Software testing also involves ensuring that the right software was created. Imagine the following conversation between a project manager and a customer:

Project Manager: "I've gone over the product with a fine-toothed comb. This cryptography engine is absolutely bulletproof, incredibly fast, and uses 8,192-bit encryption—your secrets will be safe for a trillion years."

Customer: "Actually, I just wanted to play solitaire."

Would you say that the program has met the requirements of the customer? Of course not. Even though the software has met all of the requirements of the software, doesn't crash, provides the correct answers, etc., if the software doesn't meet the needs of the customer, it's not going to be successful.

This illustrates the difference between **verification** and **validation**. Verification is ensuring that you're building the software right; validation is ensuring that you're building the right software. In other words, verification is ensuring that the system doesn't crash, that it meets the requirements, that it handles failures gracefully, etc. Validation is ensuring that the requirements meet the actual needs of the customer: Does the software do what the user wants? Are there any gaps in the requirements so that even if the software does meet all the requirements, the user will not be satisfied with the product?

Both verification and validation are part of the software testing process. Although most testers will spend much of their time concerned with verification, a software tester does not blindly test that the software meets the requirements. Testers can be thought of as defenders of the user experience, even pushing back against other internal stakeholders to develop software which meets the needs of users instead of simply meeting the bottom line.

Interestingly, as more time and resources are spent on fixing defects or improving quality in other ways, money may be saved in the long run. Developing on a system which has fewer defects, or at least which has defects you already know about, is far easier than adding features to software which fails intermittently and seemingly randomly. A system with a good automated test suite will allow you to make changes with the assurance that you have not created additional defects in so doing. This is the paradox of software quality—you may end up spending *less* money and time for a *better* product by properly testing.

2.3 A Preliminary Definition of Defect

It's important to keep in mind that not every problem found with a system is a defect. A defect is an issue that either breaks the functionality of the system as it's currently understood, or does not meet the requirements of the program. If a program operates normally and meets all of the requirements, then it does not have a defect. If the program does not meet the requirements, or does not operate normally (e.g., crashes randomly, does not respond to user input, etc.), then a defect has been found.

For example, consider a company creating a brand-new Tic-Tac-Toe implementation. The requirements are as follows:

1. The game board shall be three squares by three squares, for a total of nine contiguous squares.

2. The first player shall be allowed to mark an X in any one square.

3. The second player shall then be allowed to mark an O in any one open (that is, not already marked by an X or O) square, following the completion of the first move by the first player.

4. Players shall then take turns placing X's and O's (by the first and second player, respectively) in open squares, until there are no open squares and no row, column, or diagonal is filled in with the same marker, in which case the game is a draw; or until an entire row, column, or diagonal is filled in with the same marker, in which case the owner of that marker (X for first player, O for second player) shall be the winner and the other player shall be the loser.

This sums up the game of Tic-Tac-Toe pretty nicely. Now let's consider an instance where the first player, who should only be able to mark squares with X's, can mark a square with an O. This is a defect, because it violates Requirement 2. Even if the game is perfectly playable (let's say that the second player's marks then become X's), it's still a defect because it violates a requirement.

Now let's say that after beta testing, a user says that the game is unfair, because it forces one player to use X's and that mark is ugly. The user suggests changing the X's into W's, because W is a much more beautiful letter. Is this a defect or enhancement?

It's an **enhancement**, because the system met all of the requirements and operates normally. The fact that a user does not like it does not make it a defect! It may be very important to make this change, perhaps even more important than fixing actual defects. Enhancements are not bad, or useless, or a lesser class of complaint; they just involve modifying the existing requirements of the system.

Another example of a defect would be if the Tic-Tac-Toe board's display disappears after a player entered a mark in the center square. There are no specific requirements against this happening, but there are varying "implicit requirements" to programs, such as not crashing, maintaining a display consistent with internal state, being responsive, etc. These implicit requirements will vary based on the type of system; for example, a video game may need to be responsive 99% of the time, but a batch-processed weather forecasting program (where data is fed in, and the results returned 30 minutes later) may only need to be "responsive" in the sense that an answer will eventually come out.

There can be disagreement over whether an issue is a defect or an enhancement. Much of this disagreement can arise due to these implicit requirements. If a video game character always takes three seconds to respond after hitting a button, one might argue that this is too long, even if there isn't a specific performance requirement. It's just not a good user experience to have a three second lag all the time. However, at what point is the button response latency no longer an issue? Two seconds? One? One hundred milliseconds? Similarly, is it acceptable for a program to crash and lose data if the system runs out of memory? For a simple application running on your phone, possibly;

it may be considered a rare enough event, and with such small impact for the average user, that adding support for it would be an enhancement. For a mainframe running banking transfer software, this would almost certainly be a defect; preventing loss of data, even if not explicitly called out in the requirements, is extremely important in this domain. Being familiar with the **system under test** and its domain can allow you to perform **"seat of your pants" testing**; that is, testing for behavior that is not formally specified, but based on your knowledge of the system and domain, is to be expected..

In some scenarios, the difference between a defect and an enhancement will be a very big deal. If your company is writing avionics software for a new fighter jet, there will most likely be a very rigorous process for determining whether something is an enhancement or a defect. There will be specified requirements, arbitrators to make decisions, and people whose entire job is to draft and interpret requirements. If a company is contracted to create a program written "to the letter of the law", that company will fight to say that a request by the customer is not a defect, but something not covered by requirements, and thus an enhancement.

In other scenarios, the boundary between defects and enhancements is a bit blurry. Let's assume that you are working for a startup without much software engineering overhead, and where the only real requirement is the unstated "do whatever the customer wants or we'll go bankrupt". In that case, if the customer wants something, then it should be worked on (within reason).

While deciding which defects or enhancements should be worked on is almost always in the realm of project management instead of quality assurance, input from the QA team is often helpful to them. Software testing allows you to determine the impact of found defects, as well as the potential risks of fixing defects, making enhancements, or simply providing workarounds. Having this knowledge will allow project managers to make better-informed decisions about the direction of the product.

2.4   A Real-Life Testing Example

Let's say that you are tasked with testing a new program, "Lowerify", which takes a string and returns a lower-case version. The customer didn't give any more details, because it seemed self-explanatory—the input is text that may or may not be lowercase, the output is the same string, but any upper-case letters are turned to lowercase. The method handling this in the program has the following method signature:

```
public String lowerify(String s)
```

The customer insists that there is nothing else that you need to know to start testing. If you were tasked with testing this, though, what kinds of questions would you ask in order to develop a testing plan? In other words, what other kinds of requirements would you try to elicit from the customer?

1. What kind of character encoding will this be in—UTF-8, ASCII, EBCDIC, something else?

2. What's the expected maximum character length? Something that works well for a few words may not work so well if it's fed in ten terabytes of text.

3. What is the expected behavior if the input text is in a language other than English? Especially, what if it's a language that doesn't have the concept of uppercase and lowercase letters?

4. What should the program do if a Control-C or other cancel command occurs midway through?

5. Will this system be required to read data off the network? If so, what should occur if there is a network failure—retry, shut down, show an error message, something else?

Ensuring that you have the correct answers to these questions is part of the validation of the program. You want to test against what the user wants the program to do.

Once you've established what the user wants, however, there's still work to be done. You will need to verify that the program works under normal conditions and with a wide variety of input.

For this example, a few ideas of possible input to test that it works under a variety of cases:

1. A string of all capitalized letters, e.g., "`ABCDEFG`"

2. A string of already lowercase letters, e.g., "`lmnop`"

3. A string of non-alphabetic characters, e.g., "`78 &^% 0() []`"

4. A string of mixed capital and lowercase letters, e.g., "`VwXyZ`"

5. A string of special characters such as carriage returns and nulls, e.g., "`\r\n\0`"

6. An empty string

7. A very long string; say, the text of a long book from Project Gutenberg

8. Executable code

9. Binary input

10. Strings with EOF markers buried inside

Can you think of any other possible inputs that might cause an error or an incorrect result?

External factors could also be relevant. What happens when...

1. The system runs out of memory while processing the text?

2. The CPU is running numerous other processes, leaving the system unresponsive?

3. The network connection is lost midway through processing?

It is important to note that it would be literally impossible to perform **exhaustive testing** (testing every combination of input) on this functio. Even if we were just to test alphanumeric inputs of exactly 10 characters, and ignore all external factors, you are already looking at over 3 quadrillion test cases. Since strings can be of arbitrary length (up to the storage limits of the computer), and there are plenty of external factors to consider, an exhaustive test plan for this function would take billions of years to execute!

It's easy to see, even from this very simple example, that testing can be a very involved process, full of ambiguity and hard decisions about what to focus on. As a tester, not only will you have to resolve these ambiguities, but also determine how much effort and time should be spent on resolving them. The more energy you put into any particular aspect of testing, the less time you will have for other aspects. Keep this in mind when you are developing a testing strategy—the amount of time you have to complete the project may be flexible, but it is always finite, and there are always various priorities which you will have to juggle in order to produce quality software.

Remember that the reason behind testing software is to estimate—and if possible, reduce—the risk to stakeholders. Understanding the possible risks can itself help to reduce risk. After all, untested software which was never run could (theoretically, at least) be perfect, or it could not work at all. Testing helps calculate where between those two extremes the software *actually* is. It can help us figure out whether there are issues with the software which are trivial, or problems which should stop the product from shipping because major functionality does not work. By helping to determine the level of risk, software testers allow the other stakeholders involved to make appropriate decisions.

Chapter 3

Why Test Software?

Now that we know what software testing is, it makes sense to ask why one would want to do it. After all, you're definitely adding some extra work, since you'll have to write the tests. You'll also have to ensure that you write code that's testable, and possibly create testing frameworks for the system. Depending on how you test it, you may have to learn other frameworks or even other programming languages.

3.1 To Test Or Not To Test

Let's imagine that you're put into the role of CEO of Rent-A-Cat, Inc. A promising young project manager runs up to you in the halls, sweat dripping off of perfectly coiffed hair, clutching a printout of an Excel spreadsheet.

"Ma'am! (or sir)!" the project manager cries. "I've discovered a way to reduce our project expenses by tens of thousands of dollars! All we have to do is remove all testing resources from the team. I've got some good software developers; there's no way they'd ever make a mistake. This way, we can finally buy that gold-plated sink for the executive washroom!"

At this point, you have two options:

1. Cackle maniacally, and look forward to the feel of that distilled water on your manicured hands in the only sink regal enough for your presence.

2. Explain to the project manager the reasons for testing, and why it's important to test the software prior to release.

As you're already reading a book on software testing, I'll assume that you will choose Option 2. At first glance, though, you might think that it would make sense not to test your software. From an organizational standpoint, a corporation exists in order to enrich its shareholders. If you can reduce the cost of developing software by removing part of the software development process, then you may owe it to your shareholders to think long and hard about whether it makes sense financially to keep the test team.

Remember that a CEO is in charge of an entire corporation, not just engineering, IT or any other particular part. Even for a tech company, software testing will be a relatively minuscule part of the company in most cases. There are many other areas asking for resources, often with good reason. The marketing department is asking for more marketers, and a company that doesn't come up with good ideas for products will fail. Operations is asking for more help desk personnel; if people can't figure out how to use the product, they will stop buying it and the company will fail. All of these other parts of the company could probably use some of the financial resources currently being used to pay for software testing personnel.

All that being said, there are numerous reasons for you, as CEO, to turn down that project manager's plan.

3.2   No Software Developer is Perfect

Hands up if you've ever written a piece of incorrect code before. If you have your hand up, then you should already see why you need to test your software. (If your hand is *not* up, then I can only assume that you've never written any code before.) It's a good thing to remember that software development is one of the most intellectually complicated things that human beings do, stretching the very limits of what the human mind is capable of. Thinking in those terms, that off-by-one error you made retrieving an index doesn't seem like so much of a big deal.

According to the National Institute of Standards and Technology, software defects cost the US economy almost $60 billion in 2002.[1] That's approximately 0.6% of the country's gross domestic product. As more and more software is written, and our daily lives become more and more connected with software, this figure has probably increased dramatically by now. Even going with the low 2002 number, however, this means that software defects have caused problems worth the same as about one-third of all US agricultural output.

3.3   Catching Defects Sooner Rather than Later

The Golden Rule of Testing is that you should find defects as early as you can. If you find problems with the software early on, it is often trivial for a developer to add a fix, and nobody external to the team may ever know that for a while your application crashed if users entered numbers as their usernames. A defect such as this one that a user stumbles across in production instead may be much more damaging—the company loses money since the application is down and users are upset. In addition, it will be more difficult and costly to fix at that point. Developers will most likely be stressed, and looking for the fastest "duct tape" solution as opposed to a solid fix. Just like fixing your leaky pipes with duct tape, this solution may fall apart again at the worst possible time.

Software testing allows you to find these errors before users see them, when your team will do a better job of fixing them, with less impact to the bottom line.

3.4   Stability

Developing software is a complex process. At some times, on some teams, it can even devolve into chaos. A testing team can help alleviate this by providing stability. By ensuring that developers continue to work on software that contains fewer defects, the software can stay on a more stable footing. Additional functionality is less likely to be built on top of a shaky foundation.

A quality assurance team can also keep track of known existing defects, and allow prioritization to take place. Instead of developers and managers dropping everything and working on every recently-found defect, or ignoring any new ones while they work on old ones, a test team can help determine

---

[1] *The Economic Impact of Inadequate Infrastructure for Software Testing*, National Institute of Standards and Technology, 2002. http://www.nist.gov/director/planning/upload/report02-3.pdf.

what is worth working on at any given time. This leads to a more rigorous and smoothly-flowing software development process.

3.5 Customer Advocacy

Software developers, managers, and others working on a software project often have their own reasons for working on the project, aside from the fact that they are usually paid to work on it. Programmers may want to try a different language; designers may want to try a new user interface paradigm; project managers may want to do whatever it takes to hit the deadline. The history of software development is littered with projects that were technically interesting, or were released on time, but did not meet the needs of users.

QA engineers have a special role to play—they act as a representative of the customers and users of the software. Their role is to ensure that the customer gets high-quality software that is what the customer wants. In fact, in some organizations, software testers have the power to halt a release or allocate resources in order to ensure that the customer receives the right software, built right. Having this power depends on the domain; companies who write mission-critical or life-critical software tend to have quality assurance teams which have more power. No matter what the size of the team or the domain in which they are developing software, having somebody whose job is to act as an agent of the customer is a powerful force. Used wisely, it can help to produce software which delights the user.

3.6 An Independent, Whole-System Perspective

Developers are focused on very small parts of a system, with which they become intimately familiar. Rare is the developer who has an understanding of the entire system under development. Testers may not have depth of knowledge of any one piece of the software, but do tend to have a broad perspective of the system as a whole. They are testing various aspects of the system, trying out new functionality, and installing it on different kinds of systems.

This whole-system perspective provides a valuable counterpoint to those who are heads-down on one area of the software. Understanding how different subsystems work together, and how functionality works from a user perspective, lets QA personnel provide information on the status of the system *as a system*. This also makes testers a valuable resource when new functionality is added or modified, as they will understand how this might impact the overall system.

While other stakeholders have a direct stake in the development of the software, the role of a tester is to provide an independent view of the software. By viewing the system separately and without the biases (conscious and unconscious) of the developers and managers, software testers can provide a more realistic and objective status of the system.

3.7 Ensuring Quality

Although testing software can provide you with many valuable benefits, it is not the sole way to improve the quality of your software. One of the most well-regarded books on software engineering, *Code Complete* by Steve McConnell, lists the defect detection rates of developers using different techniques. Code reviews, formal design inspections, and software modeling have all been shown to increase the level of quality of software. **Pair programming**, where two people work at the same time at one computer, has also been shown to have remarkable positive effects on software quality. While it's easy for people to overlook their own mistakes, another person looking at the same code or text independently will often see something instantly. I know of what I speak; I overlooked numerous embarrassing typos in this book that were caught as soon as it went out for review.[2]

While quality does not only mean "reducing the number of defects", it is certainly an important part. By finding defects, software testers directly improve the quality of software. Users of the software will receive a better product

Allowing a proper amount of time for testing, development, and other aspects of the software development life cycle can also improve quality. Very few pieces of software are written perfectly, and software written under a crushing deadline may not be of acceptable quality. By providing adequate time and resources for engineers to develop the software, the level of quality will generally improve.

The choice of language, framework, and design of the program can also make a big difference in the quality of the program. While every language has its partisans, there is definitely a reason that most web applications are not written in assembly language, or that most embedded real-time software is not written with Ruby. Different languages, libraries, etc. have different benefits, and using one that is appropriate for the system you are designing will pay dividends in terms of quality.

While this book focuses on testing, it should be recognized that it is only one part of producing quality software. Quality on a modern software project is the responsibility of everybody on the team, not just the testers.

3.8   Risk

The reason for testing software boils down to minimizing risk, for everybody involved: customers, users, developers, etc. Independent testing of the software allow for objective analysis of the quality of the system. This reduces risk by providing information on the status of the system, both at a high level (e.g., "the system is ready to be released") and a low level (e.g., "if a username contains the symbol !, the system will crash"). Software development is a complex and risky process. If the CEO wants to help ensure that risk is at a minimum, it is essential that software testers are part of the team.

---

[2]For proof, see https://github.com/laboon/ebook/pull/15/.

Chapter 4

Testing Basics

Before we get deep into actually writing tests, it behooves us to make sure that we're all on the same page with the theory and terminology of testing. This chapter will provide us with the same vocabulary and the theoretical foundation for discussing testing.

4.1 Equivalence Classes and Behavior

Imagine that you are in charge of testing a new display for a car tire air pressure sensor. The air pressure reading comes in from an external sensor, and it is guaranteed that the air pressure value will be passed in to our display as a 32-bit, signed integer. If the air pressure is greater than 35 pounds per square inch (PSI), the OVERPRESSURE light should turn on and all other lights should be off. If the air pressure is between 0 and 20 PSI, the UNDERPRESSURE light should turn on, and all other lights should be off. If the air pressure reading comes in as a negative number, the ERROR light should come on and all other lights should be off.

This should be a relatively simple test. There's only one input, the type is known and all possible input and output values are known. We are ignoring exogenous factors, of course—a hardware tester would want to know what happens if, say, the wire between the sensor and display is cut, or if overvoltage occurs, or... well, use your imagination.

Where does one start when testing this? You will need to develop some inputs and expected outputs (e.g., "send in 15 PSI → see the UNDERPRESSURE light come on and all other lights go out"). You can then execute the test and see if what you see happening lines up with what you expected to see. This is the core concept of testing—checking **expected behavior** against **observed behavior**. That is, ensuring that the software does what you expect it to under certain circumstances. There will be lots of adjustments, wrinkles, and caveats to that, but the root of all testing is comparing expected behavior with observed behavior.

Your manager would like this tested as quickly as possible, and asks you to create four tests. Armed with the information that you should check expected versus observed behavior, you decide to send in -1, -111, -900, and -5 to see if the ERROR light comes on in each case, and none of the other lights do. Excited to have written your first tests, you show your manager, who frowns and says, "You're only testing one equivalence class!"

An **equivalence class** (also called an equivalence partition) is one set of input values that maps to an output value. You can think of them as different "groups" of input values that do something

21

similar. This enables testers to create tests which cover all parts of functionality, and avoid over-testing just one part (like in our example above, where the ERROR equivalence class was tested four times, while others weren't tested at all).

What are the other equivalence classes here? In order to answer this, think of all of the different kinds of output you would expect:

1. The ERROR light comes on for PSIs of -1 or less

2. The UNDERPRESSURE light comes on for PSIs between 0 and 20 (inclusive)

3. No light comes on for PSIs between 21 and 35 (inclusive) - normal operating conditions

4. The OVERPRESSURE light comes on for PSIs of 36 or greater

Mathematically, one could think of this as a mapping between a group of input values and expected output conditions:

1. [MININT, MININT + 1, ... -2, -1] → ERROR light only

2. [0, 1, ... 19, 20] → UNDERPRESSURE light only

3. [21, 22, ... 34, 35] → No lights

4. [36, 37, ... MAXINT - 1, MAXINT] → OVERPRESSURE light only

(where MAXINT and MININT are the maximum and minimum 32-bit integers, respectively.)

We have now **partitioned** our equivalence classes. Equivalence class partitioning is the act of determining our equivalence classes and ensuring that they do not overlap at all, but do cover all possible input values. In other words, they must maintain a **strict partitioning**. For example, let's say that, due to bad or misread requirements, we had generated an equivalence class partitioning such as the following:

1. [-2, -1, 0, 1, 2] → ERROR light only

2. [3, 4, ... 21, 22] → UNDERPRESSURE light only

3. [20, 21, ... 34, 35] → No light

4. [36, 37, ... 49, 50] → OVERPRESSURE light only

There are two problems here. The first is that all values less than -2 and greater than 50 are not mapped to an equivalence class. What is the expected behavior if the sensor sends a value of 51? Is that also considered an error? Is it considered OVERPRESSURE? In this case, it is **undefined**. There is often undefined behavior in a reasonably complex software system under test, but the software tester should help find these gaps in coverage and find out what should (or, at least, does) happen in these gaps.

The second, and much worse, problem is that a contradiction has arisen for values 20, 21, and 22. These belong to both the "UNDERPRESSURE" and "No lights" equivalence classes. What is the expected behavior for an input value of 21? Depending on which equivalence class you look at, it could be no lights or an UNDERPRESSURE light. This is a violation of strict partitioning, and you can easily see how problematic it can be.

It is important to note that equivalence classes do not have to be composed of cases which yield the exact same output value! For example, let's say that you are testing an e-commerce site. Sales of less than $100.00 get 10% off, and sales of $100.01 or greater get 20% off the final sale price. Even though there are going to be a wide range of output values, the output behavior will be similar for all values of $100.00 or less and for all values of $100.01 or more. Those would be the two equivalence classes; there won't be a separate equivalence class for each individual output value (e.g. $10.00 → $9.00, $10.10 → $9.01, etc.).

Now that our equivalence classes have been determined, it's possible to write tests that cover all of the functionality of this display. We may decide to send in a value of -2 to test the ERROR equivalence class, a value of 10 to test the UNDERPRESSURE equivalence class, a value of 30 to test the "No lights" equivalence class, and a value of 45 for the OVERPRESSURE equivalence class. Of course, the values were picked rather arbitrarily. In the next section, we'll see how one can choose specific values in order to maximize the chances of finding defects.

4.2 Interior and Boundary Values

There's an axiom in testing that defects are more likely to be found near the boundaries of two equivalence classes. These values—the "last" of one equivalence class and the "first" of a new equivalence class—are called **boundary values**. Values which are not boundary values are called **interior values**. For example, let's take a very simple mathematical function, the absolute value of an integer. This has two equivalence classes:

1. [MININT, MININT + 1, ... -2, -1] $\rightarrow$ For input x, outputs -(x)

2. [0, 1, ... MAXINT - 1, MAXINT] $\rightarrow$ For input x, outputs x

The boundary values are -1 and 0; they are the dividing line between the two equivalence classes. Every other value (e.g., 7, 62, -190) is an interior value; it is in the "middle" of an equivalence class.

Now that we understand what boundary and interior values are, one might ask, why is it the case that the boundaries are more likely to be defective? The reason is that it is much more likely for code to have an error near a boundary because equivalence classes are so close. Let's consider an example of the absolute value function:

```
public static int absoluteValue (int x) {
    if ( x > 1 ) {
        return x;
    } else {
        return -x;
    }
}
```

Did you see the coding error? There's a simple off-by-one error in the first line of the method. Since it's checking if the argument x is greater than one, sending in the input value 1 will return -1. Since boundary values are often explicitly mentioned in code, that's more reason for them to potentially fail or be put into the "wrong" equivalence class. Let's rewrite it correctly, now that we have found the error:

```
public static int absoluteValue (int x) {
    if ( x >= 1 ) {
        return x;
    } else {
        return -x;
    }
}
```

Much better. However, think how difficult it would be to rewrite this method so that it failed only when you pass in 57—not 56, not 58, but only 57. It's possible, of course, but much less likely. Since it's very rare to be able to exhaustively test every possible input value for a program (or even a single function), it makes sense to focus on values which are more likely to uncover defects.

Getting back to our pressure sensor display, our test manager says that we have time to test a few more values. We want to ensure that at a minimum, we test all of the boundary values, and hopefully a good sampling of the interior values. First, we'll calculate all of the boundary values, and then generate a test plan which tests all of the boundary values and some of the interior values.

Boundary values:

1. -1, 0 (Boundary between ERROR and UNDERPRESSURE)

2. 20, 21 (Boundary between UNDERPRESSURE and NORMAL)

3. 35, 36 (Boundary between NORMAL and OVERPRESSURE)

Values to Test:

1. Interior values, ERROR: -3, -100

2. Boundary values, ERROR / UNDERPRESSURE: -1, 0

3. Interior values, UNDERPRESSURE: 5, 11

4. Boundary values, UNDERPRESSURE / NORMAL: 20, 21

5. Interior values, NORMAL: 25, 31

6. Boundary values, NORMAL / OVERPRESSURE: 35, 36

7. Interior values, OVERPRESSURE: 40, 95

One could also consider **implicit boundary values**. In contrast to **explicit boundary values**, which are a natural outgrowth of requirements (such as the ones calculated above), implicit values grow out of the system under test or the environment under which the system operates. For example, MAXINT and MININT would both be implicit boundary values; adding one to MAXINT would cause an integer overflow and set the value to MININT, and decrementing one from MININT would lead to the value being MAXINT. In each case, the equivalence class would change.

Implicit boundary values can also be runtime-dependent. Suppose that we have a system with 2 gigabytes of memory free, and are running an in-memory database system. The equivalence classes for testing a function which inserts a number of rows may be as follows:

1. Negative number of rows $\rightarrow$ Error condition

2. 0 rows or table does not exist $\rightarrow$ Returns NULL

3. One or more rows $\rightarrow$ Returns number of rows inserted

There's an implicit boundary between the number of rows which fit into memory and that which don't. Whoever wrote the requirements may not have thought about this, but as a tester, you should keep implicit boundary values in mind.

4.3   Base Cases, Edge Cases, Corner Cases

Let us continue our exploration of the pressure sensor display. Going over our various test cases, we can see that they vary in how common they will be. The vast majority of the time, the pressure will be normal, or slightly over-pressure or under-pressure. Each of these is considered a **base case**—the system is operating within expected parameters for normal use.

When input values are outside normal operating parameter or are approaching the limits of what the system can handle, this is called an **edge case**. An edge case may be the tire popping and air pressure dropping to zero. Another case would be someone forgetting that they had the air hose attached to the tire, and pumping in air up to a pressure of 200 PSI, the absolute limit to which the tire is rated.

Corner cases (also called **pathological cases**) refer to situations where multiple things go wrong at the same time, or where a value is, to put it bluntly, ridiculously out of range from what is expected. An example would be a tire pressure sensor receiving a value of 2,000,000,000 (2 billion) PSI, which is quite a bit higher than the pressure in the core of the Earth. Another example would be the tire popping at the same time that the sensor fails and attempts to send an error code.

Although I have been using a simple function with relatively well-defined inputs and outputs, base cases, edge cases, and corner cases can also be specified and thought about in other kinds of operations. Consider an e-commerce site. Some base cases for testing the shopping cart might be:

1. Add an item to an empty shopping cart

2. Add an item to a shopping cart which already contains an item

3. Remove an item from a shopping cart which already contains an item

These are all on the **happy path** - a case where with valid, usual input and no problems occur. There are no errors or exceptions generated, a user is likely to do them, the system is operating well, etc. Now let us consider some edge cases:

1. The user attempts to add 1,000 items to the shopping cart at the same time

2. The user attempts to hit "remove" on a shopping cart with no items in it

3. The user opens and closes the shopping cart numerous times without doing anything

4. The user attempts to add an item which is no longer in stock

These are all things that certainly may happen, but are not "normal". They may require special error-handling (such as attempting to remove items from a shopping cart with no items, or adding an item not in stock), deal with large numbers (such as adding 1,000 items), or tax the system in an odd way (opening and closing the shopping cart repeatedly).

Finally, corner cases are cases where major disasters are occurring, or obviously bad data is sent in. A few examples would be:

1. An item that was in stock when the page loads is out of stock by the time the user clicks the "Add To Cart" button

2. The system receives a request to add 10^{80} items (approximately equal to the number of atoms in the universe) to the shopping cart

3. The memory in which the shopping cart is stored has been corrupted

Corner cases often involve a catastrophic failure of some kind (loss of network connectivity, a key subsystem crashing), entirely invalid data being sent in, or multiple failures occurring at once.

4.4 Success Cases and Failure Cases

When discussing test cases, there are two kinds of output that one would expect from a given test. First, there may be a **success case** (also called a **positive test case**); that is, the case returns an expected result given the input given to it. In general, tests following the happy path of what a user would normally do should be success cases.

Failure cases (also called **negative test cases**) are cases in which we expect the system to "fail" for some reason, such as attempting to write to a read-only disk, getting the square root of a negative number (in systems that don't work with imaginary/complex numbers), or attempting to add an invalid username to a system. In failure cases, instead of returning a correct result, the system will do... something else. What this "something else" is will vary from test to test, and with what kind of functionality is being tested. Some examples might be returning an error code or default value, throwing an exception, shutting the system down, or simply logging the error to a log file or `stderr`.

4.5   Black-, White-, and Grey-Box Testing

There are various ways of testing a system, each of which has benefits and drawbacks. We'll explore three different kinds of testing here, and go into detail on various ways to test using these three paradigms in following chapters.

Perhaps the easiest kind of testing to understand is **black-box testing**. In black-box testing, the tester has no knowledge of the internal workings of the system, and accesses the system as a user would. In other words, the tester does not know about what database is in use, what classes exist, or even what language the program is written in. Instead, testing occurs as if the tester were an ordinary user of the software.

Consider a desktop email application. Tasked with testing this, a black-box tester would test whether or not it could retrieve and send email, whether the spell check worked, whether files could be saved, etc. The tester would not check that a particular method on a class was called, or what objects are loaded into memory, or the actual calls to particular functions. If the tester wanted to ensure that emails could be properly sorted alphabetically by sender, for instance, a proper black-box test would be to click on the "Sort Alphabetically by Sender" button or menu option. A black-box tester would not know that the program was written in Java or Haskell, or whether merge sort, quicksort, or bubble sort was used. The tester *would* care about what results from those decisions, though. The black-box tester focuses on whether or not the system under test operates as expected from the user's point of view, and is free from user-facing defects.

Aspects of the system, such as what algorithm was used or what kind of memory allocation scheme is used, can be inferred by the black-box tester, but their concern is focused on the results of the system running. For example, a black-box tester might notice that the system gets extremely slow when sorting a user's inbox when the user has thousands of messages. The black-box tester may be able to infer that an $O(n^2)$ algorithm is used for sorting, and file it as a defect. However, they will not know about which algorithm was used, or any other features of the code causing the slowdown.

In regards to knowledge of the system under test, **white-box testing** is the opposite of black-box testing. In white-box testing, the tester has intimate knowledge of the codebase and directly tests the code itself. White-box tests can test individual functions of the code, often looking at much more granular aspects of the system than black-box tests.

Continuing the example of a desktop email application, white-box tests might check the actual `sort(EmailEntry[] emails)` function, sending in various values to see what the function returns or does. White-box testers would care about what happened specifically if a zero-length array or null reference were passed in, whereas a black-box tester would only care about what happens if they attempt to sort an empty list of emails in the application itself. White-box tests access the code as code—checking that return values from functions are correct, ensuring that objects are instantiated properly, etc.—instead of looking at the system from a user's perspective.

Grey-box testing, as its name implies, is a hybrid approach between white and black-box testing. Grey-box testing involves accessing the system as a user (as a black-box tester would do), but with knowledge of the codebase and system (as a white-box tester would have). Using this knowledge, the grey-box tester can write more focused black-box tests.

Let us assume that our grey-box tester is looking at testing the email sorting functionality of the mail application. Looking at the code, the tester realizes that the system uses insertion sort. Insertion sort is known to have a worst case scenario of $O(n^2)$ performance when the list is in reverse-sorted order. Thus, the grey-box tester may add a test to check that the system is still able to handle sorting a list of emails which are in reversed order. Another example would be noticing that there is no null check in the function to do a search, and checking if just hitting "enter" instead of typing something in the search bar causes a null pointer dereference, searching for "" and finding every single email, or some other unexpected behavior.

4.6 Static and Dynamic Testing

Another way of categorizing tests is to group them into **static tests** and **dynamic tests**. In dynamic tests, the system under test is actually running; the code is executed. Virtually every test we have discussed so far has been a dynamic test. Even if we don't see the code itself, the computer is running it, doing something with the input provided, and eventually providing some output.

A static test, by contrast, does not execute the code. Rather, it attempts to test aspects of the system without actually running the system. Examples of static testing would be running a **linter** (which flags "code smells" such as trying to use a variable before any value is assigned to it), or having somebody review the code manually without actually running it.

At first glance, the benefit of static testing may not be obvious. After all, how can testing software without executing it provide any additional benefits? It's as though you're deliberately removing yourself from the direct effects and looking at it from "one step away". However, since static analysis looks directly at the code, instead of at the results of the code executing, it can help to find issues of quality in the code itself.

As an example, let's consider the following two methods, both of which accept a string `toChirp` and append the string `CHIRP!` to the end of it. For example, passing in the value `foo` will return `fooCHIRP!` for each method:

```java
public String chirpify(String toChirp) {
    return toChirp + "CHIRP!";
}

public String chirpify(String toChirp) {
    char[] blub = toChirp.toCharArray();
    char[] blub2 = new char[blub.length + 6];
    blub2[blub.length + 0] = (char) 0x43;
    blub2[blub.length + 1] = (char) 0110;
    blub2[blub.length + 2] = (char) 73;
    blub2[blub.length + 3] = (char) (0123 - 1);
    blub2[blub.length + 4] = (char) (40 * 2);
    blub2[blub.length + 5] = '!';
    String boxer99 = new String(blub).concat(new String(blub2));
    return boxer99;
}
```

Both of these will return the same result for a given input. The output of both can be observed via dynamic tests, and checked against expected values. However, would anyone argue that the second method is superior? It's overly complex; it's difficult to understand what it does; the variable names are meaningless. Finding all that is wrong with the code is left as an exercise for the reader. With dynamic tests, it may be difficult or impossible to determine any difference between the two methods. However, using static testing methods such as code review, it's trivial to find issues in the second method.

Chapter 5

Requirements

Remember that validating software is ensuring that we are building the right software; in other words, ensuring that what we are creating is what the users and/or customers want. In order to validate software, we need to know what it is that users want the software to do, which can be a much more difficult task than you may think. Users often aren't able to specify exactly what they are looking for. They may think that they know exactly what they want, but when they see the implementation, immediately know that it is not. Or they may have no idea—they just want your team to build something "like a social media site, but with buying and selling, and you know, like, hot dogs? But for cats?"

One way of determining what software to build is to determine the **requirements** of the software. Requirements are statements specifying exactly what it is that a piece of software should do under certain conditions. This is more or less popular depending on the domain and the kind of software being developed. For example, when building software to monitor a nuclear reactor, there may be very specific and well-laid-out requirements. If you are working for a social media startup (hopefully not one with "buying and selling, and you know, like hot dogs... for cats", because apparently there is competition), then your "requirements" may be something your CEO scribbled on a napkin after one too many bottles of wine and one too few meetings with actual customers.

Requirements ensure that the developers know what to build, and the testers know what to test. While requirements are important, they are not inviolable! Common sense should be used when interpreting requirements, and requirements are often subject to change. Note that there are other methods of determining what software to build aside from traditional requirements, such as user stories.

In our tire air pressure example in the chapter on testing basics, we had some relatively simple requirements, although we did not mention at the time that that is what they were:

1. The ERROR light comes on for PSIs of -1 or less

2. The UNDERPRESSURE light comes for PSIs between 0 and 20

3. No light comes on for PSIs between 21 and 35 (normal operating conditions)

4. The OVERPRESSURE light comes on for PSIs of 36 or greater

These "informal requirements" show what should happen to the system under certain input values. The classic way of writing requirements is to say that the system "shall" do something. When testing, you can mentally translate the "shall" to a "must". That is, if the requirement says that the system shall do something, then the system must do it in order for you as a tester to say that the system has met the requirement. Requirements are written to be exact and should avoid ambiguity at almost all costs. Let us translate these informal requirements to something a little more in line with how requirements are written in the real world.

- *REQ-1.* If an air pressure value of -1 or lower is received by the display sensor, then the `ERROR` light *shall* be enabled, and all other lights *shall* be disabled.

- *REQ-2.* If an air pressure value between 0 and 20 (inclusive) is received by the display sensor, then the `UNDERPRESSURE` light *shall* be enabled, and all other lights *shall* be disabled.

- *REQ-3.* If an air pressure value between 21 and 35 (inclusive) is received by the display sensor, then all lights *shall* be disabled.

- *REQ-4.* If an air pressure value of 36 or greater is received by the display sensor, then the `OVERPRESSURE` light *shall* be enabled, and all other lights *shall* be disabled.

Note how much more specific this has become compared to our informal requirements listed above. Requirements engineering is a true engineering discipline, and it can be very difficult to specify a large and/or complex system. Note also how much denser and how much more text is created in an attempt to remove ambiguity. It will definitely take much more time to write down formal requirements than to scribble down a general outline of the program on a napkin. Changes are also much more difficult to make. The trade-off may or may not be worth it, depending on the domain and the system under test. Ensuring that avionics software controls the plane correctly under all conditions would probably warrant a very thorough and detailed **requirements specification** (a listing of all the requirements of a system), whereas our social media site mentioned above may not. Rigidity can provide a very good definition of a system, but at the price of flexibility.

On a side note, if you ever wonder why lawyers are paid so much, this is similar to what they do all day. One can think of the laws as a series of requirements of what a person should do to be law-abiding, what kinds of punishment to inflict in the case that a person breaks the law, how the laws should be created, etc.:

1. If an offender jay-walks on a major thoroughfare, when not at a crosswalk, and when there is oncoming traffic, and at least one vehicle found it necessary to apply their brakes, the offender *shall* be charged with a first-class misdemeanor of "Pedestrian Failure to Yield".

2. If a person jay-walks on a major thoroughfare, when the "Walk" signal is not displayed at a crosswalk, when there is no oncoming traffic, the offender *shall* be charged with a second-class misdemeanor of "Pedestrian Disobeying a Traffic Signal".

In both the law and in software testing, it's possible to "go down a rabbit hole" trying to determine exactly what the text means. The English language is full of ambiguities. For example, let's take a perfectly reasonable requirement which can be read multiple ways:

- *UNCLEARREQ-1.* The primary alarm system shall sound if it detects an intruder with a visual display unit.

Does this mean that the primary alarm should sound if the intruder is holding a visual display unit? Alternatively, does it mean that if the intruder is detected by using the system's visual display unit, the primary alarm should sound? Be sure to avoid as much ambiguity as possible when writing requirements. Although testers don't often write requirements themselves, they are often asked to review them. Ensuring that you understand a requirement and that the requirement is clearly testable will save time and headaches later on in the development process.

When writing requirements, it's important to keep in mind that requirements state what the system should do, not how it should do it. In other words, it should not specify the implementation details, but only how that system or subsystem interacts and interfaces with the world around it. This may be easier to understand with some examples from a new interstellar spaceship game:

GOOD REQUIREMENTS:

- *GOOD-REQ-1.* When the user presses the "velocity" button, the current velocity of the spaceship shall be displayed on the main screen.

- *GOOD-REQ-2.* The system shall be able to support a velocity of 0.8c (80% of the speed of light) for at least three hundred days (7,200 hours) without requiring maintenance.

- *GOOD-REQ-3.* The system shall store the last 100 coordinates of locations that it has sampled.

BAD REQUIREMENTS:

- *BAD-REQ-1.* When the user presses the "velocity" button, the system shall access memory location 0x0894BC40 and display it on the main screen.

- *BAD-REQ-2.* The system shall use a simulated antimatter-matter reaction in order to propel it to 0.8c.

- *BAD-REQ-3.* The system shall use a relational database to store the last 100 coordinates it has sampled.

Note that the bad requirements all state *how* something should be done, not *what* the system needs to do. What happens if the memory layout on the system is changed? BAD-REQ-1 would have to be changed, as well as any other requirements that may have depended on data being in a specific memory location. Why is it important to use an antimatter-matter reactor, specifically? After all, the key thing is that the spaceship can move at a specific velocity. Finally, why is it important that a relational database is used to store coordinates? From the user's perspective, all that they care about is that the coordinates are stored.

For complex or safety-critical systems (such as an actual interstellar spaceship), requirements may specify implementations. In these cases, it is not only critical that a system does something, but that it does so in a proven and specified way. For most systems, however, such requirements are overkill and would greatly limit flexibility as the software development process continues. It can also make it more difficult to test these requirements, since not only does the tester need to determine whether the expected behavior matched the observed behavior, but they also need to determine how the observed behavior occurred.

By requiring implementation details, you remove the possibility of black-box testing. Without looking at the code, how can you be sure that the system is displaying the contents of memory location 0x0894BC40? It's impossible (unless you have the incredibly specific superpower of being able to look at a RAM chip and know what is being stored and where). All tests would have to be white-box tests.

5.1 Testability

From a tester's perspective, one of the most important aspects of requirements is whether or not they are testable. From a software development life cycle perspective, "testable requirements" is another term for "good requirements". A requirement that cannot be tested cannot be shown to have been met. Let's take an example of two requirements, and try to determine which is better. Note that both are semantically and syntactically valid, and contain that all-important "shall":

1. The system shall increment the PATRONS counter by one every time the TURNSTILE sensor is activated without error.

2. The system shall do the things with the counter every time someone walks through.

Note that the first requirement is very unambiguous; it states what should be done, what input to monitor, and what behavior to expect. Specifically, whenever the TURNSTILE sensor is activated, we expect the PATRONS counter (which may be a variable, a display, or something else—it should be specified elsewhere in a complete requirements specification) to be incremented by one. The second requirement is ambiguous in several ways. What shall it do with the counter? How can it tell when someone walks through? What is it referring to that someone can walk through? It would be impossible to set up a test for this requirement.

Now that we've seen examples of testable and non-testable requirements, can we specify in detail what it means for a requirement to be testable?

In order for the requirements to be testable, they must meet five criteria, each of which we will cover individually. They should be:

1. Complete

2. Consistent

3. Unambiguous

4. Quantitative

5. Feasible to test

Requirements should cover the entire operation of the system. This is what we mean by saying that a requirements specification should be **complete**. Anything that is not covered by the requirements is liable to be interpreted in different ways by developer, designers, testers, and users. If something is important, it should be specified precisely.

The requirements should be **consistent**. That is, they should not contradict each other or the laws of the universe (or whatever domain that you are operating in). Requirements which do not contradict each other are **internally consistent**; requirements which do not contradict the world outside the system are **externally consistent**.

Here is an example of a group of requirements that is not internally consistent:

- *INCONSISTENT-REQ-1.* The system shall display "WARNING: OVERPRESSURE" on the console whenever the pressure is 100 PSI or greater.

- *INCONSISTENT-REQ-2.* The system shall turn off the console and display no further information as long as the pressure is less than 200 PSI.

What should the system do if the pressure is between 100 and 200 PSI? You can use equivalence class partitioning here to determine that the requirements are not internally consistent.

The requirements should be **unambiguous**. That is, they should specify things as precisely as possible for working in the particular domain the software is for. The acceptable level of ambiguity will vary dramatically depending on what kind of software you are developing. For example, if you are writing software for a children's game, it may be sufficient to state that a particular square should be "red". If you are describing the requirements for an interface to a nuclear reactor, the exact PANTONE® shade of red of the warning light may need to be specified.

That being said, be careful not to paint yourself into a corner with too-restrictive requirements. If your requirements state that a particular page needs to be a certain number of pixels, you may have difficulties converting to mobile devices, for example. However, requirements certainly should not be of the form:

- *AMBIGUOUS-REQ-1.* The system shall do all of the shutdown stuff whenever the "shutdown" button is pressed.

What is the "shutdown stuff"? Speaking to our friends, or amongst co-workers, we may use such ambiguous terms because the human brain is remarkably good at filling in ambiguity. However, ambiguous requirements can lead to different developers or other stakeholders interpreting them in different ways. The classic example of this is the Mars Climate Orbiter mishap, where one group of software engineers used Imperial measures and another group used metric measures. Both groups thought the correct way to return results was obvious, but they came up with different implementations.

If at all possible, the requirements should be **quantitative** (as opposed to qualitative). That is, if you can apply numbers to a requirement, you should. You should avoid using any sort of subjective terms such as "fast", "responsive", "usable", or "scrumdiddlyumptious." If you can specifically state what the system is required to do, then do so. For example, the following requirement is qualitative, and not quantitative.

- *QUALITATIVE-REQ-1.* The system shall return results extremely quickly.

What do we mean by this? It's impossible to test without defining what we mean by "extremely quickly", or what kind of results need to be returned quickly.

Finally, some common sense needs to be applied to the requirements writing. It's possible to write a requirement which may be theoretically possible to test, but for various reasons, impossible to test in the real world. A requirement like this is not **feasible** to test. Let's say that we have the following requirements for testing our air pressure sensor:

- *INFEASIBLE-REQ-1.* The system shall be able to endure pressures of up to 9.5×10^{11} pounds per square inch.

- *INFEASIBLE-REQ-2.* Under normal operating procedures (defined elsewhere), the system shall remain usable for two hundred years of continuous use.

Both of these requirements are, in fact, possible to test. In order to test the first, simply place the system at ground zero of a relatively powerful thermonuclear explosion, and determine if system quality degrades after detonation. The second requirement is even easier to meet; simply drive around with the pressure sensor for two hundred years. Since the human lifespan is noticeably shorter than that, you'll probably need a few generations of testers. Whether you make "pressure sensor tester" a hereditary position, or use a "master/apprentice" style system, is entirely up to you.

When applied to physical phenomena, it is manifestly clear how silly it would be to test these requirements. (If they don't seem silly to you, how many testers do you know who have thermonuclear weapons at their disposal? Probably fewer than five.) However, oftentimes, it's more difficult to determine that a requirement is not feasible to test when you are dealing with software. Living in a physical world, the human brain often has difficulty with determining how feasible a software requirement (which deals in the virtual world) may be to test.

5.2 Functional versus Non-Functional

Functional requirements state what a system should *do*; **non-functional requirements** state what a system should *be*.

The requirements that we have discussed so far are functional requirements; that is, they say that the software system shall do a particular action under specific circumstances. For example:

1. The system shall display the error message "User Not Found" if a user attempts to log in and the user name entered does not exist in the system.

2. Upon retrieval of a record from the database, if any field is invalid, the system shall return the string "INVALID" for that field.

3. Upon startup, the system shall display the message "WELCOME TO THE SYSTEM" to the user's console.

Functional requirements are (relatively) simple to test; they say that a specific behavior should occur under certain circumstances. There are obviously going to be complexities and variations involved in testing some of them, but the general idea is straightforward. For example, for the second requirement, tests might check for each of the various fields of the database, and different kinds of invalid values. This may be quite an involved process, but there is a plan that can be followed to develop the tests that directly grows out of the requirements.

Non-functional requirements describe overall characteristics of the system, as opposed to specific actions that are taken under specific circumstances. Non-functional requirements are often called **quality attributes**, because they describe qualities of the system as opposed to what it should do specifically. Some examples of non-functional attributes include:

1. The system shall be usable by an experienced computer user with less than three hours' training.

2. The system shall be able to support one hundred simultaneous users.

3. The system shall be reliable, having less than one hour of unanticipated downtime per month.

Non-functional requirements are often much more difficult to test than functional requirements, because the expected behavior is much more vague. This is why it is especially important to define the requirement itself clearly.

One of the key ways to clearly define non-functional requirements is to quantify them.

5.3   A Note on Naming Requirements

Back in the days of yore, when primitive engineers chiseled binary trees with stone axes, there was only one way to write requirements. It was the way that their forefathers had written requirements, and their forefathers before them, unto the dawn of civilization. This sacred method of requirements naming was as follows:

REQUIREMENTS:

1. The system shall do X.

2. The system shall do Y.

3. The system shall do Z whenever event A occurs. ...

This was simple enough for small projects. As software projects became larger and more specified, however, some problems arose with this scheme. For example, what happened if a requirement became irrelevant? There are now "missing" requirements; the list of requirements may be 1, 2, 5, 7, 12, etc. Inversely, what if software requirements needed to be added? If the list of requirements is just a straight linear ordering, those new requirements need to be put in at the end, or squeezed in between existing requirements (Requirement-1.5).

Another problem was remembering what each requirement actually specified based solely on the number. It is not very difficult for the average person to keep a list of a few requirements in their head, but this becomes untenable when there are hundreds, or even thousands, of software requirements.

Several methods were developed in order to ameliorate the issue. One method was to group all of the requirements into different sections (e.g., "DATABASE-1", "DATABASE-2") and continue the traditional numbering scheme from there. At least under this scheme, a new DATABASE requirement did not require being placed at the very end of the list of requirements, but rather placed in a location near other relevant requirements. This also gave a hint as to what the requirement referred.

Another method is to name the requirements with abbreviations of what the requirement is actually supposed to do. Prefixes and suffixes such as "FUN-" for functional and "NF-" for non-functional are commonplace.

All that being said, even more important is to use the same requirements naming convention as the rest of your team!

Chapter 6

Test Plans

Now that you understand requirements, and the basic theory and terminology of software testing, it's time to work on making **test plans**. Test plans lay out an entire plan for testing a system under test. They are then executed—that is, a person or automated testing tool goes through the steps listed in the test plan—and the results are compared to what actually happened. That is, we will be checking the expected behavior of a system (what we write down in our test plan) against the observed behavior (what we see the system actually doing).

6.1 The Basic Layout of a Test Plan

A test plan is, at its core, simply a collection of **test cases**. Test cases are the individual tests that make up a test plan. Let's assume that you are creating a test plan for testing a new app that tells you if a cup of coffee is too hot to drink. Our hypothetical app marketers really like cold coffee, and decided not to implement any functionality about reporting the coffee temperature being too low. There are two requirements:

- *FUN-COFFEE-TOO-HOT:* If the coffee temperature is measured at 175 degrees Fahrenheit or higher, the app shall display the `TOO HOT` message.

- *FUN-COFFEE-JUST-RIGHT:* If the coffee temperature is measured at less than 175 degrees Fahrenheit, the app shall display the `JUST RIGHT` message.

How would we develop a test plan for our coffee temperature app? There is one input—the coffee temperature measured—and two possible outputs, one of the set `["TOO HOT", "JUST RIGHT"]`. We can ignore for now that most people would find coffee at 45 degrees Fahrenheit to definitely not be "JUST RIGHT".

A single input value and one of two possible output values is a simple case of equivalence class partitioning, so let's partition up those equivalence classes.

- *JUST-RIGHT:* [-INF, -INF + 1, ... 173, 174] → `JUST RIGHT`

- *TOO-HOT:* [175, 176, ... INF - 1, INF] → `TOO HOT`

Our boundary values are 174 and 175, as they mark the division between the two equivalence classes. Let's also use two interior values, 135 for the JUST-RIGHT class and 200 for the TOO-HOT class. For this particular sample test plan, we will ignore the implicit boundary values of infinity and negative infinity (or the system's concept of these, MAXINT and MININT).

Using these values, and a general idea of what we would like to test, we can start to create test cases. Although different tools and companies will have different templates for entering test cases, this is a relatively standard one that can be applied or modified for most software projects:

1. **Identifier**: An identifier, such as "16", "DB-7", or "DATABASE-TABLE-DROP-TEST", which uniquely identifies the test case.

2. **Test Case**: A description of the test case and what it is testing.

3. **Preconditions**: Any preconditions for the state of the system or world before the test begins.

4. **Input Values**: Any values input directly to the test.

5. **Execution Steps**: The actual steps of the test, to be executed by the tester.

6. **Output Values**: Any values output directly by the test.

7. **Postconditions**: Any postconditions of the state of the system or world which should hold true after the test has been executed.

Don't worry if you still have some questions on these definitions. In the following sections, we will go more deeply into all of them and provide examples.

6.1.1   Identifier

Just as requirements have identifiers, test cases do as well. These provide a short and simple way to refer to the test case. In many instances, these are just numbers, but also could use more complex systems like the one described in the section on naming requirements.

Test plans are usually not as large as all of the requirements for a program; once they get big enough, individual tests plans are grouped under larger test suites. Often the identifier is just a number. If you are using automated test tracking software, then it will usually auto-number these for you.

6.1.2   Test Case (or Summary)

In this section, a summary of what the test case is supposed to test, and how, is provided. In this way, someone reviewing the test case can tell at a glance what the test is for, and why it is included. It is usually possible to determine this by a careful examination of the preconditions, input values, and execution steps, but it is usually easier for a human to just read what the test is supposed to do.

Examples:

1. Ensure that on-sale items can be added to the cart and will have their price automatically reduced.

2. Ensure that passing a non-numeric string will result in the square root function throwing an `InvalidNumber` exception.

3. When the system detects that the internal temperature has reached 150 degrees Fahrenheit, ensure that it displays an error message and shuts down within five seconds.

4. Ensure that if the operating system switches time zones midway through a computation, that computation will use the original time zone when reporting results.

6.1.3 Preconditions

A test often requires that the system be in a certain state before the test itself can be run. While one could theoretically consider putting the system into such a state as part of the execution of the test (see the section on Execution Steps, below), in general it makes more sense that certain **preconditions** must be met before the test can start. This will be necessary for many tests which are not testing mathematically pure functions.

Example preconditions include:

1. The system is already running

2. The database contains a user `Joe` with password `EXAMPLE`

3. The `SORT_ASCEND` flag is set to true

4. There are already three items in the shopping cart

Let's look a little bit further at the last example, and see why it makes more sense to have this as a precondition rather than an actual part of the test. We would like to test that adding an item when there are already three items in the cart makes the cart display four items. Describing the test in English, you can already see that one naturally does not mention adding the first three items. From the perspective of this particular test, the specific steps for adding these items is irrelevant; all that matters is that at the beginning of the test, there are three items in the cart.

From a pragmatic perspective, being able to place preconditions on the test provides both flexibility and brevity to the tests. Suppose that instead of putting the precondition that three items needed to be in the cart, we included the following execution steps in the test:

1. Search for item "1XB"

2. Select the "1XB" item

3. Click the "Add to Cart" button three times

This may work fine the first time you run the test case. However, this test is very **fragile**—there are numerous ways for it to break if the system changes out from underneath. What if the "1XB" item no longer exists? What if the Search functionality has a defect where items that start with "1" cannot be found? What if the "Add to Cart" button name has changed?

There is a drawback from a brevity standpoint, as well. We have just added three execution steps where there was only one precondition. Brevity, aside from being the soul of wit, is also helpful in ensuring that the important parts of a test are focused upon. Boilerplate text is the enemy of attention and focus.

The dividing line between preconditions and execution steps can sometimes be an art rather than a science. In general, the more safety-critical the domain, the more precise the preconditions will be. As an example, let's say that you are testing an image-sharing site, where all images are public and visible to any other users. The test case involves checking that the correct image shows up on the screen when a user goes to the correct URL. The following preconditions may be enough for this test case:

1. The user has logged in

2. The image has been posted to the URL `/pictures/foo`.

However, if we were testing banking software and were using that image display to warn of an invalid transaction, there would probably be more preconditions, and the ones that did exist would be more specific:

1. User X has logged in with password Y

2. User X has no warnings or STOP CHECK notices on their account

3. The savings account of user X contains \$0.00.

4. The checking account of user X contains \$50.00.

5. User X has no accounts with the bank other than savings and checking accounts.

6. User X has attempted to withdraw \$50.01 from the user's checking account.

In both cases, the execution steps will be the same, or at least very similar—go to a URL and check that a particular image shows up. However, the state of the system would have been much more detailed in the case of the banking software. This is not only because the system itself is much more complex, but also because a failure would be much significant for the bank system than the image-sharing system. In such a case, it makes sense to specify exactly what should happen and what should be in place before the execution steps. The more exactly you write the preconditions, the easier it will be to reproduce the same situation exactly, and as we have discussed, reproducibility is the key to fixing a problem.

6.1.4   Input Values

Whereas preconditions are aspects of the system that are set before the test is run, **input values** are those values passed directly in to the functionality under test. This difference can be a subtle one, so let's explore a few examples.

Imagine we have a sorting routine, billSort, which is estimated to be twenty times faster than any other sorting algorithm. Rather than taking at face value billSort's assertion that it will always produce the correct result, we are developing tests for it. Our particular implementation uses a global variable, SORT_ASCENDING. Depending on whether SORT_ASCENDING (a Boolean flag) is set to true or false, it will either sort ascending (from the lowest value to the highest—e.g., "a", "b", "c") or sort descending (from the highest value to the lowest—e.g., "c", "b", "a"). If we are going to test this sorting routine, setting the flag would count as a precondition, as this is something which needs to be set up before the test. The array ["a", "c", "b"] would be the input values; these values are sent directly in for testing.

Another way to think of the difference between input values and preconditions is thinking of the tests as methods. This is probably a good exercise for you to do anyway—we'll definitely be doing more of it when we get to the chapter on unit tests!

```
public boolean testArraySort() {

    // PRECONDITIONS
    SORT_ASCENDING = true;

    // INPUT VALUES
    int[] vals = [1, 2, 3];

    // New, improved billSort method! :)
    billSorted = billSort(vals);

    // Old, busted built-in Java sort. :(
    normalSorted = Arrays.sort(vals);

    // If the arrays are equal, then true is returned and the test passes
    // Otherwise, false is returned, and the test fails
```

```
    return Arrays.equals(billSorted, normalSorted));

}
```

Note that because you aren't sending the `SORT_ASCENDING` flag in to the functionality under test (specifically, the `billSort()` method), then it is not considered an input value. However, the `vals` array is passed in to the `billSort()` method, so it is considered an input value.

Isn't it possible to redesign the system so as to send in the flag as an argument to the `billSort()` method, though?

```
    // Arguments = values array, SORT_ASCENDING flag
    billSorted = billSort(vals, true);
```

This is certainly possible, and in this case one could consider `SORT_ASCENDING` an input value as opposed to a precondition. Whether something is a precondition or an input value often depends on the implementation of a program. If we were writing this in a language such as Haskell, for example, where side effects for most functions are extremely limited, functions such as this would almost never have any preconditions other than 'the program is running'.

Sorting is a mathematically pure concept, but much of what a tester tests is not so straightforward. In such cases, it can often be difficult to determine what counts as input values and what counts as preconditions. As a heuristic, if someone selects or enters a value, as part of the execution of the test case, it should be considered an input value, otherwise it is a precondition. For example, if the test case checks for a user logging in as different names, then the login name would be an input value. If the test is checking for the ability to add items to a cart when logged in as a certain user, the login name would be a precondition, as it is not entered directly in the test case, but should be done before the test even starts.

6.1.5 Execution Steps

Now that the preconditions and input values for a test case have been determined, it's time to actually run the test case. The steps taken when running the test case are called the **execution steps**, and these are what the tester actually does. Execution steps are often incredibly specific and it is critical to follow them precisely. Contrast this to preconditions where it is sufficient to achieve an end result by any means.

Let's start with a simple example. We are testing an e-commerce software system and checking that adding one item to the cart, when the cart is already empty, will display "1" as the number of items in the cart. The precondition is that the cart contains zero items. This may have been accomplished in a variety of ways: the user has never logged in before; the user is already logged in and bought any items that were in the cart, resetting the counter; or any existing items that were in the cart have been removed without being bought. From the point of view of this case, it does not matter how this point (i.e., the cart containing zero items) has been reached, only that it does.

On the other hand, the actual execution steps should be spelled out very clearly:

1. Search for item "SAMPLE-BOX" by selecting the "Search" text box, entering `SAMPLE-BOX`, and hitting the "Search" button.

2. An item labeled "SAMPLE-BOX" should be displayed. Click on the button labeled "Add Item to Cart" next to the picture of the SAMPLE-BOX.

3. Inspect the "Number of Items in Cart = x" label at the top of the screen.

Note that these steps are relatively explicit. It is important to write the steps down in enough detail that if a problem occurs, it will be easily reproducible. If the execution steps had just mentioned to "Add an item", our tester could have chosen any item from the inventory. If the problem is with the item selected (say, adding SAMPLE-PLANT never increments the number of items in the cart, but SAMPLE-BOX does), then it may be difficult to figure out exactly what the problem is. Proper defect reporting can help ameliorate this issue, but it can be prevented entirely by ensuring that the execution steps are specified correctly. Of course, it's possible to go overboard with this:

1. Move mouse cursor to pixel (170, 934) by moving right hand 0.456 inches from previous location using the computer mouse. This location should correspond with a text box labeled "Search".

2. Apply one pound of pressure for 200 milliseconds to the left button of the mouse, using your right index finger.

3. After 200 milliseconds, quickly remove pressure from the left button of the mouse. Ensure that a cursor now exists and is blinking at a rate of 2 Hz in the text box... (etc.)

In general, it's best to set the level of specification to the ability and knowledge of the people who will actually be executing the tests (or, in the case of automated tests, of the programs that will actually be executing the execution steps). If you have in-house testers that are very familiar with both the software and domain being tested, it may only be necessary to say "Set the *frobinator* to 'FOO' using the primary dial." This is specific enough that a user who is familiar with the system will unambiguously be able to follow the steps. However, not everybody will be as familiar with the system as the writer of the tests. Many times, the people who actually execute the tests are contractors, outsourced, or simply relatively new testers on the project. For an outside tester who is not familiar with "frobinization" (and surprisingly, there are a few people who are not), it may be necessary to specify what needs to be done in much more detail:

1. Open the "PRIMARY" control panel by selecting "Dials... Primary" from the menu at the top of the screen.

2. Select the purple dial labeled "FROBINATOR". Move the dial to the right from its initial position until the "STATUS" text box reads "FOO".

As a final note, there is no such thing as a *frobinator* or *frobinization*.

6.1.6   Output Values

Values that are returned directly from the functionality being tested are **output values**. When dealing with strictly mathematical functions, these are very easy to determine—a mathematical function by definition takes in some input value or values, and sends out some output value or values. For example, for an absolute value function, the function takes in some number x, and if x < 0, it returns -x; otherwise, it returns x. Testing the function with -5 and checking that it returns 5, it is obvious that the input value is -5 and the output value is 5. There are no preconditions; sending in -5 should always return 5, no matter what global variables are set, no matter what is in the database, no matter what is displayed on the screen. There are no postconditions; the function shouldn't display anything else on the screen, or write something to the database, or set a global variable.

Once again, though, computer programs don't consist solely of mathematical functions, and so we must learn to distinguish postconditions from output values.

6.1.7 Postconditions

A **postcondition** is any condition which needs to be in place after the execution steps are complete but is not an output value. Postconditions may not be directly impacted by the functionality, but may be directly caused by the functionality under test. A warning message being displayed, some data written to the database, a global variable being set, the system is still running, or that a thread was not killed are all examples of postconditions.

6.1.8 Expected Behavior versus Observed Behavior

Although we've discussed the difference between output values and postconditions, the fact is that in many cases the difference doesn't really matter, or is too academic to make much fuss about. A similar argument could be made on preconditions and input values.

The principal idea to keep in mind when writing a test case is:

```
When the system is in state X,
And the following actions Y are performed,
I expect Z to happen
```

That value Z is the crux of the test—it is the expected behavior. It is impossible to test for something if you don't know what you expect to happen. As Lewis Carroll said, "if you don't know where you are going, any road will get you there." Similarly, when writing a test case, you need to know where you eventually want the test case to go, otherwise there's no way to check that you got to where the system should be.

6.2 Developing a Test Plan

Before starting to write any test plan, one must think about the end goal. How detailed does the test plan need to be? What kind of edge cases should be checked? What are the potential risks of unknown defects? These answers will be very different when you are testing an online children's game or software for monitoring a nuclear reactor. Based on the context and domain of the software under test, even software with similar requirements may require very different strategies for designing a test plan.

The simplest—and often the best—way to develop a detailed test plan is to read the requirements and determine ways to test each of them individually. There is usually quite a bit of thought put into requirements development, and since the goal of the system is to meet the requirements, it makes sense to ensure that all of the requirements are in fact tested. It also provides a very straightforward path to generate a test plan. Here's the first requirement, write some test cases; here's the second requirement, write some more test cases; repeat until all requirements are covered.

For each requirement, you should think of at least the "happy path" for that requirement and at least one test case for that path. That is, what is a situation under normal operating parameters that will show this requirement to be met? For example, if you have a requirement that a particular button should be enabled if a value is less than 10, and disabled if 10 or greater, at a bare minimum you would want to have tests that check if the button is enabled for a value less than 10 and one that checks that it is disabled if the value is greater than or equal to 10. This tests both equivalence classes of the requirement (value < 10 and value >= 10).

You will also want to think of cases that test the various boundaries, as well as all the equivalence classes. Continuing the above example, let us assume that you have a test case for the value 5 and a test case for the value 15, thus ensuring that you have at least one value for each equivalence class. You might also want to add test cases to check the boundary between the two equivalence classes, so you add test cases for 9 and 10.

How many of these edge cases and corner cases you'd like to add, as well as how extensively you test interior and boundary values, will vary depending on the amount of time and resources that you have available for testing, the software domain, and the level of risk that your organization is comfortable taking. Remember that testing exhaustively is, for all intents and purposes, impossible. There is a sliding scale of how much time and energy one wants to put in to writing and executing tests, and no right answer. Determining a compromise between speed of development and ensuring quality is a key part of being a software tester.

Developing test cases for non-functional requirements (quality attributes) of the system can often be difficult. You should try to ensure that the requirements themselves are testable, and think of ways to quantify any test cases that you can think of for those requirements.

Unfortunately, simply having a correspondence between all requirements and a test case for each does not always mean that you have developed a good test plan. You may have to add additional tests to ensure that requirements work together in tandem, or check for cases from the user's point of view that may not map directly to requirements or flow directly from them. Even more importantly, you will need to gain an understanding of the context that the software exists in. Having domain knowledge of the field can help you understand basic use cases, how the system interacts with the environment, possible failure modes, and how users would expect the system to recover from those failure modes. If nobody on the team understands the domain of the software, it may be worthwhile to discuss the software with a subject matter expert (SME) before writing a test plan.

Understanding the programming environment that the software is written in can also facilitate writing a test plan. Although this technically veers into grey-box testing as opposed to black-box testing, since you as a tester will know some of the internal implementation details, it can provide valuable insight in knowing where potential errors may lurk. Allow me to give an example. In Java, dividing by zero, as in the code below, will throw a `java.lang.ArithmeticException`:

```
int a = 7 / 0;
```

No matter what the dividend is, if the divisor is 0, a `java.lang.ArithmeticException` is throw.

```
// All of these statements cause the same exception to be thrown

int b = -1 / 0;

int c = 0 / 0;

int d = 999999 / 0;
```

Therefore, when testing a program written in Java, you can assume that dividing by zero is essentially one equivalence class; if it occurs, then the same event should happen afterwards, whatever that event happens to be (e.g., perhaps the exception is caught and the message "Error Divide by Zero" is printed to the console).

JavaScript (yes, technically I mean ECMAScript 5, for anyone who wants to know the particulars) does not throw an exception when dividing by zero. However, depending on the numerator, when the denominator is zero, you may get different results!

```
> 1 / 0
Infinity

> -1 / 0
```

```
-Infinity

> 0 / 0
NaN
```

Dividing a positive value by zero returns `Infinity`, dividing a negative number by zero returns `-Infinity`, and dividing zero by zero returns `NaN` (Not a Number). This means that dividing by zero, despite being one "internal equivalence class" in Java programs, is three different ones in JavaScript programs. Knowing this, you would want to test that the program can handle all of these return values, and not assume that you had checked all edge cases simply because you had checked for dividing one by zero. This is an actual example from a test plan that I wrote, and it was used to find several defects.

6.3   Test Fixtures

As you write your plan, you may find that you wish to test situations which are difficult to replicate. For example, you may want to check that the coffee temperature app mentioned above works when changing time zones. It would probably be prohibitively expensive to actually move the system from one time zone to another. Remember that you are the master of this testing world! You can simply change the time zone of the system the program is running on. If you're testing that software will work in Russia, you can just change the locale settings to Russia instead of hopping on a flight. If you require ten users in the database for a test, you can just add them manually to the database. Although these fake situations may not catch all of the defects that may occur in reality under these conditions, they will tend to catch many of them.

A script or program used to put the system under test into a state that is ready for testing is known as a **test fixture**. Test fixtures can be as simple as a series of steps to type into the program, but there is no real limit to their complexity. The Lunar Landing Training Vehicle was used by astronauts on Earth to practice for landing on the Moon, using a complex feedback mechanism to simulate lunar gravity. For more examples of how testing and test fixtures helped astronauts reach the Moon, see *Digital Apollo: Human and Machine in Spaceflight* by David Mindell.

Test fixtures are often used to simulate external systems. As a personal anecdote, I was testing a subsystem that communicated with several other subsystems via JSON. At first, the other systems were manually configured at the beginning of each test case. I soon realized that this was time-consuming and error-prone. The result was `simple_respond`, a Ruby gem that would accept a given JSON file and always respond with the data in the file for any request. Instead of setting up the other subsystems—which I was not testing—I could focus on what the subsystem I *was* testing would do given certain responses. Not only did this save time and reduce human error, but the tests were no longer dependent on other parts of the system working correctly. Test fixtures like this could also be re-used when interacting with external systems, when there is no way to modify their state for a given test case.

6.4   Executing a Test Plan

Executing a test plan is called a **test run**. One way to think of test runs is as the equivalent of an object and a class. Executing a test plan generates a test run similar to how instantiating a class creates an object. The test plan is the map of where to go, whereas the test run is the voyage that the traveler makes.

Executing a test plan should be a relatively simple process, assuming that you have developed the test plan appropriately. After all, you have spent time ensuring that the preconditions are reasonable to set up, that the input values are specified, that the execution steps are detailed enough to follow, and that output values and postconditions are feasible to test. At this point, actually executing the tests should be a relatively mechanical process (and this is one of the reasons that automated testing is possible). You should be able to send someone into a room with the software and the appropriate hardware to run it on, and some number of hours later, depending on how long the test plan is, the person will come out of the room with a fully-tested system.

Unfortunately, this beautiful vision does not always come to pass. In the process of executing a test case, the test case can have different statuses. There will be a final status for each test case, although the status is liable to change during the execution of the test run. There is also often a "null" or "untested" status which means that that particular test case has not yet been executed.

Although there is no universal status repository, these are a representative sampling of the kinds of test cases that might be encountered in your testing career. The names may change, but these six provide good coverage of all the situations that your test case may be in:

1. Passed

2. Failed

3. Paused

4. Running

5. Blocked

6. Error

A **passed** test is one in which all of the expected behavior (i.e., the output values and postconditions) match the observed behavior. Colloquially, one could say that it's a test where everything worked.

Inversely, a **failed** test is one in which at least one aspect of the observed behavior was not equal to the expected behavior. This difference could be in either the output values or the postconditions. For example, if a square root function returned that the square root of 4 was 322, then that test case would be marked "failed". If a test case had a postcondition that a message `ERROR: ELEPHANTS CAN'T DANCE` appears on the screen, but the error message in fact reads `ERROR: ELEPHANTS CAN'T DEFENESTRATE`, then once again the test case has failed. Whenever a test case is marked failed, there should be a corresponding defect filed. This could be a new defect, or it could be that a known defect has caused multiple problems—for example, errors for all animals are saying that they can't defenestrate when the actual issue is that they can't dance. If there is no defect associated with a failed test case, then either the test case wasn't important enough to test, or the defect found wasn't important enough to file. If either is the case, you should rethink your test case!

A **paused** test is one that has started, but had to be put on hold for some period of time. This allows other testers and managers to know the status of a test and the progress a tester has been made. It also ensures that another tester doesn't step in and start doing the test that has already been started by another tester. A test case may be paused for quotidian reasons, like the tester going to lunch, or something directly related to the system under test, such as leaving the lab to get new test data. In any case, the assumption is that the tester will get back to working on this test as soon as he or she returns, not that the test itself cannot be executed (that is covered by the "blocked" status, below).

A **running** test is one which has started, but has not yet completed, and thus the final result is not yet known. This is usually used in cases where the test takes a long time to complete, and the tester would like other testers to know that it is being executed. Although technically all tests enter a running state for a brief period of time (when the tester is executing the execution steps), unless there is some sort of automation, this status is usually only set when the test is long-running.

In some cases, a test cannot be executed at the present time. This can be due to external factors (such as a piece of testing equipment not being available) or internal factors (such as a piece of functionality not being completed, or impossible to test due to other defects present in the system). In such cases, the test can be marked as **blocked**. This indicates that the test cannot currently be run, although it may be run in a future test run when the issues blocking its execution have been removed.

Finally, in some cases a test case simply cannot be executed, either now or in the future, due to a problem with the test case itself. In such cases, the test status can be marked as being in **error**. Tests marked as in error could have an issue with the test contradicting the requirements, such as a requirement saying that the background color of a web page should be blue, but the system under test is actually a command-line application. It could be a problem with the expected behavior of a program, for example, saying that the square root of 25 should result in "poodle". Oftentimes, a test marked "error" may be the result of a simple typo, but it could point to a fundamental problem with the development team's or testing team's understanding of the software. Test cases marked "error", unlike those marked "blocked", are not expected to be run again until the error is resolved.

6.5   Test Run Tracking

Although you could execute a test plan for fun or for your own sense of self-improvement, in most cases you want to record what the results of the test plan were. This can be done using custom test tracking software, a simple spreadsheet program, or even just a notebook. In some cases, this will be necessary due to the regulatory environment, but even if it is not required, keeping track of what tests have passed and which have not will be extremely useful.

When tracking a test run, there are several pieces of information that you will want to include:

1. The date the test was executed

2. The name or other identifier (e.g., login or ID number) of the tester

3. The name or other identifier of the system under test

4. An indication of what code was under test. This may be a tag, a link, a version number, a build number, or some other form of identification.

5. The test plan the test run corresponds with

6. The final status of each test case. Note that temporary statuses, such as PAUSED, should be changed to the final status before finishing the test run.

7. A list of any defects filed as a result of the test case, if any, or other reasons for any status that is not PASSED.

An example of a test run might be:

```
Date: 21 May 2014
Tester Name: Jane Q. Tester
System: Meow Recording System (MRS)
Build Number: 342
Test Plan: Meow Storage Subsystem Test Plan

Results:
```

```
TEST 1: PASSED
TEST 2: PASSED
TEST 3: FAILED (Filed defect #714)
TEST 4: BLOCKED (feature not yet implemented)
TEST 5: PASSED
TEST 6: FAILED (Due to known defect #137)
TEST 7: ERROR (Apparent typo in test plan; need to verify with Systems Engineering)
TEST 8: PASSED
TEST 9: PASSED
```

If a test fails, then one of two things should happen: Either a new defect should be filed, or the already-known defect that is causing the failure should be noted. A defect indicates that the system is not operating as designed; the expected behavior does not match the observed behavior. More detail on filing defects is included in the following chapter.

If a test is blocked, then the reason that it is blocked should be noted. This may be something beyond the test team's control, such as the feature not being implemented yet, or it may be something that can be ameliorated, such as not having the proper equipment. Having the rationale for the reason that a test was not completed included in the test run results not only provides valuable documentation about the status, it also may enable management or others to find a way around the problem in the future. For example, if part of the test plan requires a specific piece of hardware, having documentation that this lack of equipment is causing tests to not be run may provide an impetus for management to buy more equipment, or for other engineers to provide alternative solutions.

Tests with the status ERROR should hopefully be a rarity. If an erroneous test is found, however, it behooves the tester to note why he or she thinks that the test is in error. An idea of how to rectify it—or at least on how to get more information on it—should be included as part of the result of that test case.

Tracking your test runs allows you to see where tests are failing. If you notice that one particular area of the software is failing more often than others, perhaps you should focus more on that area. Inversely, running tests which always pass, and have been passing for years, may not be worth your time. It can also allow you to see where there are intermittent failures, so that you know what test cases are not stable. By looking over test runs over time, not only can you get a good idea of the progress and quality of the software over time, but the information you gain will allow you to generate better test plans going forward.

6.6   Traceability Matrices

Now that we have a list of requirements and a test plan to test them, what else remains? Surely, we can all go home and enjoy a beverage of our choice after a long day toiling in the data mines. However, there is one more thing to discuss on the topic. We have informally developed tests that we suppose will meet requirements, but we can double-check that our requirements and test plan are in sync by building a **traceability matrix**.

A traceability matrix is simply a way of determining which requirements match up with which test plans, and displaying it as an easy-to-understand diagram. They consist of a list of the requirements (usually just the requirement identifiers) and a list of the test case numbers which correspond to those requirements (i.e., the ones that test specific aspects of that requirement).

As an example, let's return to the requirements specification for the coffee temperature sensing application. You will note that the requirements list has changed a bit—this is not uncommon when developing software!

- *FUN-COFFEE-TOO-HOT.* If the coffee temperature is measured at 175 degrees Fahrenheit or higher, the app shall display the TOO HOT message.

- *FUN-COFFEE-JUST-RIGHT.* If the coffee temperature is measured at less than 175 degrees Fahrenheit, but more than 130 degrees Fahrenheit, the app shall display the JUST RIGHT message.

- *FUN-COFFEE-TOO-COLD.* If the coffee temperature is measured at 130 degrees Fahrenheit or less, the app shall display the TOO COLD message.

- *FUN-TEA-ERROR.* If the liquid being measured is actually tea, the app shall display the message SORRY, THIS APP DOES NOT SUPPORT TEA.

We write down the identifiers of the requirements, and leave a space for the test plan identifiers:

```
FUN-COFFEE-TOO-HOT:
FUN-COFFEE-JUST-RIGHT:
FUN-COFFEE-TOO-COLD:
FUN-TEA-ERROR:
```

Now look through the completed test plan, and determine which test cases correspond to testing these specific requirements. For each test case which does, write down its identifier next to the requirement:

```
FUN-COFFEE-TOO-HOT: 1, 2
FUN-COFFEE-JUST-RIGHT: 3, 4, 5
FUN-COFFEE-TOO-COLD: 6, 7
FUN-TEA-ERROR: 8
```

It's easy to see that for each requirement, there is at least one test covering it. If there were another requirement, say,

- *FUN-COFFEE-FROZEN.* If the coffee is in a solid and not a liquid state, then the app shall display the message THIS COFFEE CAN ONLY BE EATEN, NOT DRUNK.

and we tried to create a traceability matrix, it would be very easy to see that there were no tests checking for this requirement:

```
FUN-COFFEE-TOO-HOT: 1, 2
FUN-COFFEE-JUST-RIGHT: 3, 4, 5
FUN-COFFEE-TOO-COLD: 6, 7
FUN-TEA-ERROR: 8
FUN-COFFEE-FROZEN:
```

Likewise, traceability matrices can allow us to determine if we have any "useless" tests which are not testing any specific requirements. For example, let's say that we have created a "Test Case 9":

```
IDENTIFIER: 9
TEST CASE: Determine if app properly reads poodle temperature.
PRECONDITIONS: Poodle is alive and in reasonably good health, with a normal poodle
    body temperature of 101 degrees Fahrenheit.
INPUT VALUES: None
EXECUTION STEPS: Point sensor at poodle for five seconds.  Read display.
OUTPUT VALUES: None
POSTCONDITIONS: "POODLE IS OK" message is displayed upon screen.
```

Our traceability matrix will once again have a gap in it, but this time on the requirements side. Test case 9 does not match up with any of the requirements, and may be a superfluous test:

```
FUN-COFFEE-TOO-HOT: 1, 2
FUN-COFFEE-JUST-RIGHT: 3, 4, 5
FUN-COFFEE-TOO-COLD: 6, 7
FUN-TEA-ERROR: 8
???: 9
```

Occasionally, in the "real world", there may be some tests that do not officially line up with a specific requirement. For example, if a systems engineer did not put in a requirement for reliability, the test plan may still include a test for ensuring that the system works even when running for an entire day. This is certainly not a best practice, but it does happen occasionally. If this occurs, the best course of action would be to create a requirement for reliability that it can be tested against.

Of course, a traceability matrix provides a very simple overview of the test coverage. The fact that every requirement has been tested does not mean that each requirement has been tested thoroughly. For example, what if the system has issues with extremely hot coffee? The highest temperature we checked for was 200 degrees Fahrenheit, but it may fail at 201 degrees Fahrenheit. There's no verification in the traceability matrix itself that the tests are good, either. If we had tested whether or not the system was meeting the FUN-COFFEE-TOO-HOT requirement by dunking the system in ice water, but said that that test case lined up with the FUN-COFFEE-TOO-HOT requirement, there's no way tell just by looking at the traceability matrix.

Traceability matrices are a good way to double-check your work and report to others outside of your team how well covered the system is from a test perspective. In time crunches, you or your manager may decide that certain parts or functions of the system are more important to test than others, and so you may not even write tests for these less-important aspects. Again, this is not a good practice, but at least you can use a traceability matrix to keep track of where the gaps in your testing coverage are.

Customers and management, especially in highly regulated fields such as defense contracting and medicine, may also require traceability matrices as a way of proving that the systems have been tested to at least a baseline level.

Chapter 7

Breaking Software

Thus far, we have focused on how to develop test plans, but there has been little discussion of what to test, outside of ensuring that the software meets the requirements. While this is not the worst approach to testing software, it leaves out important aspects in regards to verification, especially in checking for more obscure edge cases.

The reason one tests is to find defects; in order to find defects, you may have to venture a bit from the happy path, where everybody enters data in the format you like, systems have infinite memory and CPU, and your zero-latency networks are always connected. You'll have to traverse through the dark woods where people try to enter "FORTY-SEVEN" instead of "47", where the program runs out of memory midway through a computation, where a horror movie villain stands poised above the Ethernet cable with a sharpened hatchet.

Maybe not that last one. However, you will have to think of ways to test for the operation of a system when things aren't quite perfect. Consider this chapter a way of priming your testing brain for how to cause failures and find the cracks in the software under test.

7.1 Errors To Look For

1. **Logic Errors**: A logic error is an error in the logic of the program. The developer understood what needed to be done, but in the process of converting the system from its description to its implementation, something went wrong. This could be as simple as accidentally replacing a greater-than (>) with a less-than (<), or as complicated as an intricate interaction between numerous variables.

   In order to check for logic errors, you should ensure that the expected result occurs for a variety of inputs. Boundaries—explicit and implicit—are often a rich vein to be mined for defects. Try other kinds of interesting input as well, such as special characters, exceedingly long strings, and improperly-formatted data. Input that comes from other systems or users will often send strange or incorrect data. It's good to know what happens when your system receives it.

   For complex output (e.g., generating a large web page from a template), it may not be feasible to check the output directly. However, you can check that there are valid properties of the output, and that those properties are expected. For example, you can check that the generated page data can be parsed and that it displays and shows data correctly. You can also look at the data from a higher abstraction level—instead of checking that there is an HTML <strong>

tag around every occurrence of the word "cat" on a page, it may be easier to look at the page, search for cat, and check that each time it is displayed, it is in bold.

2. **Off-By-One Errors**: Although technically a logic error, these are so common that they will be addressed separately. An off-by-one error is when a program does something wrong because a value is off by just one unit. This is the reason that there was a focus on determining boundary values in a previous chapter—boundary values are a focused way of looking for off-by-one errors. Why are these so common? Let's imagine a very simple method which returns whether or not a person is a minor, which consists solely of the statement"return personAge <= 18;".

Did you spot the error? At least in the United States at the time of this writing, you are no longer considered a minor once you reach 18. By using <= instead of <, the method will return that the person is still a minor when they turn 18. This minor mistake can happen in all sorts of ways—thinking that an array is 1-indexed instead of 0-indexed, confusing a "greater than or equal to" sign with "greater than", using ++i when you should have used i++, etc. These are also often less visible than other errors, since they will only show up for specific values. When testing, check the boundary values and you are likely to run across some off-by-one errors.

3. **Rounding Errors** and **Floating Point Errors**: Computer systems often use floating-point variables to represent decimal numbers such as 1.1. These are often much more efficient than using arbitrary-precision or rational values, but this efficiency comes with a cost—loss of precision. For example, assume that the system under test is using IEEE 754 single-precision 32-bit floating point values. Entering 1.1 as a value does not mean that the value is stored as 1.1. Instead, it's stored as 1.10000002384185791015625, because there are a literally infinite number of decimal numbers, and they all need to be stored in 32 bits. Whenever you try to map an infinite amount of values to a finite space, there's going to have to be multiple values that share the same representation. If you remember your discrete math, this is the Pigeonhole Principle in operation. That value just happened to be the closest possible value to 1.1. Mapping multiple values to the same representation is essentially saying that values will be rounded.

"That's fine," you may think, "that's such a small amount of difference between the actual value and the represented value. I can't imagine it would make a difference." What happens when you multiply it by another floating point number, though? The difference may be magnified. And then multiply it by another floating point, and another... soon you may be dealing with values that are not at all close to what they are supposed to be! Although a gradual drifting of values is not guaranteed to happen, since some represented values may be higher and some lower than the actual value, it is certainly possible.

This is one of the reasons that there is a Currency data type in many programming languages; imagine a bank getting these kinds of calculations wrong. Using floating-point values could cost them vast amounts of money. And it could be even worse, no imagination necessary: read up on the Patriot Missile Defense Failure of 1991. Accumulated floating point errors resulted in an American base's failure to detect an incoming Scud missile during the Gulf War, causing 28 deaths and around 100 injuries.

In other cases, there may also be a deliberate loss of precision due to rounding, or to a program taking the ceiling or floor of a number. For example, at some point a program may have to convert a decimal value to an integer, and the programmer has many choices in how to do this. The conversion could always round down (e.g., 4.8 becomes 4, dropping everything to the right of the decimal point), it could always round up (e.g., converting 4.3 to 5), or it could use the rounding we all learned in elementary school, rounding up if the number if 4.5 or greater and rounding down otherwise. Which is the correct path to take? It depends on the program and the expected output, and it's easy to get wrong.

In order to check for rounding and floating point errors, try testing with different decimal values as input. Ensure that the final output does, in fact, match the expected output within the range of error. If the input data is going to interact with other data, check what happens when there is a large amount of data. These kinds of errors will often be compounded, and thus easier to detect, when there are large amounts of data.

4. **Integration Errors**: When errors exist at the interface between two different parts of a system, this is known as an integration error. These interfaces can be class boundaries, package boundaries, or interprocess boundaries, all the way up to boundaries between large, multi-computer systems. Because interfaces are often where there are splits between teams or individuals working on different parts of a system, they are a target-rich environment for defects. Teams tend to communicate better with other members of a team; after all, they are working on similar pieces of the system and will often get rapid feedback whenever there is a problem when working on their particular subsystem. When interacting with other teams, miscommunication is more likely, and that creates opportunities for double-checking that the system is working correctly and that the assumptions that were made are correct. Even if there is a well-defined interface specification, there are opportunities for misunderstandings of the specification or errors in implementing it.

As a tester, a focus on testing how systems integrate will pay great dividends. Ensuring that systems interoperate correctly is often difficult for developers to do, since they tend to be focused on the specific aspect of the software they are working on, as opposed to having a holistic view of the system.

5. **Errors of Assumption**: It is, for all intents and purposes, impossible to completely define most systems using requirements. If you were to define a system that precisely, you would have basically written the program. Therefore, developers will often make assumptions about how the program is supposed to behave. However, these assumptions may not be in line with what the customer requires, or how other systems expect the system to act. Some common examples to check for include:

   (a) How should the system display errors?

   (b) How should data be displayed or otherwise output?

   (c) Are there any requirements on formatting of files?

   (d) What systems need to be supported?

   (e) What other systems will this interact with?

   (f) What sort of interfaces will be necessary?

   (g) What kind of user experience and user interface is expected?

   (h) How will the system be accessed? By whom?

   (i) What kind of terminology, acronyms, etc. are used?

   (j) What are valid ranges or limits for data?

   (k) How will data be input? In what formats?

If you assume that all weight input comes in as pounds, what happens when someone else assumes that it is in kilograms? Was an assumption made that output is in ASCII, but some data is input in UTF-8, thus causing data to be lost upon display? Did a software engineer write a program that uses a command-line interface when the customer actually wanted a GUI? Are output files written using CSV (comma-separated values) when downstream users expect them to be tab-separated? All of these are assumptions in the development process that can lead to defects when the system is used.

There also may be common requirements for a given domain, of which the software developers are not aware. After all, software developers tend to be software developers, not subject matter experts on the domain of the software they are writing. That is not always the case, of course, but often enough there will be a disconnect between the knowledge of the person developing the system and the eventual customer.

As a tester of software, you can and should help to bridge that gap. Understanding what the customer requires, as well as how developers are writing the software, can allow you to see discrepancies and know what to look for when you are developing test plans. It also can help you prioritize and strategize when you are determining what features and edge cases to check. For example, if you know that a particular kind of file that your system operates on is rarely over 50 kilobytes when your program is used, you can focus on testing small files instead of the edge cases inherent in dealing with extremely large files.

6. **Missing Data Errors**: Whenever data comes in from an external source to the program (e.g., from a CSV file, or an API endpoint, or from direct user input on the terminal), there exists the chance that necessary data will be missing. This may be as simple as a user accidentally hitting Enter when asked for input, or as complex as a missing attribute somewhere deep within a large JSON response. In all cases, though, the system should deal with it appropriately. Always assume that anything external may or may not send you all of the data that you need.

   What to do when data is missing is going to vary by program and by domain. In some cases, your program can safely ignore it; in others, it should be flagged or logged, or the user alerted; in rare instances, the correct thing to do is shut down the entire system. However, you should know how a system is supposed to respond to missing data, and determine that the system actually performs that way when it encounters it.

7. **Bad Data Errors**: Even more problematic than Missing Data Errors are Bad Data Errors. While there is only one item to check for a given attribute when looking at Missing Data Errors, there are almost infinitely many possible ways for data to be "bad". This data could be generated internally, but the most likely cause of bad data is data coming from an external system which has different assumptions, uses a different format, has been corrupted or modified in some way, etc.

   (a) *Data is too long:* Perhaps the system can only handle up to a certain amount of data. What happens if the input data is longer than that?

   (b) *Data is too short:* On the other hand, what if the system operates strangely with very small amounts of data? This won't be as common as problems with data being too long, but it is often a cause of inefficiency (e.g., a system always allocating a megabyte for every input by default, even if it's only a few bytes long).

   (c) *Data is formatted incorrectly:* What happens if your program expects comma-delimited data, and it receives tab-delimited data? What happens if your program expects a JSON string, but it receives XML?

   (d) *Data is out of range:* What happens if your software is asked for the 593rd State of the United States? What happens if the temperature is listed as -500 degrees Celsius (which is below absolute zero, and thus impossible in this universe)?

   (e) *Data has been corrupted:* Are there any safeguards when accepting data that checks that data is legitimate and has not been modified? Although data corruption is less of a problem than it used to be, there could still be errors such as someone opening a file in a text editor on a different operating system, causing all linefeed characters to be converted to an unexpected character.

(f) *Data is not consistent:* What happens if input data contradicts itself? For example, if you are receiving data and it has two listings for user ID 723, one with the name "John Doe" and one with the name "Jane Doe"? Do you know what the expected behavior should be in this situation?

(g) *Data is unparseable:* What happens if you receive data that cannot be parsed, because it is missing a closing > or), or has a circular reference? Does the system give an appropriate error message, or even know that it is stuck in an infinite loop?

Tracking down bad data problems can be difficult, since there are so many ways that things can go wrong, and oftentimes only a very particular configuration of bad data will cause a problem. While it's certainly possible to write test data that is problematic in different ways, a more efficient way is to use **fuzz testing**—sending in randomly generated data (which may or may not conform to the expected input in different ways) and ensuring that the system still operates correctly. See the chapter on Stochastic Testing for more information on fuzz testing.

8. **Display Errors**: While a system may compute the correct value, it may be displayed incorrectly. This may be a problem when a number or string is too large to be displayed in full (e.g., displaying the result of 1 / 3), and so characters are cut off. In other cases, there may be no cut-off, so that the display of a value causes problems by overwriting or otherwise distorting other aspects of a display. If you are displaying values on a chart, an outlier on the X or Y axes may either not be displayed, or be displayed well off the chart, causing issues for other aspects of the display. Graphics may be displayed incorrectly, or the wrong bitmap or color may be used. Certain characters printed to a display may cause the terminal to freeze, or a bell to beep, or cause other issues with the display. Improperly escaped HTML may cause your rendered web page to no longer appear.

Whenever data is displayed, check not only that the value was computed properly, but also that it is being displayed properly. By sending in data that contains odd characters, or extremely large or small values, or that is missing some normally-expected value, you can ensure that all the time spent determining the right value to display is actually seen by the user.

9. **Injection Errors**: A subset of Bad Data Errors, Injection Errors are when executable code or other instructions are passed in to a program. If a program can be tricked into executing these instructions, the consequences can be dire, including loss or corruption of data, unauthorized access to a system, or simply causing the system to crash.

An especially common issue is not dealing with escapes or odd characters properly. An escape code which is not caught by the interface that the data is entered in may be used by another subsystem that does recognize it, or vice-versa. Characters may be used for different purposes by different subsystems or language. For example, Java strings can have null characters inside of them, whereas a null character indicates "end of string" for C strings.

In order to test for these, determine what happens when various kinds of code are passed in to the program. This doesn't have to be Java (or whatever language the system itself is written in). A web application might execute JavaScript code on visitors' browsers. Many systems use SQL for database updates and queries, and arbitrary SQL code can change or delete data. The injected code could be assembly at the end of a long input—a trick often used to take advantage of a buffer overflow vulnerability (see the chapter on Security Testing for more information). Checking all of these potential issues involves testing a wide variety of inputs, and there are adversaries who stand to gain personally from you missing a single point of entry for their malicious programs.

10. **Network Errors**: Although computers are becoming more and more networked all the time, network connectivity is not yet ubiquitous or trouble-free. The system should continue to work even if network connectivity is temporarily lost. Some systems, of course, require network connectivity to work (running ssh or a web browser would be rather boring if you could not connect to any other systems), but they certainly should not crash or freeze without it.

Perhaps the most dramatic example of testing against network errors is the "hatchet test" (alluded to above), in which a tester takes a hatchet and chops the cable connecting the system to the network. This can be simulated, with slightly less chance of injury, by unplugging the cable or turning off the wireless connectivity in the middle of the program's operation.

Loss of connectivity is not the only possible issue that a network-enabled program could encounter. You may also wish to check what happens when there is extremely high latency or extremely low bandwidth. Often, a program may assume that as long as there is connectivity, that it must be good connectivity, and the system will become unusable when the connection exists but the connectivity is very poor. Another scenario to check is when network connectivity is spotty (connecting and disconnecting frequently), which may cause problems which are not seen when there is one long interruption of service. A network connection with a high rate of packet loss may provide a good test, especially if you are using UDP or another connectionless protocol. For a real test, you may want to add corruption to the line. In all of these situations, and other network problems, the system should degrade gracefully instead of failing hard.

11. **Disk I/O Errors**: Data inside your program lives in a nice, little, prepared world. Data outside your program is vicious and uncontrolled, red in tooth and claw, following no law but Murphy's. If you're reading a file off a disk, perhaps the file you are trying to read doesn't exist. Perhaps it does exist, but it's of the wrong format. Perhaps it's of the right format, but it's corrupted. Perhaps you're trying to write to it, but it's read-only. Perhaps another user has opened it in the meantime. Perhaps it's in a directory to which your user does not have access. Perhaps you had access to that directory when the program started, but not now. Perhaps the file exists, but is empty. Perhaps the file is several hundred megabytes and you only expected it to be a few kilobytes. The list of things goes on and on.

You should be checking that if your system needs to access the disk, it is prepared for these eventualities. One possibility is to have a special testing subdirectory filled with all sorts of odd files, and whenever a new function would read a file, run it against these examples. These odd files would hit all of the variations mentioned above, as well as domain-specific oddities such as files whose internal structure was self-referential, or contained missing data, etc.

12. **Interface Errors**: Systems often need to communicate with other systems, and they will need some sort of interface to do so. This interface may be more or less well-defined, from simply accepting text as input and providing text as output (such as with most Unix utilities such as `more` or `grep`) up to complex binary formats. However, this interface does need to be defined at some level, and there exists the possibility that the definition is specified ambiguously, or different parts of the definition contradict each other, or each side of the interface team had different assumptions when creating it (see Errors of Assumption, above). There also exists the possibility that it was just programmed incorrectly!

These interfaces do not have to be inter-process or inter-computer. They can be as low-level as an interface between two classes. The interface to a method is usually easy to understand; in Java, for instance, it's trivial to see what the following method accepts as arguments and what it outputs, even without comments:

```java
public boolean greaterThanTen(int a, int b) {
    return (a + b) > 10;
}
```

In the previous instance, you can see that the method accepts two integers, and returns a Boolean. It's also relatively easy to determine what the method does, even without comments. Although it's always possible to write obfuscated code (intentionally or unintentionally), and rely on side effects and global variables, the average programmer's brain tends to be decent at understanding things at the method level. As soon you go up to the class level, it can be more difficult to tell how things interoperate, and why. No longer are you looking at the language itself, focusing on keywords like `for`, `if`, and `return` that are as familiar as your childhood blankie. Instead, you are seeing a sort of "meta-language" of the class, which will be new to you. You're working at a higher level of abstraction, and it gets even worse as you move up to higher and higher levels. The cure is to define and design the interfaces well, but what may make sense to one person is likely to cause another to throw their hands up in despair. Interfaces also tend to demarcate the line between developers or teams of developers. Thus, they also mark a fertile ground for misunderstanding, and where there is misunderstanding, there too are defects.

When testing, you should spend time exploring the interfaces in the system. These are areas where communication may have broken down, or where people on differing sides made different assumptions. What happens when you try to pass in unexpected values? What happens if an expected value is not sent in, or more values are sent in than expected? What happens if data is out of range, or too large?

13. **Null Pointer Errors**: You may be lucky enough to be working in a language in which the concept of a null pointer does not exist, but if you are programming in Java you are probably more familiar with these than you care to admit. Any time that an object might be null, there needs to be an explicit check to ensure that it's not before trying to access it. In a 2012 talk on the history of the concept of null, Franklin Chen noted that in languages like Java, any object is always of *two* possible types—the object itself, or a null version of itself.[1] You can't assume, for example, that if you have an `Integer` object, it's actually an `Integer`; it might be a null object masquerading as integer.

    This can be relatively easy to look for if you are doing white-box testing and can see the code itself. If you're performing black-box testing, though, you can still think of cases where an object may not exist. What happens when you try to search for an object in a database that doesn't exist? What happens when you don't enter anything in a text box? What happens when you give an invalid ID? For many programs, the behavior necessary to operate under these conditions must be explicitly programmed. Any time that a common behavior must be checked for explicitly, there is a chance that the programmer forgets to do it or does it incorrectly.

14. **Distributed System Errors**: Testing a system which runs concurrently on multiple servers comes with its own set of issues. In many cases, there is not a "true" copy of data (one place where the data is expected to always be correct, as opposed to places which contain "copies" which may be out-of-date or incorrect). Not only must you worry about testing it with different hardware and software setups, but also check different network topologies and different combinations of hardware and software setups. Different levels of bandwidth and latency may cause defects to manifest themselves. Times and timestamps may differ from one system to another, multiple people may be modifying the same data from different machines, different machines may have different concepts of the current state of the data, etc. There are numerous situations where determining what the expected behavior should be is difficult, if not altogether impossible.

---

[1] For an in-depth look at the "billion-dollar problem" of null pointers, watch Franklin Chen's talk, *nil: Historical, Theoretical, Comparative, Philosophical, and Practical Perspectives*, at http://franklinchen.com/blog/2012/09/06/my-pittsburgh-ruby-talk-nil/.

When testing a distributed system, you should spend time checking that systems are synchronizing correctly; data should be coherent, at least eventually. Ensure that the system works whenever different aspects of the system change, and especially when individual systems break down (as they almost certainly will at some point—the more machines you have running your code, the more likely at least one will have a failure). Read Peter Deutsch's *The Eight Fallacies of Distributed Computing*[2]—don't worry, it's a very quick read—and think of what assumptions you and the developers of the system have made... and then break those assumptions.

15. **Configuration Errors**: There are two different ways that configuration errors can manifest themselves. First, the administrators of a system can configure a software system in many different ways. For example, when setting up a Rails application, there are numerous configuration options in various YAML files that you can set. Many applications have configuration settings, command-line switches, or other ways of modifying how they operate, and they sometimes override or interact with each other in strange ways.

    Secondly, if a system is reachable online, the users of a system may have set up their personal computers in many different ways. There are many web browsers, for instance, from full-featured ones released by major companies and organizations, to small text-based browsers. These browsers have various levels of compatibility with standards. Users will be running them on different operating systems, with different hardware, and different software and plug-ins. Some users keep JavaScript enabled all the time, others don't; some users block third-party applications or advertisements; some users don't display images; some users send a "Do Not Track" request and some don't; the list goes on and on. There always exists the possibility that a problem lies with a specific configuration.

    Will your system perform properly under every possible configuration that users use to access it (e.g., with different browsers, with JavaScript disabled, with images disabled, etc.)? Does it give proper information on the problem if it is configured incorrectly? Does it provide sensible defaults (or warn the user, depending on the requirements and domain) if a configuration value is missing or invalid? Do certain settings override others in ways that are non-obvious, or cause problems when set in certain combinations?

16. **Accessibility Errors**: Oftentimes, systems will work properly when used by a user using a standard configuration, but not when a user is using a non-standard input or output device. These are often necessary for users who cannot access a system using the standard keyboard-mouse-monitor input/output setup; for example, blind users who use a braille terminal for reading output from their computer. If your software does not work correctly with these systems, then people who depend on them may have no other way to use your software.

    Be sure that you provide multiple methods of input and output, or at a bare minimum can at least accept and output raw text of some sort. Not all users can use a mouse, or can view graphics. Don't assume that the setup that you have will work for everyone who uses the software.

7.2   The List Goes On and On

This chapter is not a complete list of how to break programs and find defects. It's not even a fairly comprehensive list. The fact is, computers do exactly what you tell them to do, and one of the challenges of writing software is telling the computer exactly what to do under all sorts of circumstances. While many of these circumstances are relatively common across programs (such as dealing with missing files or network connectivity), many other errors will be specific to the domain

---

[2] *The Eight Fallacies of Distributed Computing*, https://blogs.oracle.com/jag/resource/Fallacies.html.

you are working in, or the program you are writing. As a tester, you will need to keep an open mind and constantly be thinking of ways in which defects can manifest themselves in the particular program under test.

As you are doing so, remember to keep in mind that you are not the user. You, as a tester of the software, are going to be familiar with the system under test—if not at first, then eventually. In many cases, you will be more technically competent in general than the person using the software. The users are not going to use the software the same way as you do, and things which seem obvious to you will certainly not be obvious to them. It is important to keep in mind the kind of mistakes that the users will make, the kind of input the users will provide, and the kind of output that the user will expect to see.

Chapter 8

A Test Plan Walkthrough

Let's walk through developing a test plan for a given list of requirements for a cat-weighing system called *catweigher* (if you want clever names for programs, this is not the chapter to find them in). This extremely useful program will accept one argument indicating the cat's weight in kilograms, and let us know if the cat is underweight, normal weight, or overweight:

```
$ catweigher 1.7
Cat Weighing System
Cat is underweight

$ catweigher 83
Cat Weighing System
Cat is overweight
```

As the test cases are developed, take note of the trade-offs that are made, and how decisions about which test cases to include are made. Also note how we use the ideas which we explored in earlier chapters—especially in equivalence class partitioning and thinking of failure cases—to make a well-rounded test plan.

8.1 Examining The Requirements

1. *FUN-PARAMETER:* The system shall accept a single parameter, `CATWEIGHT`, which can only be a single positive floating-point value or positive integer. If the parameter is not one of these two kinds of values, or if there is not exactly one parameter, the system shall immediately shut down with only the message "Please enter a valid parameter."

2. *FUN-STARTUP-MESSAGE:* Upon startup, the system shall display "Cat Weighing System" upon the console.

3. *FUN-UNDERWEIGHT:* If `CATWEIGHT` is less than 3 kilograms, then the message "Cat is underweight" shall be displayed upon the console.

4. *FUN-NORMALWEIGHT:* If `CATWEIGHT` is equal to or greater than 3 kilograms and less than 6 kilograms, then "Cat is normal weight" shall be displayed upon the console.

5. *FUN-OVERWEIGHT:* If `CATWEIGHT` is greater than or equal to 6 kilograms, then "Cat is overweight" shall be displayed upon the console.

6. *NF-PERF-TIME:* The system shall display the appropriate message within two seconds of the program being executed.

Although this is a relatively simple program, with only a small set of requirements, there is already some ambiguity. In real-world applications, you can expect much more. This will often necessitate discussions with systems engineers, requirements analysts, and/or customers to resolve the various ambiguities. The particular ambiguity in this case is that in FUN-PARAMETER, it says that the system should immediately shut down with *only* the message "Please enter a valid parameter" if an invalid parameter is entered. The next requirement, FUN-STARTUP-MESSAGE, says that the message "Cat Weighing System" should be displayed upon startup; it does not mention whether or not this includes times when invalid parameters were entered. In other words, should the expected behavior be:

```
$ catweigher meow
Please enter a valid parameter
```

or:

```
$ catweigher meow
Cat Weighing System
Please enter a valid parameter
```

We should determine what the expected behavior is before writing a test plan. This can be done by checking with the appropriate requirements analysts, systems engineers, product owners, or whoever is in charge of requirements. If you are working on a less formal team, the correct path forward may be to make an assumption. However, these assumptions should be noted as part of the test plan! If one must make assumptions, they should at least be delineated clearly somewhere. In general, however, you should avoid making assumptions; you want to know what the expected behavior is as precisely as possible. In this case, let's assume that we went to the project manager (of course *catweigher* has a project manager) and determined that "Cat Weighing System" should not be displayed if the parameter is not valid. In other words, the first string of output is correct.

8.2   Plotting Out the Test Plan

I have found that a top-down approach of the requirements of the program is of the most help in creating a test plan. By a "top-down approach", I mean that a general outline of the test plan will be generated first, and then specific details can be filled in. This contrasts with a "bottom-up approach", where the specific details of small sections are filled in first, and as more and more small details are filled, a larger picture gradually emerges.

Looking at the requirements, I can mentally divide them into three sections:

1. Input (accepting the parameter):
    (a) FUN-PARAMETER
2. Output (displaying messages and results):
    (a) FUN-STARTUP-MESSAGE
    (b) FUN-UNDERWEIGHT
    (c) FUN-NORMALWEIGHT
    (d) FUN-OVERWEIGHT
3. Performance:

(a) NF-PERF-TIME

How did I determine how to sort these out? I looked for requirements which were related to each other and put each in a "cluster". The program you are testing will probably not have these exact same clusters (unless you also happen to be working on a cat-weighing program... in which case, lucky you). For larger programs, these clusters will often revolve around specific features (e.g., shopping cart, item display, and checkout in an online shopping application) or different sub-systems (e.g., user interface, enemy artificial intelligence, and graphics for a video game). There is really no "right answer" as to how to cluster requirements together for testing, and as you understand the system better, the clustering may change. However, by providing a general outline, you can start to get a handle on testing the system holistically.

Looking specifically at the test plan outline we developed here, it is apparent that the second section, Output, has - by far - the most requirements listed. This does not necessarily mean that it will take the longest amount of time to test, or involve the most work. In fact, as FUN-STARTUP-MESSAGE is very simple and unchanging, and the three other requirements involve mathematically pure functions, the tests themselves will probably be relatively easy to write. In real-world instances, some requirements may take orders of magnitude longer to test than others! Performance and security requirements, among others, can be much more difficult to test than the length of their requirements would suggest.

8.3 Filling Out the Test Plan

Let's start with the first section, Input. I notice that there are several possible use cases here:

1. The user enters one valid parameter

2. The user enters no parameters

3. The user enters one parameter, but it is invalid

4. The user enters two parameters (one extra)

5. The user enters many more parameters than

In the last four cases, the expected behavior is the same; the system shuts down and the message "Please enter a valid parameter" is displayed. In the first use case, the system will continue on and have behavior governed by other requirements. You can already see here that it's important to have a view of the entire system, instead of looking at requirements solely in and of themselves. This becomes more and more difficult as the number of requirements grows and the system under test becomes more complex.

Use cases 1, 3, 4, and 5 all have multiple variants which could be tested. There are numerous values for valid parameters, in the first case, which will have different behaviors as enumerated in the other requirements. There are an essentially infinite number of single invalid parameters, anything from negative values, to imaginary numbers, to random strings of any length. For the fourth use case, there could be two valid parameters, or two invalid parameters, or one valid and one invalid. For the fifth use case, the only limit to how many parameters the user can enter is up to the operating system; he or she can enter two, three, four or more. The second use case has no variants; there are no different ways to enter no parameters; there are no different flavors of null.

Depending on the importance of the cat-weighing program, we can decide if we want to test all possible use cases, and how many variants of the particular use case we want to test. At a bare minimum, you probably want to test the happy path, that is, the expected use case that a user will follow, which in our case is the user entering one valid parameter. Since users often forget the

format of arguments, we should also check for invalid input with the correct number of arguments.
We will probably also want to test the boundary values around the proper number of arguments,
since those will be the most common failure mode for this requirement. Users may forget to enter
an argument, or they may type on extra one in. Less often, the user may think that many more
arguments are required. All of these cases besides the happy path can be considered failure cases,
since the expected behavior is to cease execution as an invalid value or set of values has been entered:

```
IDENTIFIER: VALID-PARAMETER-TEST
TEST CASE: Run the program with a valid parameter.
PRECONDITIONS: None
INPUT VALUES: 5
EXECUTION STEPS: At the command line, run "catweigher 5"
OUTPUT VALUES: N/A
POSTCONDITIONS: The program exits and displays normal output for a 5 kilogram cat.
    The program does not display "Please enter a valid parameter".
```

The FUN-PARAMETER requirement has four failure cases which I'd also like to add tests for.
These are outside the happy path, as they indicate that the user is not using the program correctly.
However, in such cases, we still need to ensure that the system is following the requirements. Let's
add additional test cases for the three failure modes:

```
IDENTIFIER: INVALID-PARAMETER-TEST
TEST CASE: Run the program with an invalid parameter.
PRECONDITIONS: None
INPUT VALUES: "dog"
EXECUTION STEPS: At the command line, run "catweigher dog"
OUTPUT VALUES: N/A
POSTCONDITIONS: The program displays "Please enter a valid parameter" and exits
    without further output.


IDENTIFIER: NO-PARAMETER-TEST
TEST CASE: Run the program without passing in a parameter.
PRECONDITIONS: None
INPUT VALUES: None
EXECUTION STEPS: At the command line, run "catweigher"
OUTPUT VALUES: N/A
POSTCONDITIONS: The program displays "Please enter a valid parameter" and exits
    without further output.


IDENTIFIER: TWO-PARAMETERS-TEST
TEST CASE: Run the program with two parameters).
PRECONDITIONS: None
INPUT VALUES: 1 2
EXECUTION STEPS: At the command line, run "catweigher 1 2"
OUTPUT VALUES: N/A
POSTCONDITIONS: The program displays "Please enter a valid parameter" and exits
    without further output.


IDENTIFIER: TOO-MANY-PARAMETERS-TEST
TEST CASE: Run the program with too many parameters (specifically, four parameters).
PRECONDITIONS: None
INPUT VALUES: 5 6 7 8
EXECUTION STEPS: At the command line, run "catweigher 5 6 7 8"
```

OUTPUT VALUES: N/A
POSTCONDITIONS: The program displays "Please enter a valid parameter" and exits
    without further output.

At this point, there's a reasonable amount of test coverage for this requirement. On to the next one, FUN-STARTUP-MESSAGE, which it turns out is very simple to test. There are two possibilities—that the system has been passed in a set of valid parameters, and that it was not passed in a set of valid parameters. In the first case, the startup message should be displayed; in the second case, it should not, as we determined by resolving the ambiguity in the message requirements earlier:

IDENTIFIER: STARTUP-NO-MESSAGE-TEST
TEST CASE: Run the program without passing in a parameter,
    startup message should not appear.
PRECONDITIONS: None
INPUT VALUES: None
EXECUTION STEPS: At the command line, run "catweigher"
OUTPUT VALUES: N/A
POSTCONDITIONS: The program does not display the message "Cat Weighing System"
    upon the console before exiting.

IDENTIFIER: STARTUP-MESSAGE-TEST
TEST CASE: Run the program passing in a valid parameter,
    startup message should appear.
PRECONDITIONS: None
INPUT VALUES: 5
EXECUTION STEPS: At the command line, run "catweigher 5"
OUTPUT VALUES: N/A
POSTCONDITIONS: The program displays the message "Cat Weighing System"
    upon the console before displaying the cat's weight status.

We now have both possibilities covered. Note that the postconditions focus on the specific aspect of output to be tested, instead of checking all of the output. For example, STARTUP-MESSAGE-TEST only checks that the message is displayed, instead of what the specific weight status of a 5-kilogram cat would be. Although it seems like a minor issue to include more detail—and might even catch a defect or two—this could lead us down a rathole in more complex programs. Imagine if we decide to change the definition of "overweight" in the future. If you think this is far-fetched, it has already happened for humans, at least in the United States. In 1998, tens of millions of people suddenly became "overweight" due to the National Institutes of Health's redefinition of the term.[1] How easy this would be to happen to our poor cats as well! If it did, we would have to go through all of our tests one by one, ensuring that even unrelated tests did not accidentally depend upon the old weight status definitions. By keeping our tests focused on the specific expected behavior, we ensure that our test suite does not become fragile.

It would be simple to add more edge cases, such as additional invalid and valid inputs, running on different operating systems, running with other programs in the background... the list goes on and on. However, discretion is the better part of valor. Spending too much time on a simple requirement like this would in all likelihood be a suboptimal use of resources. Of course, there is always the chance that displaying a message is of the utmost importance, such as a legal requirement or safety notice. In such cases, obviously more attention would be focused on it. While this may seem like I am avoiding giving clear rules for how much emphasis to place on each requirement, the point I

---

[1]For more information, you can read the CNN news story at http://www.cnn.com/HEALTH/9806/17/weight. guidelines/, or see the original NIH paper, *Clinical Guidelines on the Identification, Evaluation, and Treatment of Overweight and Obesity in Adults* at http://www.ncbi.nlm.nih.gov/books/NBK2003/.

want to get across is that there are no clear rules. As a tester, you will have to decide how much to focus on each requirement, subsystem, feature, or other aspect of the system under test. This will vary based on domain and the particular software project, and you may get it wrong. I can provide examples and heuristics, but no book can replace the grey matter between your ears.

8.4   Determining Focus

Let's move on to the three weight requirements: FUN-UNDERWEIGHT, FUN-NORMALWEIGHT, and FUN-OVERWEIGHT. This seems like a perfect time to partition the inputs and outputs into equivalence classes, as explained earlier:

- < 3 kg → Underweight
- >= 3 kg and < 6 kg → Normal Weight
- >= 6 kg → Overweight

Let's assume that cats are weighed in increments of one-tenth of a kilogram. This can be verified by discussing with the systems engineers or other appropriate stakeholders. We can select the explicit boundary values: 2.9, 3.0, 5.9, and 6.0 kg. Now let's add an interior value from each equivalence class: 1.6 kg for Underweight, 5.0 kg for Normal Weight, and 10 kg for Overweight. We'll also want to add in implicit boundary values, say 0 and 1,000. This final value assumes that 1,000 kilograms is the theoretical upper bound for a cat before it collapses into a black hole, which is my understanding of physics (note that the author is not a physicist). Finally, let's check some corner cases: a negative number (-13) and a non-numeric string (quackadoodle_doo). Note how much more emphasis is put on determining a variety of input values for these requirements compared to the startup message. Since determining the weight status of the cat is the core of this application, more testing emphasis is given to it:

```
IDENTIFIER: UNDERWEIGHT-INTERNAL
TEST CASE: Run the program passing in an underweight cat with a weight of 1.6 kg.
PRECONDITIONS: None
INPUT VALUES: 1.6
EXECUTION STEPS: At the command line, run "catweigher 1.6"
OUTPUT VALUES: N/A
POSTCONDITIONS: The console shall display "Cat is underweight".


IDENTIFIER: UNDERWEIGHT-LOWER-BOUNDARY
TEST CASE: Run the program passing in a weightless cat with a weight of 0 kg.
PRECONDITIONS: None
INPUT VALUES: 0
EXECUTION STEPS: At the command line, run "catweigher 0"
OUTPUT VALUES: N/A
POSTCONDITIONS: The console shall display "Cat is underweight".


IDENTIFIER: UNDERWEIGHT-UPPER-BOUNDARY
TEST CASE: Run the program passing in an underweight cat with a weight of 2.9 kg.
PRECONDITIONS: None
INPUT VALUES: 2.9
EXECUTION STEPS: At the command line, run "catweigher 2.9"
OUTPUT VALUES: N/A
POSTCONDITIONS: The console shall display "Cat is underweight".
```

IDENTIFIER: NORMALWEIGHT-INTERNAL
TEST CASE: Run the program passing in a normal weight cat with a weight of 5 kg.
PRECONDITIONS: None
INPUT VALUES: 5
EXECUTION STEPS: At the command line, run "catweigher 5"
OUTPUT VALUES: N/A
POSTCONDITIONS: The console shall display "Cat is normal weight".

IDENTIFIER: NORMALWEIGHT-LOWER-BOUNDARY
TEST CASE: Run the program passing in a normal weight cat with a weight of 3 kg.
PRECONDITIONS: None
INPUT VALUES: 3
EXECUTION STEPS: At the command line, run "catweigher 3"
OUTPUT VALUES: N/A
POSTCONDITIONS: The console shall display "Cat is normal weight".

IDENTIFIER: NORMALWEIGHT-UPPER-BOUNDARY
TEST CASE: Run the program passing in a normal weight cat with a weight of 5.9 kg.
PRECONDITIONS: None
INPUT VALUES: 5.9
EXECUTION STEPS: At the command line, run "catweigher 5.9"
OUTPUT VALUES: N/A
POSTCONDITIONS: The console shall display "Cat is normal weight".

IDENTIFIER: OVERWEIGHT-INTERNAL
TEST CASE: Run the program passing in an overweight cat with a weight of 10 kg.
PRECONDITIONS: None
INPUT VALUES: 10
EXECUTION STEPS: At the command line, run "catweigher 10"
OUTPUT VALUES: N/A
POSTCONDITIONS: The console shall display "Cat is overweight".

IDENTIFIER: OVERWEIGHT-LOWER-BOUNDARY
TEST CASE: Run the program passing in an overweight cat with a weight of 6 kg.
PRECONDITIONS: None
INPUT VALUES: 6
EXECUTION STEPS: At the command line, run "catweigher 6"
OUTPUT VALUES: N/A
POSTCONDITIONS: The console shall display "Cat is overweight".

IDENTIFIER: OVERWEIGHT-UPPER-BOUNDARY
TEST CASE: Run the program passing in an overweight cat with a weight of 1000 kg.
PRECONDITIONS: None
INPUT VALUES: 1000
EXECUTION STEPS: At the command line, run "catweigher 1000"
OUTPUT VALUES: N/A
POSTCONDITIONS: The console shall display "Cat is overweight".

IDENTIFIER: WEIGHTSTATUS-INVALID-NEGATIVE
TEST CASE: Run the program passing in an invalid negative weight cat of -13 kg.

```
PRECONDITIONS: None
INPUT VALUES: -13
EXECUTION STEPS: At the command line, run "catweigher -13"
OUTPUT VALUES: N/A
POSTCONDITIONS: The system shall not display any cat weight status,
    and the program will exit.

IDENTIFIER: WEIGHTSTATUS-INVALID-STRING
TEST CASE: Run the program passing in an invalid string argument.
PRECONDITIONS: None
INPUT VALUES: "quackadoodle_doo"
EXECUTION STEPS: At the command line, run "catweigher quackadoodle_doo"
OUTPUT VALUES: N/A
POSTCONDITIONS: The system shall not display any cat weight status,
    and the program will exit.
```

This can seem like a quite a bit of typing for the tests and their relative importance! Remember, though, that the amount of documentation required will vary based on your company, legal requirements of the system under test, etc. While this is a relatively in-depth test plan, a plucky start-up may have a simple paragraph listing of various inputs to try and no formally expected behavior of the software. The onus may be on the tester to realize what is the proper behavior. While this is going to put more work and require more mental effort on the part of the tester, as well as be ripe for human error to occur, the trade-off is that the test plan will be much more flexible and quick to develop. In software testing, as in all software engineering, there are very few "absolutely right" answers, just selecting the correct trade-offs.

There is also some overlap between the last two test cases (WEIGHTSTATUS-INVALID-NEGATIVE and WEIGHTSTATUS-INVALID-STRING) and the previous test cases checking the requirement FUN-PARAMETER. Although they are looking at slightly different aspects of the system, they are doing it through the same black-box methodology. An argument could definitely be made that they are unnecessary, although white-box testing might show that different parts of the system are tested by each of the various test cases.

Depending on the culture of the company and what is expected from the test plan documentation, we could compress the test cases so that each test case describes multiple values. While I don't recommend this process—it's relatively easy to copy and paste, and having more test cases allows them to be more specific —it does save time when writing. It also allows each test case to cover more "territory", but adds an additional step to determining where the problem lies if a test case is seen to fail. Caveats aside, let's show an example of compressing the three "underweight" test cases into one:

```
IDENTIFIER: UNDERWEIGHT-INTERNAL
TEST CASE: Run the program passing in values that mark the cat as underweight.
PRECONDITIONS: None
INPUT VALUES: 0, 1.6, 2.9
EXECUTION STEPS: At the command line, run "catweigher n", where n is equal
    to one of the input values.
OUTPUT VALUES: N/A
POSTCONDITIONS: For each of the input values, the string "Cat is underweight"
    shall be displayed upon the console.
```

8.5 Test Cases for a Non-Functional Requirement

There's an entire chapter on performance testing later, but for now, let's just go through a very simple performance test. We want to check that the system completes calculation and information display within two seconds. An easy way to verify this is by using the Unix tool `time`, which will tell you how long it took for a command to execute. Although the standard tool will give you several different results, focus only on the "real" time which measures how long something actually took according to the clock on the wall (the other kinds of time that the tool measures will be discussed in the chapter on performance testing).

We want to check that various values will all be calculated and the program exited within 2 seconds. Several values are tested, in case calculations for one equivalence class are much more time-consuming than others:

```
IDENTIFIER: PERFORMANCE-RUNTIME
TEST CASE: Run the program passing in various values and time it, ensuring
     each iteration takes less than two seconds.
PRECONDITIONS: Program has no known functional defects
INPUT VALUES: 0, 1.5, 5, 7.5, 10
EXECUTION STEPS: At the command line, run "time catweigher n", where n is equal
     to one of the input values.
OUTPUT VALUES: N/A
POSTCONDITIONS: For each of the input values, the real time measurement as
     measured by the time command will be less than 2.000 seconds.
```

Note the addition of a precondition here. This test case will not be considered valid unless all of the functional defects have already been fixed. After all, it does not matter how long a program takes to run if it won't give you the correct cat weight status! This does not mean that the test case cannot be executed ahead of time, but that the results should not be considered valid unless the software is functionally correct. This is one of the big problems with performance testing; it is often difficult to do until the program is functionally complete, or at least close to it.

Chapter 9

Defects

We've spent quite a bit of time up to this point learning how to find defects. This makes sense, since one of the key goals of testing is to do exactly that. However, we have not yet completely defined what a defect is or discussed what to do about them once they are found.

9.1   What is a Defect?

A defect is any sort of error in a program which causes the system under test to do one of the following:

1. Not meet the specified requirements (functional or non-functional)

2. Return an incorrect result

3. Stop execution unexpectedly (system stability is an implicit requirement in all systems under test)

The most obvious kind of defect is a system failing to meet requirements. If the requirements state that the program should do something, and the program does not do it, then that is a defect. As discussed in the chapter on requirements, though, anything written in natural language is bound to have some ambiguities. The developer who implemented the feature may have had a different understanding of what the requirement actually meant than the tester.

An example of a system returning an incorrect result would be a spreadsheet program showing that the value of 2 + 3 is 23, or a drawing program where every time the user clicks on the color red, the drawing tool starts drawing in blue. These may or may not be specified by the requirements (and thus may or may not overlap with the first kind of defect).

The last kind of defect is one common to all programs—a program should not cease execution ("die") unexpectedly. That is, if the intent of the user or the original writer or installer of the program is that the system should be running at some point in time, that program should be running at that point in time.

Software may "shut down hard" without it necessarily being a defect. For example, sending a SIGKILL (via `kill -9` or a similar command) to a Unix process causes the program to cease execution without running any of its shutdown routines. However, it did not die unexpectedly— the user wanted it to do so and even sent it a message telling it to do exactly that! The reason that the user had to send a SIGKILL to the process may be a defect, but the fact that it stopped running under these circumstances is not a defect. If the system dies due to a segmentation fault, an untrapped division by zero, or dereferencing a null pointer, these are all considered defects. They should never happen in a program, even if the requirements do not specify that "the program shall run without any null pointer exceptions".

Finally, note that the word "**bug**" is often used interchangeably with the word "defect". They mean exactly the same thing, but "bug" is much more colloquial. In this book, the word "defect" will be used, except in those cases where the author forgot to do so.

9.2   The Defect Life Cycle

Upon discovering a defect, the tester (or whoever else finds the defect) should **report** it. Reporting may have different meanings depending on the organization and the severity of the defect. At its root, it means that the specifics of the defect should be marked down in a location where it can be reviewed in the future, by stakeholders of the project—other testers, developers, management, etc. In most cases, teams will have some sort of defect-tracking software, but defect reporting could be as simple as marking down the error with old-fashioned pen and paper.

When testing software, it is important to keep track of as much information as is practical, for a variety of reasons. The first is that the more information is available, the more likely it will be that the defect is reproducible. Imagine that you have a system failing only when certain environment variables are set, but you don't specify that in the defect report. When the developer assigned to fix the defect goes to work on it, they may just mark it as "works for me", since the system worked as designed no matter what the developer did. Without knowing about those environment variables, there's no way for the reproduction of the defect to take place.

On the other hand, it's possible to take this too far. There is usually no need to mark down every process running on the system whenever a typo is discovered. Exactly how much to write down for a defect will vary based on the defect and domain in which you are working. However, there are certain pieces of data which are useful in many cases. The following section will outline a defect template so that these items are not forgotten. By reminding the filer of the defect to include certain information, the filer is much more likely to not miss any important steps or information, thus minimizing superfluous communication about the defect in the process of fixing it. Checklists and templates like this are extremely powerful tools for situations where the costs of failing to do something are high.

When a defect is reported, its life is just beginning. Just as software development as a whole has a "software development life cycle"—going from requirements, to design, etc., all the way to maintenance, support, and eventual "end-of-life"-ing of the software—defects also have a "defect life cycle". The defect life cycle is as follows:

1. Discovery

2. Reporting

3. Triage / Assignment

4. Fixing

5. Verification

When a tester or other user first encounters and recognizes a defect, this is the "Discovery" stage. In some cases, nothing can happen after this—the user ignores the defect or decides that it's not worth investigating further. However, for a professional tester, this should not be the case—the job of a tester is to determine the quality of the software, and this includes finding and reporting defects.

The second stage is filing the defect, usually in some sort of standardized way. This involves spending some time and figuring out exactly what the tester did to expose the issue, what was expected to happen, and what was observed to happen. Remember that the role of the tester is to discover the issue and how to reproduce it, not to figure out the root cause of the problem in the code. This can be done—and often is, depending on the technical knowledge of the tester—but it is not the primary role. If a tester looks too deeply into the codebase, he or she may be tempted to write what needs to be done to fix the defect as opposed to focusing on what the defect actually is. Remember, similar to requirements, a defect should be focused on *what* is wrong, not *how* to fix it.

After a defect is filed, somebody must determine whether or not to spend resources to fix it, and if so, how to prioritize what may be a large number of defects. This is called **triaging**. The word "triage" comes from a medical term for prioritizing the order that patients should be treated based on how badly they've been wounded or how ill they are. It is often done when there are large numbers of casualties at once, too many for medical personnel to take care of all of them. For instance, after a major natural disaster, a hospital may be overrun with patients, some of whom have minor injuries, others with serious injuries, and some who are critically wounded and unable to be saved. In such cases, the hospital may triage the incoming patients and immediately treat those with serious but treatable wounds, but deprioritize working on those with minor injuries and those whom they are unlikely to be able to heal no matter what they do.

Although a dramatic triage like this is rare in the medical world, in the software development world it is extremely common. There are usually far more defects known than the developers have time to fix. Relevant stakeholders decide which defects can be fixed given the amount of resources available, and prioritize according to how quickly they can be fixed and how much pain they are causing to users of the software. In some organizations, developers are responsible for choosing which defects to work on, determining for themselves which will be easiest to fix and resolve the most pain for the users of the software. This kind of system works best when the developers deeply understand the needs of the user, for example when the project is itself a software development tool which they are users of.

After the defect is assigned to a developer or group of developers to work on, the developer fixes it. Oftentimes, an automated test will be added to cover the case where the defect occurred, so as to avoid it happening again in the future. As the developer is very close to the software being written, however, the final determination on whether or not a defect has been fixed is not up to them. In the same way that a person has trouble seeing typos in a paper that they have written themselves, a developer may not see that a different error was introduced by the fix, or that some edge cases were not covered. Mandatory code reviews can help ameliorate this somewhat, but usually a tester is used for the final verification that a defect has been fixed. Since one of the key aspects of a tester's job is to be an independent observer of the quality of the software, they can provide a more objective and unbiased determination of whether or not the defect has been fixed appropriately.

Thus, after the defect has been fixed, the software should be returned to the test team to verify that it has been fixed. The developer or developers may not have tested all the different edge cases, or they may have caused other issues with their fix. The tester can independently verify that the fix did indeed resolve the defect without causing other defects in the process. In some cases, of course, other defects may arise, especially if the first one was occluding others. For example, if there is a typo in the "welcome" page which appears after login, but a defect has prevented users from logging in, the tester should still verify a fix that allows users to log in. The fact that there is a typo on the welcome page has been exposed by the ability to log in, but it is not related. Even a defect which causes related defects may sometimes be verified. Continuing the example of a login not working, if a fix comes in that allows users to log in, but never checks the password, this may be seen as an improvement and a second defect filed for the password issue.

9.3   A Standardized Defect Template

This is not an industry standard defect reporting template, but I have found it to be very useful. It ensures that all of the major aspects of a defect, once found, have been reported. By acting as a kind of checklist for what to put down for a defect, it helps to ensure that a tester will not forget anything (that big blank space after a line has a way of showing up in most people's visual fields). Note that although there is no identifier specifically listed here, it will often be automatically added by whatever defect tracking software you are using. If you are not using defect tracking software, and don't want to, then you can add an IDENTIFIER field.

Without further ado, here is the template:

```
SUMMARY:
DESCRIPTION:
REPRODUCTION STEPS:
EXPECTED BEHAVIOR:
OBSERVED BEHAVIOR:
IMPACT:
SEVERITY:
WORKAROUND:
NOTES:
```

9.3.1   Summary

The **summary** is a one sentence or so summary of the defect found. It's useful when people are scrolling through long lists of defects, or to make sure that people understand the gist of the defect. Some examples of good summaries would be:

1. Page background is red, should be blue

2. In-app calculator displays -1 for result of sqrt(-1)

3. System exits with SEGFAULT error when user selected

4. Adding three or more items to a cart at the same time clears out other items

All of these describe the problem succinctly but precisely, with only enough detail to indicate the problem. Superfluous commentary does not belong in this section. Remember that the summary will often be glanced at along with perhaps hundreds of other defect summaries, especially if you are presenting to management. There is a reason why most books written today have snappy titles, as opposed to titles such as *The Egg, Or The Memoirs Of Gregory Giddy, Esq: With The Lucubrations Of Messrs. Francis Flimsy, Frederick Florid, And Ben Bombast. To Which Are Added, The Private Opinions Of Patty Pout, Lucy Luscious, And Priscilla Positive. Also The Memoirs Of A Right Honourable Puppy. Conceived By A Celebrated Hen, And Laid Before The Public By A Famous Cock-Feeder.* Yes, that is a real book, written by an anonymous author and published in 1772.

You should be very careful not to overgeneralize in this section. If the user cannot search on one particular page, then do not mark the summary as "Search is broken". If one calculation reliably gives an incorrect answer, do not describe the defect as "Math is not working". Before filing the defect, try to figure out how far the problem extends.

9.3.2   Description

In the description, the defect is described in more detail. The goal is to allow an in-depth under-standing of what the issue and why the behavior is, in fact, a defect. This is usually a few sentences long, although if the defect is more complicated or requires expository information to understand, it may be longer.

In this section, you can also go more into detail about the boundaries of the issue than in the summary. For example, you may have noted in the summary that "Taxes not calculated correctly with items which cost over $100.00". In the description, you can note that you tested this with items costing $100.01, $200.00, and $1000.00, and in each case taxes were less than half of what they were supposed to be. This will allow others to know what was tried and have a better idea of the boundaries of the defect.

9.3.3   Reproduction Steps

Remember that once you have found a defect, that somebody is probably going to try to fix it. It may be you, or it may be somebody else, but the first step to fixing something is being able to reproduce it. The **reproduction steps** are the specific steps that one must take in order for the defect to manifest itself.

When someone brings a problem to a developer to be fixed, the order of operations is as follows:

1. The developer attempts to replicate defect.

2. If the developer cannot replicate the defect, they will write on the defect report that "it works on my machine" and stop working on defect.

3. Otherwise, the developer will write some code hoping to fix it.

4. The developer replicates the reproduction steps that caused defect.

5. The tester notes on the defect report whether or not the defect has been fixed. If not, the process goes back to step 3.

You will notice that there is a bit of a premature exit at line 2 if the developer cannot replicate the defect. You will also note the first appearance of the bane of many testers, the excuse that "it works on my machine!" Development and production machines are often very different—in installed programs, libraries, perhaps even operating systems. A defect appearing in production or in a test environment but not a developer's system is a very real and very common problem. Just as often, though, the tester has simply not specified the reproduction steps as precisely as possible. As a tester, you can help minimize the problem of hearing "it works on my machine!" by writing down reproduction steps in a detailed and unambiguous way.

This includes writing down any relevant steps and preconditions before the actual steps which directly caused the defect to occur. For example, if a certain environment variable needs to be set before starting the program, or a particular garbage collection flag was passed in, or even that the system was running for six hours before the particular test steps occurred. Determining what is and is not relevant is a difficult process. As you gain experience testing projects in your particular domain, and understand the system under test more, you will be able to use your testing "sixth sense" to determine this. Before you have hit that point, it usually makes sense to err on the side of "too much information" rather than too little.

It is imperative to write down specific values and steps, especially if there is more than one way to do things. Never write that one should "Enter an invalid value"; instead, write that one should "Enter -6 once the > prompt appears." Note that in the latter example, the tester is providing a specific instance of an invalid value, as well as saying where and when it should be entered. Just like when writing test cases, you should imagine that the person executing these is an automaton with a general understanding of the system. Tell that automaton exactly what to do and remove as much ambiguity as is possible.

9.3.4 Expected Behavior

The core concept behind testing, and one which we will refer to again and again throughout this book, is checking that the expected behavior of a system matches the observed behavior. It makes little sense to test something if you don't know what should happen. In the **expected behavior** field, the tester should note what the system was expected to do after the execution steps are executed.

Once again, the more specific the behavior listed, the easier it will be for developers and other testers to reproduce the issue, and eventually fix it. One should never write down that "the system should return the correct value"; instead, write that the "the system should return 6".

Aside from saving people from calculating the correct value themselves, another benefit of writing down the expected behavior so precisely is that the tester or test case may not be expecting the correct behavior! In this case, someone can view the defect and determine that it's actually invalid— the software is performing as intended. This can happen when the requirements are ambiguous or the reporting tester simply makes a mistake.

9.3.5 Observed Behavior

Opposed to the expected behavior field is the **observed behavior** field. This describes what actually happened after the execution steps were executed. Just as in all of the fields of the defect report template, this should be filled in as precisely as possible. If necessary, some detail should be added explaining why it is different from the expected behavior (for example, if it is a long string with only a single letter in the middle modified).

9.3.6 Impact

The tester should have some idea of what impact this will have on the user base. In the **Impact** field, this can be specified.

Be careful not to overgeneralize or editorialize in this section. Let's say that a video game background color changes from blue to purple when the player jumps. A factual way of describing the impact is that "User will see background color change, but gameplay is unaffected." An editorialized version would be "User will hate this game and everybody who made it, because the stupid background becomes a stupid color when the stupid user does something stupid." In general, if you find yourself using the word "stupid" or other derogatory words in your defect reports, there is probably a better way to express the issue.

Keep in mind that, when possible, this should note what the impact is on the user base as a whole, not just a particular user. For example, if a problem occurs on all browsers, that will make it more serious than the same problem which only affects users of one particular browser. If a defect only happens to power users editing system configuration files, then it is probably of less importance than if it happens mostly to new users of a system. The power users are more likely to be accepting of problems resulting from their modifications than new users. By indicating how the defect impacts the user base, the defect can be more effectively triaged.

9.3.7 Severity

Related to the Impact field is the **Severity** field, which contains the defect reporter's initial impression of how severe the issue is. This can either be explained qualitatively (e.g., "this is really, really, bad. Really, really, really bad." or "This isn't much of an issue, to be honest") or a standardized scale can be used in order to be more quantitative. The latter is far more popular, but will usually vary from organization to organization. It may be something as simple as a numeric scale, with "1" being a very minor issue and "10" being an absolute showstopper. However, oftentimes there will be gradations with descriptors.

An example rating system is explained below:

1. **Blocker**: This is a defect so severe that the system cannot reasonably be released without either fixing it or devising a workaround. Examples of blocker defects would be the system not allowing any user to log in, or a system that crashes whenever somebody presses the "A" key.

2. **Critical**: Although the system could still be released with a defect of this magnitude, it severely impacts the core functionality of the program or makes it almost unusable. Alternatively, a defect that normally would be marked as a blocker, but that has some sort of workaround, could be classified as critical.

3. **Major**: This is a defect which causes a relatively severe problem, although not so severe as to entirely hobble a system. It has a good chance of being noticed by any user using the feature where the defect exists.

4. **Normal**: This is a defect which inconveniences the user, or a more severe defect with an easy and straightforward workaround.

5. **Minor**: The defect might or might not be noticed, but does not cause much issue for the user, or has a simple and straightforward workaround.

6. **Trivial**: The defect would probably not even be noticed, unless someone is looking specifically for it. An example would be a small typo, such as a transposition of letters, in a large block of text.

7. **Enhancement**: Sometimes a defect isn't really a defect; it's something that the users want, but is not specified by the requirements or is otherwise not in the scope of the current project. In such a case, the defect can be filed as an enhancement. Alternatively, a tester may think that a problem is a defect, but management may overrule them and mark it as an enhancement.

Grading the severity of defects is often more of an art than a science, although there are some heuristics for determining how severe an issue is. Depending on the domain of software in which the tester is working, as well as the organization's own rules for testing, the severity of a defect may be marked dramatically differently. Even within organizations, there can be conflicts between engineers, managers, testers, and other stakeholders on exactly how severe a defect is.

Severity should not be mistaken for priority. Severity is how severe the problem is, whereas priority marks what order the organization would like to see the problem fixed. For example, a typo on the home page of a web application is of low severity, as it does not impact the functionality of the software. However, it reflects poorly on the company that created it, and will require only a modicum of developer time to fix. In such a case, its priority would be very high. Alternatively, a defect could of low priority, but high severity. An example would be a serious performance issue with database reads, where they are so slow that it makes the system completely unusable to the user after a half-hour of work. This is a very severe problem. However, if fixing it will be a very time-consuming process, and database optimization is already planned for later in the project, it may be of low priority. With all else being equal, though, defects of a higher severity are usually of higher priority than ones of a lower severity.

9.3.8 Workaround

The **workaround** field describes how the defect can be avoided, or at least ameliorated. Assuming a defect where special characters don't work in passwords, the workaround is to only use alphanumeric characters in passwords. It is important to note that workarounds are not always *good* workarounds; they may involve not using certain functionality. For example, if the word count feature of an editor is not working, the workaround may be to not use word count, or to use a different program (e.g., `wc -w` in Unix systems). This may cause the user some distress or inconvenience, but it does allow the functionality to be accessed.

In some cases, there may not be any sort of workaround, or at least not a known one. If the system is crashing at seemingly nondeterministic times, it would be impossible to list a workaround except the trivial case of "don't use the software". This is generally not accepted as a workaround. This does not mean that a workaround does not exist, only that one is not known; there may be a setting or input value which is causing the issue, but the testing team just has not uncovered it. If no user can log in to a web application, or the server refuses to start, or a system consistently gives wrong results to every query, then there may be no workaround, as the system is entirely unusable. In such cases, the severity of the defect is inevitably BLOCKER or its equivalent.

9.3.9 Notes

I like to think of this field as the "miscellaneous" field. It's where everything which might be useful for tracking down a defect, or that may or may not be relevant, goes. It is also a good place for putting data which is too long to fit in any of the other sections, which should be relatively short and easy to grasp for developers, managers, other testers, and anyone else who may have to look at this defect and try to understand it, but may not be as familiar with that section of the software as the original tester.

What exactly goes here will vary by the type of software you are testing, but it will usually be technical details of the program or its environment, or factors which may or may not be relevant. Some examples include:

1. Stack traces

2. Copies of relevant sections of the program log

3. System or environment variables

4. Technical specifications of the system where the defect was discovered (e.g., operating system, CPU, amount of RAM, etc.)

5. Other applications running on the computer at the same time

6. Particular settings, flags, or arguments passed into the program

7. Suspicious or notable behavior of other programs

8. Copied error message text

9.4   Exceptions to the Template

For some defects, fields may be intentionally left blank. For example, the defect may be relatively simple and not include any extra detail, so the Notes field may be marked "N/A". In many cases where the expected behavior is obvious, this field can also be marked "N/A"; if the Observed Behavior is "System crashes", it would be obvious to most reviewers that the Expected Behavior is "System does not crash." As a best practice, it's better to write "N/A", "None" or some other signifier, so that others who look at the defect report are not under the impression that the tester just forgot to fill in some fields.

In other cases, the field may be marked by "Unknown" or a similar marker that indicates that the filer of the defect does not know what the field should be. For example, if the system crashed randomly, with no error message or other output, and the tester is unable to reproduce it, the Reproduction Steps field may be marked "Unknown". If requirements are ambiguous or contradictory, the expected behavior field may be marked "Unknown". If the tester is not sure what impact the defect would have on the end user, e.g., because the problem is deep in the infrastructure of the system, the Impact field may be marked "Unknown".

Depending on how much focus is spent on testing in an organization, some of the fields may be omitted, or some added. For example, in some organizations, testers may not have the domain knowledge to be able to determine the impact or severity of a defect. At a minimum, any defect report should include reproduction steps, the expected behavior, and the observed behavior. Anything beyond that is the icing on the defect cake.

9.5   Defect Examples

In this section, several examples of defects will be provided.

Note that a defect report provides a description of the defect, not what should be done to fix it. In the first example, there are numerous ways that the defect could be resolved—the default error message for an HTTP 500 Internal Server Error screen may be changed to include a message such as "Press the back button to retry", or a null check could be added to the code so that the exception is never thrown, or additional error handling could occur inside the exception handler. From the point of view of someone filing a defect, it doesn't matter; the problem is that the defect exists, and it is the job of the filer to report it accurately, not to say how it should be fixed. This is similar to writing requirements, which are supposed to say what should be done, not how to do it.

- SUMMARY: Site returns 500 error when username is blank
- DESCRIPTION:

   When a user attempts to log in and fills in a password, but does not fill in a username, the system returns a 500 error page (see NOTES section for text of page).

   This was attempted with numerous passwords. It does not occur if no password is filled in.

- REPRODUCTION STEPS:

   Preconditions: User is not logged in

   1. Using any web browser, navigate to root page of app

   2. In the text box labeled "Password", type `foo`

   3. Ensure that the text box labeled "Username" is blank

4. Click the "Login" button

- EXPECTED BEHAVIOR:

User sees error page with "Please fill in both username and password" message

- OBSERVED BEHAVIOR:

User sees 500 error.

- IMPACT:

A user who forgets to type in their username, but does type in the password, will not see the expected error page.

- SEVERITY:

Normal—This is an edge case, but the user may not know to hit the back button to retry logging in.

- WORKAROUND:

Ensure username field is not blank when logging in.

- NOTES:

The text of the page shown is:

`500 Internal Server Error`

`We're sorry, something went wrong.  Please try again later.`

The server logs report the following error:

`Caught NullPointerException in LoginProcedure, Line 38`

- SUMMARY: "Invisible wall" on level 12 of Amazing Bulgarian Plumber

- DESCRIPTION:

On level 12, three blocks to the right from the first Anaconda Plant, there are three blocks stacked on top of each other. However, they are the same color as the background and thus invisible to the user. Per the requirements, there should be no invisible obstacles for players of the game.

- REPRODUCTION STEPS:

1. Start on level 12

2. Go to the right three screens

3. Jump over Anaconda Plant

4. Move three blocks to the right

5. Attempt to move one further block to the right

- EXPECTED BEHAVIOR:

Player can move onto block

- OBSERVED BEHAVIOR:

Player cannot move, as invisible blocks are in the way

- IMPACT:

  Player of game may be confused by inability to move

- SEVERITY:

  MAJOR—This is specifically called out by the requirements, and is quite annoying to the player of the game.

- WORKAROUND:

  Jump over invisible blocks, once you know that they are there

- NOTES:

  None

- SUMMARY: Users cannot log in to system

- DESCRIPTION:

  When attempting to log in to the system with all user and administrator accounts, the same error message is given: "Login failed, perhaps you mistyped your password?"

- REPRODUCTION STEPS:

  1. Go to login page of system

  2. Type `TestUser1` in "Username" text box

  3. Type the password for TestUser1 in "Password" text box

  4. Click the "Login" button

- EXPECTED BEHAVIOR:

  Welcome page is shown

- OBSERVED BEHAVIOR:

  Error message is displayed "Login failed, perhaps you mistyped your password?"

- IMPACT:

  No users will be able to use the system

- SEVERITY:

  BLOCKER—As it is, the system is unusable to all users.

- WORKAROUND:

  None

- NOTES:

  If you do not know the password for TestUser1, please see the QA Lead.

  The logs do not show any unusual messages when attempting to log in.

Chapter 10

Smoke And Acceptance Testing

10.1 Smoke Testing

My father is a plumber. Before connecting the pipes in a new building to the water main, he sends smoke through the pipes, and looks around to see if any smoke has escaped from the pipes into the building. Why does he do this? Well, if there are any leaks, it's much easier to clean up smoke (since you just let it dissipate) than water. It's much more noticeable if smoke is filling up a room, compared to checking if there is any wetness behind the walls. It's much faster than inspecting all of the piping inch by inch, yet provides similar information. Once the smoke test has been passed, the water can come in and further, more specific testing—e.g., ensuring the correct pressure at different floors—can commence.

Smoke testing in software is similar. **A smoke test** involves a minimal amount of testing that can be done to ensure that the system under test is ready for further testing. It can be thought of as a guard to further testing—unless the system can perform some minimal operations, you don't move on to running a full test suite. This is usually a small number of tests, checking that the software can be installed, that major functionality seems to work, and that no obvious problems appear.

For example, if you are testing an e-commerce site, you may check to see that a user can access the site, search for an item, and add it to their shopping cart. The full test suite would check numerous edge cases and paths, as well as all of the ancillary functionality such as recommendations and reviews. As another example, smoke testing a compiler might involve checking that it can compile a "hello, world" program and that the resulting executable does in fact print out "hello, world". It would not include checking what happens when there are complex Boolean expressions, or if a referenced library is missing, or whether an unparseable program will produce the appropriate error message. It just determines that the system is able to perform basic functionality. This is often useful when a system should either work entirely or not at all, such as when installing a piece of software on a new architecture. If the code is compiled incorrectly, there is a good chance the software will fail to start. Smoke testing will allow us to bypass all of the work of setting up an appropriate test environment if the software simply doesn't work at all.

Why bother performing a smoke test before a full test suite? Wouldn't you eventually find all the same problems without it? In all likelihood, yes, but the key word is "*eventually*". Smoke testing allows you to determine whether the software is even worth testing before running the full test suite on it. There is often a cost associated with setting up a system for testing, such as installing software on servers and clients, looking up test plans, and generating test data. If the software is so broken that it doesn't even support basic functionality, then smoke testing can prevent you from spending time doing all of the other work involved in running a full test suite.

As a real-life example, I once worked in a location where we had weekly releases of software. Each week, the new version of the software would have to be installed in a lab consisting of approximately fifteen different computer systems. Installing the software and updating the testing data for the new version—even with a custom-built over-the-network script—usually took several hours. However, occasionally that week's version of the software had so many defects, or such bad ones, that it was essentially untestable. Errors such as constant data corruption or an inability for users to login could make testing that version more trouble than it was worth. Instead of determining this *after* a morning of installing and upgrading, we were able to run a quick smoke test and find them first thing in the morning. This gave the testers extra time to work on something else (e.g., developing test scripts or automation tools) and the developers earlier notice that there was a problem with the software. This often resulted in fixes for the defects sooner, meaning that testers could get back to testing the software.

Smoke testing can be either **scripted** or **unscripted**. In unscripted testing, an experienced tester or user just "plays around" with the software for a little while before the actual testing occurs. This is usually done by someone experienced with the software, so as to ensure that the most important functionality is tested, known defects have been fixed, and the software generally behaves as it should. Scripted testing means that there is a specific test plan that specifies the test cases to be executed. While scripted testing provides a much more regulated environment and helps to keep track of what has been shown to work, unscripted testing is much more flexible and allows testers to check different aspects of the software for different releases.

An even milder version of smoke testing is **media testing**. This is a check that all the relevant files have been written to the storage medium correctly and can be read. It's just a final double-check that the CD was not corrupted before sending it to the customer, or that the files that were put on the server were written to the correct directory. This can be as simple as checking that the files on the medium are bitwise equivalent to the files in the original location, or could involve some very minor work after that, such as putting the CD in a drive and ensuring that you can start installing the software.

10.2   Acceptance Testing

Smoke testing checks if the software is ready to be tested; in other words, can the software be accepted by the testing team in order to perform some other work on it? It is a subset of **acceptance testing**. Acceptance testing is any kind of testing that checks that the system is acceptable to continue to the next phase of its life cycle, be it testing, or delivery to a customer, or making it ready for a user.

Depending on the domain, acceptance tests may be scripted or unscripted. For large contracting companies or complex projects, there are often several test plans verifying that multiple parts of the system operate correctly, and metrics for quality (e.g., no more than three major defects will be found during the test period) which must be met. For smaller programs, it may be as simple as allowing the customer or user to sit down with the software for a few minutes and give a thumbs-up or thumbs-down.

Since software developers are usually also not domain experts in the field of the software they are writing, there are many opportunities for a system to be developed which does not meet the needs of the customer. Even if the requirements are spelled out clearly, there are often ambiguities and assumptions specific to the domain. For example, to a software developer, a zero-based index makes perfect sense—many popular programming languages enumerate arrays starting with 0, and few Java developers would write a `for` loop as:

```
for (int j=1; j <= 10; j++) { ... }
```

However, for many non-programmers, having 1 reference the second element of a list is very confusing!

Formal acceptance tests are usually determined ahead of time and agreed upon by both the developer of the software and the customer. If all the tests pass—or the two parties come to a compromise agreeable to both—then the software is said to be accepted by the customer. Other possible solutions may be a partial payment, payment to be paid after certain defects are fixed, or an understanding that there is a certain level of quality that does not involve all tests passing (e.g., all major tests pass, and at least 95% of minor tests).

Operational testing, also called **field testing**, is testing the system under real-life (operating) conditions. Often, a problem is not found, or even thought of, during the development process or when checked piece-by-piece. Operational testing can find these overlooked errors by actually running the system in a real-life environment. For example, every piece of a new avionics system may be tested using the techniques described in this book, but the system won't have undergone operational testing until the airplane that the software is running on is actually up in the air. Often, operational testing is the last kind of testing to occur on a system, ensuring that the system will in fact operate correctly under real-world conditions. This can be an expensive method of testing, both from a setup standpoint and a risk standpoint. For example, if the avionics system fails and the plane does not fly correctly, the costs of failure are extremely high; even if it works correctly, using a plane for several hours is probably going to be orders of magnitude more expensive than buying time on a computer for simulations and integration tests.

Another kind of acceptance testing is **user acceptance testing**. Commonly used in Agile environments, user acceptance testing (UAT) checks that the system meets the goals of the users and operates in a manner acceptable to them. Usually, a subject matter expert (SME—a non-developer with understanding of the domain the software is written for) is given a number of tasks to perform. The SME is given no instructions as to how to do the tasks by the person doing the testing; it is up to the SME to figure out how to use the software (using appropriate documentation or other supporting material) to complete the tasks. If testing a new web browser, for instance, a user acceptance test may pick a skilled web surfer (if that term is even used anymore) as a subject matter expert. The SME may have three tasks—navigating to a popular search engine's homepage, bookmarking a page, and returning to a bookmarked page. Members of the team may watch the SME perform these tasks, but are not to explain or help in any way. Restraining members of the team from helping can be a difficult task, as those who develop the software have a high level of knowledge about the system and want to show users "the best way" to do things. However, allowing the SME to attempt the tasks without any help will allow you to see what parts are difficult for users in that domain who will need to use the software on their own.

One can think of **alpha testing** and **beta testing** as kinds of acceptance tests. Although the terms can have slightly different meanings in different domains, they both involve having independent users or teams using the software under development. In all cases, alpha testing precedes beta testing, if any alpha testing is done. Alpha testing involves a very small, select group of customers—often those of high value or with high technical skill—using the software. In some cases, it may actually not be a customer doing the testing, but a testing group external to the group that developed the system. Beta testing involves a broader release of the software to a variety of customers. This often occurs after alpha testing for large, well-tested software projects. However, there is nothing to stop a team from skipping alpha testing entirely and sending software straight out to a large group of people—perhaps the entire customer base—with the understanding that the software is a beta version. Google is famous for doing this; Gmail, for example, was technically a beta release for the first five years of its existence, during which time millions of people used it. If you are less concerned with having more defects being known to the outside world, beta testing can be a fast way to get quite a bit of usage data and defect reports from a large number of users.

With online systems, oftentimes beta testing can be "mixed in" with regular usage of the system. You can have a specific subset of users—say, those who have shown an interest in trying new features, or customers important for revenue, or even a random sampling—have access to the new functionality you wish to beta test. Usually, you want to either clear it with these customers or make sure that they know that the functionality they are using is not considered complete.

A related concept to acceptance testing is **dogfooding** or **eating your own dogfood**. Despite the somewhat disturbing name, this means that the team that is developing the software is also using the software. This is useful in situations where the system under development is something either common to computer users (e.g., an operating system or text editor) or programmers in particular (an IDE or compiler). It is usually not possible until later stages of the project, when enough functionality has been completed so as to allow a relatively smooth user experience—it wouldn't make sense to dogfood a program whose main functionality hasn't even been developed yet. Dogfooding allows extremely fast discovery of defects, since the entire team is using the software, not just the testers. Even if other members of the team are not specifically looking for defects in a system, the fact that there are a large number of people using it—and using it in similar ways as other users would—means that more defects are likely to be found. They will also tend to be especially clustered in areas that users are using, allowing for additional metrics to be gathered (both for usage and defect density in different subsystems). As an added bonus, developers who are using the software have additional incentives to ensure quality in their codebase!

Chapter 11

Exploratory Testing

We've determined how to understand requirements, develop a test plan, and find defects in a variety of different ways. There has been an underlying assumption for everything we have done so far—that we know what the behavior of the program is supposed to be, or at least that somebody does. Sometimes, especially at the beginning of development before ideas and software have fully crystallized, nobody may know what should happen under specific circumstances. These may be input values that no systems engineer thought about, or the software being used for a different purpose than intended, or usability aspects that were not considered when the system was being designed. Situations may also arise where there is no time in the schedule for a formal test plan, or for the kind of software being developed, it is seen as unnecessary. Finally, testers may want to check out parts of the system in order to understand them, and find defects only incidentally.

Under such circumstances, you will want to use **exploratory testing**. This is defined as testing without a specified test plan, where the main goal is to learn about and influence the development of the system, as opposed to specifically determining whether the observed behavior is equal to the expected behavior. Exploratory testing allows the tester to follow their own path, thinking of edge cases on the fly or following leads if something seems like it may cause a problem. It also allows the tester to learn by doing, instead of reading design documentation or code, which is often a much more effective way to understand a system.

11.1   Benefits and Drawbacks of Exploratory Testing

Exploratory testing is sometimes referred to as *ad hoc* testing, but that term can imply carelessness and sloppy work. However, exploratory testing isn't careless, it's just less rigid. There is often much thought put into determining whether exploratory testing is appropriate and even more thought put into determining the next things to explore.

Exploratory testing is often the first experience a tester may have with a new feature or system. Step-by-step instructions—to be added as execution steps to a test plan—may not be determinable only by reading design documents. Often, some initial exploratory testing is done to understand how things have been implemented. As a tester gains experience with the system, there may be even more exploratory testing, as they better understand the nooks and crannies which were not covered by their initial test plan. Occasionally, there's just nothing for a tester to do, and so they spend some time hunting for defects off the beaten path of tests based solely on test plans.

By spending some time in the weeds—where test plans have not yet tread—a tester may discover quirks in the system that might never be caught by more formalized testing. Additionally, exploratory testing will often uncover more defects, by operating much more quickly. More time spent on actual testing, as opposed to the minutiae of looking up test plans, writing down test statuses, etc., means that more time is spent finding defects and less time is spent developing documentation around those defects.

Exploratory testing also provides a side benefit, as the tester will learn about the system more quickly than with formal testing. Mindlessly following a test plan does not allow for much of the back-and-forth that characterizes learning in humans. Just as you will find it difficult to learn to play the piano simply by reading a book, you will find it more difficult to understand the system under test by simply reading and executing test plans.

There is very little overhead involved in installing the software or accessing the system and just trying to find defects, unlike the steps involved in developing and writing out a test plan and executing it. If you have half an hour to find as many defects as possible in some software, you aren't going to spend the first twenty-five minutes writing up preconditions and postconditions and execution steps, only to run a few tests at the end. This also means that it's very easy to run an updated test, even if the software has been dramatically modified; simply do some more exploratory testing! There are no test plans to update aside from the one in the tester's head, whereas a test plan (or even worse yet, an automated test) might require quite a bit of modification to work whenever the original program is changed.

There are some downsides to exploratory testing. After all, there is a reason that test plans are developed in the first place. The first downside is that it is unregulated, meaning that there is no real plan ahead of time to determine what to test. Trying to explain to non-testers exactly what is going to be tested and why can be difficult, and even trying to explain retroactively may not be easy. While deep in testing some software, you may have a perfect mental model of what you are doing and the reasons behind it, but this is often lost once you are finished.

Much of the responsibility for what exactly to test will be in the hands of the tester when doing exploratory testing. A diligent tester who understands the system well will do a much better job of discovering defects than a tester who does not understand the system or is lazy. If the testers were both following the same test plan, then assuming that the second tester is at least diligent enough to do the tests and write down the correct results, then the amount of coverage will be well-known and approximately equal for them both. Providing a formalized testing plan thus often hinders experienced testers, while helping inexperienced testers who may need guidance to understand what to test.

Another problem that may arise when doing exploratory testing is that the defects found may not be reproducible. It could be that the reason something failed ten minutes into an exploratory test is because the tester did something slightly different than the last time in the first minute of testing. Trying to repeat all of the steps without knowing what the difference was can be an exercise in frustration, if not actually impossible. With formalized testing, assuming that the tester has followed the steps, this is much less of a problem.

It's difficult to gauge how much coverage the system under test has received when using exploratory testing. Unless the tester is recording exactly what is being done, via screen capture software, software logging, or manually, there may be many parts of the system where you're not sure how well-tested it is. There is very little to analyze since there are so few test artifacts. If you are working in a safety-critical domain, or one in which there is the necessity of documenting what has been tested, relying solely on exploratory testing will not serve you well.

Testing as a field has relied more and more upon automation as time goes on, and there have been no signs of that slowing down. However, since exploratory testing relies so much on the skill of the tester and their familiarity with the system under test, it's basically impossible at this point to automate it. Barring any unforeseen advances in artificial intelligence, you will still require human beings to perform exploratory testing.

11.2 Guidelines for Exploratory Testing

Here are the two simple steps for exploratory testing:

1. Use your best judgment.

2. If in doubt about what to do, see step 1.

Exploratory testing assumes that you, as a tester, understand the system, or at least are understanding the system better as time goes on. After all, if you are writing a test plan before you test a feature, by definition that's the time that you'll be the least knowledgeable about that system. You will learn more and more as time goes on and you interact with the system more. It also assumes that you will be able to recognize a defect even if it you are not doing a strict matching of observed behavior against expected behavior. This means that there should be more frequent communication with engineers, system designers, and others to determine whether or not a given behavior is, in fact, expected.

How does one go about performing exploratory testing? This is going to depend on the particular system under test, but some broad guidelines can be given. The first guideline is to check that frequently used and important tasks can be completed and behave correctly. It matters little if the system handles a strange corner case if none of the simple base cases work! Check the happy path and make sure that it works correctly before heading off into the unhappy weeds.

Once you have determined that key basic functionality is operating correctly, think of edge cases as you go along. If asked to enter a number, what happens if the number is negative, or you don't enter anything, or you enter a series of control-character sequences? If you should enter the name of the file, what happens if that file doesn't exist, or is improperly formatted? If you don't have an idea of where things can go wrong, review the chapter *Tips for Breaking Software* and see if any of the errors listed are possible to reproduce in your system.

Check what happens when different functionality interoperates. If the system under test has the capability to read in a file, perform some operations on it, and save the result to disk, what happens if you try to overwrite the result to the original file? What happens if one part of the system has a setting for "Sort Ascending" and another has it set for "Sort Descending"—do these conflicting sort orders show up as problems elsewhere? If a system is performing a complicated rendering while also attempting to download data from the network, can race conditions occur?

Put yourself in the developer's shoes. Even if you are not a programmer yourself, you can imagine what kinds of scenarios may not have been thought of by somebody who was focused solely on a specific feature and getting a particular method working correctly, with a project manager constantly asking for status updates. Under such situations, many things may slip through the cracks. The developer may not have checked for null pointers, or integer overflow, or what would happen if threads never end. Using this knowledge, you can try to reproduce such situations from the user side, by entering in zero-length strings, or using extremely large numbers that would overflow a 32-bit integer, or attempting to read very large pieces of data from the database.

Don't be afraid to follow your intuition. If you notice something that seems a little off, or funny, or unexpected, then you may want to try other ways to cause it and see if there is something that relates them. You may also have ideas which would not come to you if you were just developing a test plan. This is the time to try things out.

Finally, even though exploratory testing is a much less formal process than generating and executing test plans, you will want to write down defects that you find as soon as you can, and in as detailed a manner as possible. The longer you wait, the more details you will forget. Additionally, the longer you use the system, the more likely it will be that you find yourself in a state where it's impossible to reproduce the error. Determining the steps which caused the defect and writing them down should override trying to find more defects. After all, if you don't note what the defects are and provide enough information for a developer to fix them, then there really is no point to doing testing at all. You can also use the reproduction steps you've figured out to add a more formal test later.

Chapter 12

Manual versus Automated Testing

So far, we have focused mostly on manual testing; that is, we actually develop and run the test cases ourselves. If you've done any manual testing, though, you'll know that it is time-consuming and often extremely boring for the tester who has to follow a script (it's much more fun to follow a script when acting than when running software). If only there were some sort of machine which can be used for running repetitive tasks!

If you're testing software, then chances are very good that you have a computer available to help you with the tests, since you probably have a computer available to you to run the software that you're testing. There are numerous tools to help you test the software more effectively and efficiently.

With automated testing, you write the tests, using some sort of programming or scripting language or tool, which are then executed by the computer. These tests can check aspects of the program as specific as individual return values from methods all the way up to how an entire graphical interface should look on a screen.

12.1 Benefits and Drawbacks of Manual Testing

12.1.1 Benefits of Manual Testing

1. *It's simple and straightforward.* There's a reason that this book discussed manual testing first; it's easier to understand the concepts of testing without worrying about the particular syntax or quirks of tools or languages being used. You're using the same software setup, or at least a very similar setup, as the user. Most people, even ones who are not very technical, can follow a well-written test plan. Most non-technical people would have great difficulty understanding a JUnit test, however.

2. *It's cheap.* At least from a naïve perspective, there's no additional up-front cost. It's very easy to perform informal testing even without writing a test plan—just run the software and try thinking of base cases and edge cases on the fly.

3. *It's easy to set up.* If you can get the software to compile and run—which hopefully you will be able to do anyway, since software which can't run is usually not appreciated much by users—then you have everything that you need to do some basic manual testing. Creating test harnesses, setting up test drivers, and all of the other related work for running automated tests can be bypassed.

4. *There is no additional software to learn, purchase, and/or write.* Although there are free options available for testing tools, keep in mind that purchase price is not the only price you pay when using a software product for development. There is time to be spent on learning how the tool works, the syntax of any scripting language it uses, and working around the inevitable bugs that it contains. Researching the most appropriate testing tool to use, having test engineers learn to use it, and writing (and debugging) the scripts for it can all reduce the amount of time available for actually running the tests and thinking about test design.

5. *It's extremely flexible.* If a user interface changes, it's relatively straightforward to modify the test plan. If you are doing exploratory testing or other testing outside of a test plan, as long as the tester knows about the change, they can modify the steps taken. Even if the tester does not know about the interface changes, it may be possible for a human being to figure out the differences just by using the software. This is not possible in automated testing; if an interface changes, then any automated tests exercising that interface will usually fail unless the testing code has been changed to expect the new interface. This may be a benefit, though; automated tests are far more rigid, which means that they may be better at catching unanticipated modifications. Humans may not even notice certain changes and just "go with the flow."

6. *You are more likely to test things that users care about.* Manual testing can only be done on the software running as a user would run it; it's a form of black-box testing. By doing this, the tester is seeing the software the way a user sees it, and will tend to use the software in similar ways. Not only does this mean that testers will gain an understanding of how the software is used, and gain domain knowledge in the area, it also means that the focus will be on aspects of the software that users care about. Users do not care about specific values returned from specific functions buried deep within the code; they care if the final results are correct. In manual testing, your focus will almost automatically be on the functionality of the software that the users care about the most, because the testers will also be users.

7. *Humans can catch issues that automated testing does not.* Automated tests will find failures for anything that they have been written to check. However, if they are not written to check some aspect of the software, even if it would be easily noticed by the human eye, they will not note it as a failure. As an example, imagine a simple word-counting program. Automated tests check that it gives the correct answer in response to all sorts of different input. However, it also sends some additional escape characters to the terminal that changes the screen's background color to purple. This would be immediately recognizable and filed as a defect by a human tester, but unless there are automated tests checking specifically for background color of future output, it will go unnoticed.

12.1.2 Drawbacks of Manual Testing

1. *It's boring.* Have you ever spent an entire day pressing a button, then writing down the result, then pressing a button, then writing down a result, *ad nauseam*? It's a great way to burn out and alienate employees. If that's not your goal, however, you want to keep the amount of boring tasks down to a minimum.

2. *It's often not repeatable.* If a tester does something slightly out of the ordinary and finds a defect, he or she may not be able to reproduce the exact steps that caused the defect to show itself. This is to some extent ameliorated by well-defined and well-specified test plans, but even if you have extremely granular instructions, you may find it difficult to reproduce the *exact* steps taken to get to a certain point. For example, imagine a test case for a web browser test plan. One of the execution steps is to "open a new tab". However, there are multiple ways to do this; does the tester select the New Tab option from the menu, or use a keyboard

shortcut, or right-click on a link and open it in a new tab? Perhaps the defect only occurs under one of these situations. With automated tests, you will be able to re-run the test very precisely, using the same steps each time.

3. *Some tasks are difficult or impossible to test manually.* Let us assume that you are testing the performance of a system where one of the requirements states that there should be less than a 50 millisecond delay between receiving a request and returning a response. Since human reaction time is more than four times the maximum delay, even if the display is instantaneous, it would be impossible to check manually. There may be other aspects of the program which are invisible to the user, but only directly testable via programs or other tools, such as the number of threads running or the value of a variable.

4. *Human error is a possibility.* Every time you have a person do something, there is a chance that that person will make a mistake. In the case of executing a test case, a human being could read the instructions incorrectly, misunderstand them, write the test status down in the wrong place, or otherwise run the test incorrectly. The longer that you have somebody performing manual testing, the more likely that an error like this will occur. Other organizations have figured this out long ago—truck drivers and airplane pilots, for example, have limitations on how long they can operate their vehicles without taking a break. While an automated test could theoretically perform different execution steps than the ones it is programmed to do, the chances of it doing so are extremely remote. Computers are very good at doing exactly what you tell them to do, and doing it over and over again.

5. *It is extremely time- and resource-intensive.* Testing personnel manually pressing keys, clicking buttons, or doing anything else with the software limits them to the speed that an ordinary user would do those things. Even that is a theoretical maximum, as testers must also read and follow the test plan, double-check that they performed the steps correctly, mark down statuses, and perform overhead work when they manually test. Running manual tests can be multiple orders of magnitude slower than well-written automated tests, even performing the same actions. Running 1,000 test cases manually may take a week for a team of testers to do; it may take less than 10 minutes on a desktop computer. This means that either much of testers' time will be spent on monotonous tasks, or others will have to be hired to run the tests.

6. *It limits you to black-box and grey-box testing.* It is essentially impossible to do white-box testing manually for programs written in many popular programming languages. You will not be able to test individual methods or functions, but only in how they interact with the rest of the system. Depending on how complex the program is, this may make it much more difficult to find defects, since you will not be able to operate on nearly as granular a level.

12.2 Benefits and Drawbacks of Automated Testing

12.2.1 Benefits of Automated Testing

1. *There is no chance of human error during test execution.* If there is one thing at which computers are great, it's performing the exact same operations over and over again. Write a program to draw a circle, the circle drawn the first time the program is executed will look exactly like the one thousandth circle. This is not the case with humans—some circles will be shakier, some will be larger than others, some may look close to perfect and some will be marred with imperfections. Similarly, an automated test will perform the exact same set of execution steps each time—it won't accidentally perform the tests in the wrong order, it won't click on the wrong button, it won't accidentally mark down the wrong status.

2. *Test execution is extremely fast.* Computers can execute and check results much faster than any human being can. This not only allows tests to be run more quickly, but also allows for more possible test runs, and thus more tests.

3. *It is easy to execute, once the system is set up.* Setting up a system to run a manual test can be a laborious process. Software must be installed, test tracking software must be set up, appropriate data may need to be loaded into the database. With most automated testing solutions, running a test suite is as simple as clicking a button on the IDE or running a command from the command line. This not only helps minimize the amount of busy work done by testers, it allows faster iteration time between development and testing of code.

4. *It is easily repeatable.* As mentioned earlier, relying on automated tests minimizes the chance of human error. Even without "errors", though, having tests be almost perfectly repeatable reduces the incidence of non-deterministic errors (that is, errors that only occur sometimes when running the test, not every time that the test is run). By performing exactly the same steps in exactly the same order, the chance that a test will fail "randomly" is lessened, although not completely eliminated. As a side note, these "random" failures almost certainly have a root cause, it's just that you as a tester have not discovered it yet.

5. *It is simple to analyze the process.* Finding patterns in test failures is much easier to do when all of the test case statuses are stored and can be re-run numerous times. If past test runs are stored, it's even possible to determine which test cases and kinds of test cases are finding defects, and which are just always passing, because the aspects of the system they are testing have not changed much or just contain very few defects.

6. *It is less resource-intensive.* Running a thousand tests on your local computer may make it unusable for ten minutes, but that certainly is preferable to having the entire test team work on it for a week. Computing power is getting cheaper and cheaper every year; the same cannot be said of engineers' time.

7. *It is ideal for testing some aspects of the system which manual testing is bad at testing.* Parts of the system which are not directly user-facing, such as internal variables or data written to a database, at a minimum require extra work to check when manually testing. They may even be impossible.

8. *It scales very well.* Adding automated tests often results in a sublinear increase in time, since much of the time for automated tests often consists of setup time. That is, adding five test cases to an existing plan consisting of five cases will most likely result in an execution time that is much less than twice the original test plan. Adding additional manual test cases can often result in a superlinear increase in time in run execution, since humans running through the test cases manually will not be able to maintain a consistent speed, and will tend to slow down the longer that they spend running tests themselves. More and more time will be needed to double-check results as their mental energies are exhausted.

12.2.2   Drawbacks of Automated Testing

1. *It requires extra setup time up-front.* Once you understand the basic concepts of writing a test plan (which hopefully readers of this chapter have already learned in the preceding chapters), it's relatively straightforward to start writing a test plan and determining test cases for a piece of software. However, if you are writing automated tests, not only will you have to ensure that the code that is written is testable, you will also have to set up testing libraries and a testing framework, as well as potentially learn new syntax, terminology, and paradigms. Even if it's a framework that you have used before, there will be some time spent setting it up for the specific system under test.

2. *It may not be able to catch some user-facing defects.* Even if you know to look for them, the testing framework and libraries that you are using may not be able to check for certain defects or kinds of defects. For example, suppose you have a custom-built framework for the graphical user interface of your application. This framework can tell you the content of a window and if it is visible, but not its location. If the system does not display the window in the correct location, you have no way of knowing with an automated system. This can be somewhat ameliorated by using industry-standard frameworks and display systems, but sometimes one or both of these is not a possibility.

3. *It requires learning how to write automated tests, as well as additional tools and frameworks.* Writing automated tests is a skill that is very different from manual tests. Although the logic and theory are similar, writing automated tests requires even more emphasis on being exact as well as ensuring that interactions with the system itself are spelled out in detail.

4. *It requires more skilled staff.* Although manual testing can be done without extensive technical knowledge, automated tests require at least a basic understanding of computer programming or scripting. Testing staff will have to either already be familiar with the testing framework used for the system under test, or time and resources must be spent for them to learn it. During the time that they spend learning the system, they will not be very effective in producing tests or finding defects with them.

5. *Automated tests only test what they are looking for.* While humans running tests may easily notice that there is a problem with some part of the program even if they are not specifically looking for it, computers will do no such thing. If you have not written a test to check that entering 5 + 5 on the calculator should equal 10, then when it equals 11, no error will be reported.

6. *Tautological tests and other bad tests may creep in.* Very large test suites can often accumulate cruft, since they may not be looked at by human eyes for long periods of time. As long as the tests pass, they stay in the code; meanwhile, small modifications and fixes may creep into the codebase. Over time, this could result in some **tautological test cases** (that is, tests that will always pass because they are checking statements that are always true, such as 1 == 1). Or, some tests may become no longer necessary (e.g., checking parts of the program that are no longer used or are inaccessible to users). Without explicit work to ensure that the tests remain up to date, you may find that your computer is spending more time testing than is strictly necessary.

12.3 The Real World

Of the two options, manual and automated testing, which is better? "Better" is a loaded term, of course; numerous other factors will come into play when making a decision. One of the interesting things about software testing is that automated and manual tests do not have much overlap; things that manual testing is good at doing, automated testing tends not to be good at doing, and vice-versa. There are certainly a few things that neither traditional automated testing or manual testing are good at catching, such as security testing or probing for many edge cases. We'll discuss some variations in testing in later chapters that can fill in the weaknesses of the traditional kinds of testing we are discussing now.

The decision on whether or not to use manual or automated testing for a particular system, subsystem, or requirement will be influenced by a variety of factors:

1. *How important* are the tests?

2. *How much of an impact* does user interface or other "intangible" aspects have on the finished product?

3. *How often* will the tests be run?

4. *How experienced* is the test team?

5. *What is the schedule* for testing?

6. *How difficult* is it to automate the tests?

In general, the vast majority of testing, from a strict "number of tests run" perspective, will be automated tests of one sort or another. Running a well-designed unit test can take as little as a few microseconds of computer time; even the simplest manual test will require much more time than that for even very simple test cases. Automated tests are much easier to run more often and more quickly. All else being equal, it is better to have more tests that are faster and more frequent than it is to have fewer tests that are slower and less frequent.

When should you, as a tester, automate tests? If a test can be automated in a reasonable amount of time, you should almost always automate it. Doing so streamlines your testing and development process, guards against human error in future test runs, and makes your life less boring. However, there are occasional issues which prevent you from writing automated tests; parts of the system may not have a testing framework, a time crunch absolutely prevents you, or you just can't get the automated tools to work under certain conditions you would like to test. In these cases, it may make sense to simply perform a manual test and come back later to automate it. A bit of warning, though—in the majority of cases, "later" never comes, and you're stuck performing a rote and repetitive task for the foreseeable future.

In the "real world" of software development, virtually all organizations that I'm familiar with use a mixture of manual and automated tests for their applications, with the emphasis almost always falling more heavily on automated testing. Overall, automated testing provides many benefits for modern software development, especially being able to quickly run tests after changes are made to ensure that no regression defects have occurred. Although there is certainly an up-front cost to adding an automated testing framework, for non-trivial projects, the benefits you get from allowing the computer to do the testing work for you will quickly outweigh those drawbacks. On the other hand, releasing software relying solely on the automated tests—without ever checking how the software actually runs for a user—is done only by those organizations whose software is very far removed from user experience, who have an extremely high level of confidence in their automated tests, and/or which are especially foolhardy.

Chapter 13

An Introduction to Unit Testing

In the last chapter, we discussed the benefits and drawbacks of automated testing compared to to manual testing. Now, we'll start to dive in to a specific kind of automated testing, unit testing, which will enable you to test the code directly. Unit testing can help you to ensure that individual methods and functions operate in an expected manner.

13.1 Unit Tests: The Very Idea

What are unit tests? In a nutshell, they test the smallest "units" of functionality, which in traditional object-oriented programming, usually means methods, functions, or objects. It's the ultimate in white-box testing; in order to properly write unit tests, you'll need to understand the implementation of a system at a very deep level. They allow you to check that the methods that you write do exactly what you intend them to do, given a specific input.

Some examples of unit tests are checking that:

1. A `.sort()` method returns [1, 2, 3] when you pass in [3, 2, 1]

2. Passing in a null reference as an argument to a function throws an exception

3. A `.formatNumber()` method returns a properly formatted number

4. Passing in a string to a function that takes an integer argument does not crash the program

5. An object has `.send()` and `.receive()` methods

6. Constructing an object with default parameters sets the `default` attribute to true

As you can see, these functions are all testing aspects of the software which are not directly visible to the end user. A user is never going to be in the position of looking at a particular method or object. They won't care about what methods an object has, or what value variables are set to, or what happens when a null pointer is passed in as an argument. They will be able to see the *results* of those things happening, of course, but they won't be able to specifically see the code that caused it.

Unit testing is usually done by the developer writing the code. The developer is intimately familiar with the codebase and should know what data needs to be passed in, which edge cases and corner cases exist, what the boundary values are, etc. Only occasionally will a white-box tester have to write unit tests in the absence of a developer.

Despite this, it's very important to understand unit testing, even if you are not a developer. In many organizations, software testers help with unit testing procedures. This doesn't have to mean writing them; it could be developing tools to help make writing unit tests easier, or verifying that unit tests are testing what the developer thought they were testing, or ensuring that the tests are appropriate and cover all essential cases.

We have seen earlier that the user will never directly see the aspects of the software that unit tests are testing. What's the point, then? Wouldn't it make more sense to just test everything from a user perspective? That way, we'd only catch defects that impact the user. We wouldn't have to waste time worrying about things at a low level. It would probably be more time efficient if we didn't have to write unit tests, right? Unfortunately, that's not the case. There are numerous reasons for writing unit tests in addition to systems-level tests. Note, though, that there are many kinds of defects which unit tests are not very good at catching, which is why unit testing should be only part of your testing strategy.

1. *Problems are found earlier.* Unit tests are normally written along with the code itself. There's no need to wait for (usually longer-running) systems tests to run, for a manual test to be developed, or for a build to get into the hands of the testers. The developer finds problems while still developing. Like most things, the sooner a problem is found in a process, the cheaper, faster, and easier it will be to fix.

2. *Faster turnaround time.* If a problem is found, there's no need for a build to occur, or to get into testers' hands. The developer finds a problem when executing the unit test suite, and can immediately go back and start fixing it. If the developer has to wait for a tester to look at the software, file a defect, and get assigned that defect, it may be quite a while before the developer actually fixes it. In that time, he or she may have forgotten some implementation details, or at the very least will have probably swapped out some of the information and will require time for a context shift. The faster a defect can be found, the faster it can be fixed.

3. *Faster runtime than systems-level tests.* A well-designed unit test will have few to no dependencies on other libraries, classes, files, etc. This means that they can be extremely fast, with many tests taking a few milliseconds or less to execute. By focusing on very specific parts of the code, that part of the code can be tested numerous times without the extra setup and execution time caused by other aspects of the system.

4. *Developers understand their code.* Writing tests allows the developer to understand what the expected behavior of the function is. It also allows the developer to add tests for things that he or she knows might be problematic for a specific function. For example, a developer may know that a sort function may not sort numeric strings correctly, because certain flags need to be set to ensure that it treats them as numbers instead of strings. If we are sorting by numeric value, 1000 is bigger than 999. However, if the function treats input as strings, 999 is "bigger" than 1000. If you do not understand why this is, think of numbers as just strange-looking letters, where A = 0, B = 1, C = 2, etc. In this case, 1000 would be equivalent to BAAA, and 999 would be equivalent to JJJ. BAAA (1000) would come before JJJ (999) in the dictionary, but if we view them as numbers, 1000 (BAAA) would come after JJJ (999). A black-box tester may not realize that this is what is happening "under the hood" and so not think to test this particular edge case.

5. *Living documentation.* The tests provide a kind of "living documentation" to the code. They explain what a codebase is supposed to do in a different way than the actual code and any comments or documentation for the software. Failing tests are updated; they are either removed or changed as the software itself changes. Unlike traditional documentation, if unit tests are executed on a regular basis (such as before being merged to baseline), then it's impossible for the tests to become obsolete. Obsolete tests generally do not pass, and this is a giant indicator

to get them fixed.

6. *Alternative implementation.* One way to think of tests is as a different implementation of the software. In a sense, a program is just a listing of what a computer should do given certain input—*IF* `foo` is less than five, *THEN* print out "`small foo`". *WHEN* a new bar object is created, *SET* the `baz` variable to false. A comprehensive test suite provides a similar service, saying what the program should do in a slightly different way. There's always room for error, but if you're implementing it twice, once as a test and once as code, then there's less chance that both will be written incorrectly.

7. *Able to tell if code changes caused issues elsewhere.* Programs nowadays can be rather large and complicated, and it's not always easy—or even humanly possible—to know whether a change you're making will have unintended consequences elsewhere. The author has lost count of how many times he has meant to, say, change the background color of a screen, and caused a stack overflow in some recursive function elsewhere in the code which required the background color to be green for some reason. However, by having a relatively complete test suite, the developer can check easily if he or she is breaking anything obvious elsewhere in the codebase. It's not foolproof, but it certainly makes it easier to avoid problems.

13.2 An Example in Natural Language

Before diving into the code, let's examine a unit test in natural language. Let's say that we're implementing a `LinkedList` class, and we would like to test equality. When we make two lists that have the same data in them, they will show as equal, even though they are not the exact same `LinkedList` object. How could we specify a test for this case?

"Create two linked lists, *a* and *b*, each with data for the nodes equal to $1 \rightarrow 2 \rightarrow 3$. When they are compared with the equality operator, they should be seen as equal."

We can see that there are three steps here, which correspond to some of the steps in a manual test. This should not be surprising. After all, the basic concepts of testing do not change, despite the level of abstraction of a particular test. The steps are:

1. *Preconditions:* First, we need to generate the preconditions of the test. If you recall from several chapters back, the preconditions are those conditions which must be met before the actual test starts. In this case, the preconditions are that we have two different linked lists, named *a* and *b*, and that they contain the exact same data, $1 \rightarrow 2 \rightarrow 3$, all of which are the same data type.

2. *Execution Steps:* These make up the behavior we intend to test in the unit test. In our example, the equality operator is applied between the two linked lists *a* and *b*, and will return a Boolean value.

3. *Expected Behavior:* Remember that the key principle to testing software is that expected behavior should equal observed behavior. The unit test should specify what the expected behavior is, then check if it's equal to the observed behavior (i.e., the actual result of the test). In the world of unit testing, this is called an **assertion**—the test *asserts* that the expected behavior is equal to the observed behavior. In our case, our test will assert that the returned value of comparing the two linked lists is true.

13.3   Turning Our Example Into a Unit Test

It would be entirely possible to unit test this in a "manual" fashion. Just generate a quick program which creates a linked list a, creates a linked list b, applies the equality operator to both of them, and finally checks if the result of that value is true. If it is, print out "test passed!"; otherwise, print out "test failed!". However, usually we use a testing framework to automate much of the work and ensure that we are testing in a consistent and coherent manner.

For this book, we will be using the JUnit unit testing framework.[1] JUnit is an instance of the xUnit testing framework, which originally came from SUnit, a testing framework for Smalltalk. As a side note, Smalltalk is one of those languages that was years ahead of its time. If you want to see what the future of software engineering will be like, one of the best things to do is to go look at what cool features languages had twenty years ago that were considered too slow or too immature or too "academic". Usually, these cool features will come back into vogue years later, with the community of whatever language they've ended up in loudly trumpeting their novelty (see: garbage collection, macros, metaprogramming).

Fuddy-duddy rants aside, the JUnit test framework allows us to create unit tests that have much of the "behind-the-scenes" work taken care of. The developer can then focus on generating the test logic and understanding what is being tested, instead of wasting time writing out conditionals printing "yay, test passed" or "boo, test failed".

Although we will be covering JUnit, as it is a popular and easy-to-understand testing framework, it is far from the only unit testing framework in existence. Among many other Java testing frameworks, there are TestNG, a more fully-featured framework; JTest, which includes the ability to automatically generate unit tests; and cucumber-jvm, which helps to write tests in a more human-readable format. All of these have their benefits and drawbacks. If you're interested in finding more potential unit testing frameworks, just do a web search for "unit testing frameworks *your language of choice*".

Keep in mind, though, that the particular implementation of testing framework you use isn't nearly as important as the concepts you learn and can apply. When you are reading this chapter, worry less about the syntax, and more about understanding the concepts of unit testing. Think about how aspects of unit testing are both similar and different to concepts that you have already learned in manual testing.

The following is an implementation of a unit test checking for linked list equality, as per above. Don't worry if you don't understand all of the code; over the next few sections it will be explained thoroughly.

```
import static org.junit.Assert.*;

public class LinkedListTest {

    @Test
    public void testEquals123() {
        // Preconditions - a and b both have 1 -> 2 -> 3
        LinkedList<Integer> a = new LinkedList<Integer>( [1,2,3] );
        LinkedList<Integer> b = new LinkedList<Integer>( [1,2,3] );

        // Execution steps - run equality operator
        boolean result = a.equals(b);

        // Postconditions / Expected behavior - assert that result is true
```

---

[1] Available from http://junit.org.

```
        assertEquals(true, result);
    }

}
```

Looking over this test, it is easy to see the parallels with a manual test. There are some preconditions to set up the test, some execution steps to run the test, and some postconditions, where we can check the observed behavior against the expected behavior. As mentioned in an earlier chapter, the key concept to keep in mind when testing software is that some behavior is expected under some circumstances, and when those circumstances are reached, a test should check that the observed behavior is in fact the expected behavior. While unit tests check smaller units of functionality than most black-box tests, the core concept remains the same.

Whenever a test fails, the particular test failure will be displayed on the screen. We expect that tests should normally pass, so they are usually indicated with just a ".". If you are using an IDE or other graphical representation of the test, failing tests will often be colored red and passing tests will be colored green.

13.3.1 Preconditions

Before the test can be run, you need to set up the necessary preconditions for the test. These are similar to preconditions in a manual test, only instead of focusing on the system as a whole, you focus on setting things up for the particular method to be called. In the example above, the unit test is going to check that two linked lists with equal values (specifically $1 \to 2 \to 3$) will be regarded as equal by the .equals method of a linked list object. In order to test that two linked lists are equal, first we must created the two linked lists, and set their nodes to the same set of values. This code simply creates them and puts them into variables a and b. We will use these two linked lists in the next phase of the unit test.

13.3.2 Execution Steps

Here is the actual equality check. We determine whether or not a.equals(b) is true or not, and put the Boolean result in the variable result.

13.3.3 Assertions

Remember that assertions are checking the expected behavior against the observed behavior of the execution steps. Specifically, we are using the assertion assertEquals, which checks that the value in result should equal true. If it does, the test passes and we can say that under these circumstances, the .equals() methods works correctly. If it does not, then the test fails.

There are a variety of assertions one can use. Some can be interchanged; for example, instead of asserting that result should be equal to true, we could instead have directly asserted that result should be true. In Java:

```
assertTrue(result);
```

A list of some of the most commonly-used assertions, along with some trivial examples of their usage, include:

1. *assertEquals*: Assert that two values are equal to each other, e.g. assertEquals(4, (2 * 2)).

2. *assertTrue*: Assert that the expression evaluates to true, e.g. `assertTrue(7 == 7)`.

3. *assertFalse*: Assert that the expression evaluates to false, e.g. `assertFalse(2 < 1)`.

4. *assertNull*: Assert that a value is null, e.g. `assertNull(uninitializedVariable)`.

5. *assertSame*: Assert not only that the two values are equal, but that they point to the exact same object. Example:

```
Integer a = Integer(7);
Integer b = Integer(7);
Integer c = a;
assertSame(a, b); // False; values are same, but point to different object
assertSame(a, a); // True; both are the same reference to the same object
assertSame(a, c); // True; these are different references to the same object
```

Additionally, there are several "not" variants of these assertions, such as `assertNotEquals`, which will check that the original assertion is not true. For example, `assertNotEquals(17, (1 + 1))`. In my experience, these are used much less often. You want to check for a specific *expected* behavior, if at all possible, not that it's *not unexpected* behavior. Checking that something does not exist could be an indication that the test is fragile or not thought through. Imagine that you have written a method which will generate 19th-century Romantic poems. You know that these poems should never start with the word "homoiconicity", so you write a test to that effect:

```
@Test
public void testNoLispStuff() {
    String poem = PoemGenerator.generate("19th_Century_Romantic");
    String firstWord = poem.split(" ");
    assertNotEquals("homoiconicity", firstWord);
}
```

When your poem starts with "Behold", "Darling", or "Limpid", this test will pass. However, it will also pass if the poem starts with "%&*()_" or "`java.lang.StackOverflowError`". Tests should, in general, look for *positive* behavior as opposed to the absence of *negative* behavior. Imagine testing that a "welcome" box does *not* show up on a web page. If the URL for the page returns a 500 `Internal Server Error`, the test will still pass. Think very carefully about failure cases when testing for the absence of a particular behavior.

13.3.4   Ensuring that Tests are Testing What You Expect

One of the simplest ways to do this is to first ensure that your tests fail! While we'll go into detail on a development strategy that always calls for tests to fail first in the chapter on Test Driven Development, a quick change to a test can often prove that it's not just passing all the time because you're mistakenly asserting that `true == true`, for example.

Perhaps even worse, you may be testing something entirely different than what you think you are testing. For example, let's assume that you are testing to ensure that negative values work in your brand-new absoluteValue() method. You write a test:

```
@Test
public void testAbsoluteValueNegatives() {
    int result = absoluteValue(7);
    assertEquals(result, 7);
}
```

This is a perfect valid and passing test. However, due to a typo, it's not actually testing anything about negative numbers. There is nothing which will check that you entered what you thought you entered; the computer always does what it is told, not what you *meant* to tell it.

You also need to ensure that you understand what the method is supposed to do, or you may be testing for behavior that is expected by you (as a developer/tester), but it is not expected by the user (or the requirements of the software). For example, let us consider the following test, which is a rewritten version of the one above.

```
@Test
public void testAbsoluteValueNegatives() {
    int result = absoluteValue(-7);
    assertEquals(result, -7);
}
```

If you don't understand what should happen when the method accepts a negative value (in this case, that it should return the value without the negative sign), then you'll write a perfectly incorrect method which returns a perfectly incorrect value, but your tests will all pass because you are checking to see if it will return an incorrect value. Remember that tests are not magical; they need to be told what the expected value is. If you are expecting the wrong value, then when the observed value matches that wrong value, the test will pass. Tests are not infallible. You still need to use your own wits to ensure that they are checking everything correctly.

In some cases, you may not be testing anything at all! A JUnit test only fails if an assertion fails. If you forget to add an assertion, then the test will always pass, no matter what sort of execution steps you add to it.

In the linked list equality test above, what could you change to ensure that your tests are testing what you think they are testing?

What if you changed the first linked list, *a*, to contain the data $1 \rightarrow 2$?

```
@Test
public void testEquals123() {
    LinkedList<Integer> a = new LinkedList<Integer>( [1, 2] );
    LinkedList<Integer> b = new LinkedList<Integer>( [1, 2, 3] );
    boolean result = a.equals(b);
    assertEquals(true, result);
}
```

Or $7 \rightarrow 8 \rightarrow 9$?

```
@Test
public void testEquals123() {
    LinkedList<Integer> a = new LinkedList<Integer>( [7, 8, 9] );
    LinkedList<Integer> b = new LinkedList<Integer>( [1, 2, 3] );
    boolean result = a.equals(b);
    assertEquals(true, result);
}
```

Or you changed the equality check to an *inequality* check?

```
@Test
public void testEquals123() {
    LinkedList<Integer> a = new LinkedList<Integer>( [1, 2, 3] );
    LinkedList<Integer> b = new LinkedList<Integer>( [1, 2, 3] );
    boolean result = !(a.equals(b));
```

```
        assertEquals(true, result);
    }
```

In all of these instances, the test should fail. You can then rest a little easier, knowing that your test isn't tautological (always passing, no matter what the code does) or testing something other than what you think it is testing.

You want your test to fail at first, so you know that when it passes, you have actually fixed the issue which you are testing. There's still no guarantee that your changes fixed it - after all, your assertion itself may be incorrect! - but it is much more likely.

13.4   Problems With Unit Testing

Unit testing with the techniques we've learned up to this point will get us far, but won't get us all the way. Just using the assertions and testing code that we've gone over, there's no way to check, for example, that a particular string will be printed out, or that a window will appear, or that another method is called... all very important things. After all, if all methods did was return different values with different input, never displaying them to the user or interacting with the environment in any way, we'd have no way of knowing what was happening with our programs. Our only output would be the generally increasing noisiness of the fan and heat of the CPU.

Any behavior aside from returning a value is called a **side effect**. Displaying a window, printing some text, connecting to another computer over the network—all of these are, from a terminological perspective, side effects of computation. Even setting a variable or writing data to disk are side effects. Functions and methods without side effects that only receive input from parameters are called **pure**. Pure functions will always return the same result given the same input values, and may be called an infinite number of times without modifying any other aspects of the system. Functions and methods that *have* side effects, or that may present different results based on something other than values passed in as parameters, are **impure**. Some languages, such as Haskell, make a strong differentiation between pure and impure functions, but Java does not.

An example of a pure function would be a mathematical function, such as the square root function, as in the following Java code:

```java
public double getSquareRoot(double val) {
    return Math.sqrt(val);
}
```

Assuming no floating-point rounding errors or errors of that nature, the square root of 25 will always be 5, no matter what global variables are set, no matter what time or date it is, no matter what. There are also no side effects from calling a square root function; it's not as though a window pops up every time your system calculates a square root.

An example of an impure function would be printing out statistics from global variables, or any method which outputs something to the console or screen, or depends upon variables that are not specifically passed in. In general, if you see a method with a void return, it's probably impure—a pure function with a void return type would be absolutely useless, since the returned value is its only way of communicating with the rest of the program. Here is an example of an impure function, which allows users to go to a cat café (that is, a place where you can drink coffee and pet cats):

```java
public class World {

    public void goToCatCafe(CatCafe catCafe) {
        System.out.println("Petting cats at a Cat Café!");
```

```
        catCafe.arrive();
        catCafe.haveFun();
    }
}
```

Pure functions are usually easier to test, because passing in the same values will always return the same value, and it's easy to test for input and output with standard unit test procedures. Impure functions are more difficult, since you may not have a return value to assert against. Additionally, they may depend upon or modify parts of the code outside of this particular method. Here's an example of an impure method which would be very difficult to test, since its dependencies and output are not localized. In the following code, all variables prefixed with _global are defined and set external to the method:

```
public void printAndSave() {
    String valuesToPrint = DatabaseConnector.getValues(_globalUserId);
    valuesToSave = ValuesModifier.modify(valuesToPrint);
    writeToFile(_globalLogFileName, valuesToSave);
    printToScreen(_globalScreenSettings, valuesToPrint);
}
```

Contrast this to the square root function, where we know what exactly we're passing in. Since the passed-in value is the only value the function has access to, and the only value we care about is the one that is returned, it is easy to check the results of specific calculations. In the printAndSave() method, though, there are dependencies on several external variables. Running this code once may cause everything to work properly; running it again, when those variables are set to different values, may cause everything to fail. It's difficult to know where all to check for the expected behavior. It's writing something to a file, it looks like, but we'll need to figure out the file name and location based on the value of the variable at a particular point in time. We'll also need to figure out what the _globalUserId is to determine what the right values are, and how it will be displayed by looking at the value of _globalScreenSetting. In any of these cases, they could be set by a large number of external factors, and the values of the output depend on things that we may not have direct control over. All of these come together to make testing impure methods a much more difficult task.

This does not mean that impure functions are bad! As we've seen, they're absolutely necessary if you want to do anything other than make your processor warm. After all, printing anything to the screen is technically a side effect. However, by keeping as many functions pure as possible, and limiting impure functions to certain areas, you will make testing the system much easier. You can think of this process as "quarantining" the impure functions, so that you know where difficulties in testing might lie.

13.5   Creating a Test Runner

Assuming we have the correct jar files downloaded, it possible to manually compile individual unit test classes, as in the command below. Note that the particular version and location of the jar files may differ on your system.

Compilation:

```
javac -cp .:./hamcrest-core-1.3.jar:./junit-4.12.jar FooTest.java
```

Note that this works with OS X and Unix systems. Replace ":" with ";" on Windows machines (java -cp .;./junit-4.12.jar;./hamcrest-core-1.3.jar TestRunner) . If you are using Windows 7, you will also need to put the classpath argument entirely in quotes (java -cp

".;./junit-4.12.jar;./hamcrest-core-1.3.jar" TestRunner). Don't use "~" or other short-cuts when referring to the path that the `junit` and `hamcrest` jar files live. Your Java files may compile but then won't run - apparently the -cp option in `javac` parses paths different than `java`.

You can then add your own `public static void main` to each individual class to run each individual test, and specify each test method to run.

However, you can imagine that this would get tedious as we add additional tests, and adding a `public static void main` method to each of these files to run all of the individual unit tests. What you will find is that a better solution is to create a **test runner**. A test runner will set up an environment and execute a selection of unit tests. If you are using a build system or an IDE, this test runner will usually be created and updated for you automatically. However, I believe it is useful to show how to create one's own test runner, as you may be in charge of creating a new one, or you may work on a system which is not being developed with an IDE, or a customized build tool which does not include automatically running tests.

Here is an example of a simple test runner program which will execute all methods with an `@Test` annotation in any of the specified classes. If there is any failure, it will display which tests failed; otherwise, it will let the user know that all of the tests have passed.

```java
import java.util.ArrayList;

import org.junit.runner.*;
import org.junit.runner.notification.*;

public class TestRunner {
    public static void main(String[] args) {

    ArrayList<Class> classesToTest = new ArrayList<Class>();
    boolean anyFailures = false;

    // ADD ANY MORE CLASSES YOU WISH TO TEST HERE

    classesToTest.add(FooTest.class);

    // For all test classes added, loop through and use JUnit
    // to run them.

    for (Class c: classesToTest) {
        Result r = JUnitCore.runClasses(c);

        // Print out any failures for this class.

        for (Failure f : r.getFailures()) {
        System.out.println(f.toString());
        }

        // If r is not successful, there was at least one
        // failure.  Thus, set anyFailures to true - this
        // can never be set back to false (no amount of
        // successes will ever eclipse the fact that there
        // was at least one failure.
```

```
        if (!r.wasSuccessful()) {
        anyFailures = true;
        }

    }

    // After completion, notify user if all tests passed or any failed.

    if (anyFailures) {
        System.out.println("\n!!! - At least one failure, see above.");
    } else {
        System.out.println("\nALL TESTS PASSED");
    }
    }
}
```

This simple test runner will execute all tests in any classes added to the `classesToTest` list. If you would like to add additional test classes, just follow the template above and add them to the list of classes to test. You can then compile and execute your test suite with the following commands:

```
javac -cp .:./hamcrest-core-1.3.jar:./junit-4.12.jar *.java
```

```
java -cp .:./hamcrest-core-1.3.jar:./junit-4.12.jar TestRunner
```

Chapter 14

Advanced Unit Testing

Although you can go relatively far with the skills learned in the last chapter, there are still aspects of unit testing which won't be possible with those techniques. In this chapter, we'll go further in depth on how to construct more complex test cases.

14.1   Test Doubles

A unit test should be a localized test; that is, it should check the particular method or function under test, and not worry about other aspects of the system. If there is a test failure, we want to make sure that the failure is due to the code in that particular method, not something else which that method relies upon. Software is often interconnected, and a particular method which relies upon other methods or classes may not work correctly if those other units of code do not work correctly.

In the following method, we will have fun at a duck pond. Calling `.haveFunAtDuckPond()` with a `Duck d` will feed the duck `numFeedings` number of times. The method will then return the amount of fun, which is directly in proportion to how many times the duck is fed. The duck will quack each time that it is fed. Note that we are feeding the duck pieces of regulation duck chow. Don't feed ducks bread, it's not actually good for them! If a null duck is passed in, or the number of feedings is zero or fewer, then it simply returns 0 as the amount of fun (null ducks and negative feeding are both equally not fun). Let us further assume that the implementation of `Duck` is faulty, and calling the `.quack()` method results in a `QuackingException`:

```
public int haveFunAtDuckPond(Duck d, int numFeedings) {
    if (d == null || numFeedings <= 0) { return 0; }
    int amountOfFun = 0;
    for (int j=0; j < numFeedings; j++) {
        amountOfFun++;
        d.feed();
        d.quack();
    }
    return amountOfFun;
}
```

Even though the code in this method works perfectly for all inputs, it requires that a working duck be present. Otherwise, any non-negative number of feedings with a valid duck will cause an exception to be thrown. If we see a unit test for this particular method failing, we will naturally think that the problem is in this method. Only after examining it will we understand that the problem actually lies elsewhere. How can we test this code when the code it depends upon doesn't work?

I wouldn't have asked the question if I didn't have an answer—**test doubles**. Test doubles are "fake" objects which you can use in your tests to "stand in" for other objects in the codebase. This has numerous benefits aside from hiding pieces of the codebase that don't work. Test doubles also allow you to localize the source of errors. If our tests for `haveFunAtDuckPond()` fail, then the problem should lie in that particular method, not in one of the classes or methods that the method depends upon.

JUnit does not support test doubles directly, but there are libraries that you can install alongside JUnit that do. For the next few sections, we will use a library called Mockito to enable doubles, mocks, verification, and stubbing. I know we haven't defined these terms yet, but isn't it exciting to know what's coming next?

In order to use Mockito, you will need to ensure that you have both the mockito and objenesis jars in your classpath, along with any required JUnit jars. If you use the Makefile from the previous chapter, and have downloaded the appropriate jar files, this should work for you automatically. If you are using an IDE or a build tool (such as Gradle or Maven), this may also already have been taken care of. If you are not using the test runner from the last chapter, you should review the documentation for your build tool to ensure that you have set it up correctly.

You should then add the line `import static org.mockito.*` to your test class files in order to access all of the tools in the libraries. As a reminder, using `import static` instead of `import` will allow us to access the static members of the mockito classes without explicitly referring to them. If you like, you can use a regular `import` statement, but this will mean that you will need to preface all of your

Here is an example of using a test double with JUnit and Mockito to test a method which relies on a test double object. Note that Mockito calls all test doubles "mocks", even if they don't use the capabilities of a mock object (described later in the chapter):

```
// Class to test
public class Horse {

    public int leadTo(Water w) {
        w.drink();
        return 1;
    }

}

// Unit test for class
import static org.junit.Assert.*;
import static org.mockito.*;
import org.junit.*;

public class HorseTest {

    // Test that leading a horse to water will return 1
    @Test
    public void testWaterDrinkReturnVal() {
        Horse horse = new Horse();
        // We are making a test double for water
        Water mockWater = mock(Water.class);
```

```
        int returnVal = horse.leadTo(mockWater);
        assertEquals(1, returnVal);
    }

}
```

We have now created a "fake" object instead of passing in an actual instantiation of the Water class. Water is now "quarantined" and cannot cause a failure in our code. If the test fails, it's the fault of this particular method. Therefore, whenever there is a failure, we'll know exactly where to look in the codebase to determine the issue. Whenever you use doubles, however, you are also dependent upon your assumptions of how the code you depend upon is supposed to work in the actual program. There is nothing stopping you from, say, creating test doubles that have a method that the actual class does not. In this case, your tests will work fine but the actual program will not.

Doubles can also be used to speed up the execution of tests. Think of a Database object which writes information out to a database and returns the status code. Under ordinary circumstances, the program needs to write out to disk and perhaps even access the network. Let's say that this takes one second. This may not seem like an incredibly long time to wait, but multiply it by all the tests that access the database. Even a relatively small program may have hundreds or even thousands of unit tests, adding minutes or hours to the amount of time each test run takes.

You should never, ever, ever use a double for the current class under test! If you do this, you're no longer testing anything, really, as you are creating a fake object for the actual thing that you are testing.

Test doubles should be used, as often as possible, when the code that you are unit testing uses a different class than the class under test. Sometimes it will be difficult to do. In order to minimize issues, you should pass in the object as a parameter whenever possible, as opposed to relying on member variables or global variables. Even worse, and more common, are methods that generate and use objects entirely internally. It is often not possible to use test doubles for these methods. Let's take a look at an example of this:

```
public class Dog {

    DogFood _df  = null;
    DogDish _dd  = null;
    DogWater _dw = null;

    public void setUpDogStuff() {
        _dd = new DogDish();
        _df = new DogFood();
        _dw = new DogWater();
    }

    public int eatDinner() {
        _df.eat();
        return 1;
    }

}
```

If we were to write a test for this class, we have no way of making doubles for the objects internal to the class! Even if we then refactored setUpDogStuff() to accept DogDish, DogFood, and DogWater parameters, we would be forced to work with additional items when all we care about is DogFood.

Let's refactor the method a bit to make it somewhat more amenable to test doubles:

```
public class Dog {

    DogFood _df = null;
    DogDish _dd  = null;
    DogWater _dw = null;

    public void setDogFood(DogFood df) {
        _df = df;
    }

    public void setDogDish(DogDish dd) {
        _dd = dd;
    }

    public void setDogWater(DogWater dw) {
        _dw = dw;
    }

    public int eatDinner() {
        _df.eat();
        return 1;
    }

}
```

If we wanted to test this, we would have to create an object and set the value separately from the actual test execution:

```
public class DogTest {

    @Test
    public void eatDinnerTest() {
        Dog d = new Dog();
        d.setDogFood(mock(DogFood.class));
        int returnVal = d.eatDinner();
        assertEquals(1, returnVal);
    }

}
```

This is better, but still not ideal, as extra statements are still required to set up the test. If, instead, we just pass in DogFood as a parameter to the method, like so:

```
public class Dog {

    public int eatDinner(DogFood df) {
        df.eat();
        return 1;
    }

}
```

The test would then look like:

```
public class DogTest {

    @Test
    public void testEatDinner() {
        Dog d = new Dog();
        int returnVal = d.eatDinner(mock(DogFood.class));
        assertEquals(1, returnVal);
    }

}
```

This will enable much easier and much more focused testing. You'll also note the code has several other benefits aside from increased testability. It's easier to read and understand, it's shorter, and there are fewer chances for errors. In the original version, it would be very easy for a programmer to forget to set the _df variable to a DogFood object at some point, causing a null pointer exception whenever the dog tried to eat. While still possible, this is less likely when you are passing in the object directly to the method. We'll discuss more of the benefits of writing testable code—and why testable code is good code, and vice versa—in a later chapter.

14.2   Stubs

If doubles are fake objects, stubs are fake methods. In the above examples, we didn't care what calling .eat() on the DogFood object did; we just didn't want it to call an actual DogFood object. In many cases, though, we expect a certain return value when a method is called. Let's modify the .eat() method on DogFood so that it returns an integer indicating how tasty the dog food is:

```
public class Dog {

    public int eatDinner(DogFood df) {
        int tastiness = df.eat();
        return tastiness;
    }

}
```

If we were just using df as a normal test double, then there is no telling what df.eat() will return. Specifically, the answer varies by test framework—some will always return a default value, some will call out the real object, some will throw an exception. This should just be a piece of trivia, though—you shouldn't call methods on a double object unless you have stubbed them. The whole reason for making a test double is so that you have an object that you have specified, instead of relying on external definitions. So let's say that our doubled DogFood object has a (scientifically determined) tastiness level of 13. We can specify that whenever the .eat() method is called on our doubled object, then just return a value of 13. We have made a **stub** of the method:

```
public class DogTest {

    @Test
    public void testEatDinner() {
        Dog d = new Dog();
        DogFood mockedDogFood = mock(DogFood.class);
```

```
        when(mockedDogFood.eat()).thenReturn(13);
        int returnVal = d.eatDinner(mockedDogFood);
        assertEquals(13, returnVal);
    }

}
```

Now when the mockedDogFood object has its .eat() method called, it will return the value 13. Once again, we have quarantined the other methods by re-creating fakes of them that act as we think they should. In some languages, although not Java, we can even stub methods that don't exist. This allows us to not only test classes that have errors, but even ones that don't have all of their methods written yet.

14.3 Mocks and Verification

"Yes, yes, this is all fine," I can hear you saying, "but you didn't answer the original question! We are still dependent on asserting on a value that is returned from a method, and thus won't be able to test methods without a return value!" Remember the impure method goToCatCafe that we wanted to test in the last chapter:

```
public class World {

    public void goToCatCafe(CatCafe catCafe) {
        System.out.println("Petting cats at a Cat Café!");
        catCafe.arrive();
        catCafe.haveFun();
    }

}
```

There is no return value and thus nothing on which to assert. The only way to test this method is to ensure that the .arrive() and .haveFun() methods on the catCafe object were called. We can do this using a special kind of test double called a **mock**. A mock object will allow you to assert that a particular method was called on the mocked object. In the above instance, instead of asserting that a particular value is returned (since no value is ever returned), you instead can make "meta-assertions" that .haveFun() and .arrive() are called. This is called **verification** since you are *verifying* that a method has been called. Note that this kind of verification has nothing to do with the kind of verification that means "checking that the software is right". They are two different concepts that happen to share the same word.

Here is how we might test that method using verification.

```
@Test
public void testGoToCatCafe() {
    CatCafe cc = mock(CatCafe.class);
    World w = new World();
    w.goToCatCafe(cc);
    verify(cc.arrive());
    verify(cc.haveFun());
}
```

Note, in this case, that there is no traditional assertion (e.g., `assertEquals`). The assertions are "hidden" inside the `verify()` call. If verification fails, the test case will fail just as it would with a simple assertion.

You may want to check that is called a certain number of times. Let's assume that we have a method `.multiPet()` which will allow you to easily pet the same cat numerous times, based on a passed-in integer.

```
public void multiPet(Cat c, int numTimes) {
    for (int j = 0; j < numTimes; j++) {
        c.pet();
    }
}
```

Using the `times()` method along with verification, you can check that if you call `multiPet(c, 5)`, that the cat C will be petted 5 times, or if you call it with the numTimes argument equal to 900 that cat will be petted 900 times (lucky cat!).

```
/**
 * Check that if we call multiPet with a valid cat and a numTimes
 * argument of 5, that cat will be petted 5 times.
 */

@Test
public void testMultiPet5() {
    World w = new World();
    Cat c = mock(Cat.class);
    w.multiPet(c, 5);
    verify(c.pet(), times(5));
}
```

Conversely, you may also want to check that a method is never called. Let's imagine another CatCafe-related method in our `World` class, `.petCat()`.

```java
public void petCat(Cat c, boolean gentle) {     if (gentle) {           c.pet();
} else {           // Do nothing - don't pet cats without being gentle!
```

In this case, we want to test that if the `gentle` variable is true, `.petCat()` will be called, otherwise it will not be called. We can create two unit tests for each of these equivalence classes.

```
/** * Check that attempting to pet a cat while being gentle will * cause the cat to be petted one
time. This is done by verifying * that c.pet() is called one time. */
```

```
@Test public void testPetCatGently() { World w = new World(); Cat c = mock(Cat.class);
w.petCat(c, true); verify(c.pet(), times(1)); }
```

```
/** * Check that attempting to pet a cat without being gentle will * not cause the cat to be petted.
This is done by verifying * that c.pet() is never called. */
```

```
@Test public void testPetCatNotGently() { World w = new World(); Cat c = mock(Cat.class);
w.petCat(c, false); verify(c.pet(), never()); } "'
```

We could also replace the `never()` method call with `times(0)`, as they are equivalent.

In summary, verify is used to make an assertion on the executed code. That is, unlike a traditional assertion which checks that a value is correct, a `verify` call asserts that a method was called (or not).

Note that we did not test whether or not the `System.out.println()` call worked. We will see how to do this later in this chapter, in the section *Testing System Output*.

14.4   Fakes

Sometimes, you need to have a test which depends on an object, and will require complex or non-performant behavior. In this case, you can use a **fake**. A fake is a special kind of test double which acts similarly to the regular object. However, it is written to be a part of the test, meaning that it runs faster and simpler. For example, you may remove any parts of the code which write to disk (always a slowdown when writing tests). You may have it perform a simpler calculation rather than a very time-consuming one. You may reduce that object's dependencies on other objects.

Fakes require more work to create than a simple test double, since they are a "lite" version of an object instead of simply specifying its external behavior. However, this allows you to perform more intricate tests than the relatively simple ones possible with test doubles. Suppose your DuckPond class is as follows:

```
public class DuckPond extends Pond {

    private int _funLevel = 0;

    public void haveFun() {
        _funLevel++;
    }

    public void haveUltraFun() {
        int funMultiplier = super.retrieveUltraLevelFromDatabase();
        _funLevel += funMultiplier * _funLevel;
    }

    public int getFunLevel() {
        return _funLevel;
    }

}
```

Let's set aside any issues one might have about how this code is written, and how it might be refactored to make it more testable. In this case, calling haveUltraFun() requires querying the database, which is called from a method from DuckPond's superclass. However, this also modifies the `_funLevel` variable, based on the value it received from the `retrieveUltraLevelFromDatabase()` call. The value of the variable `_funLevel` is going to depend both on that call to the database as well as how many times `haveFun()` and `haveUltraFun()` have been called. While it would be possible to just make a test double that returns specific values, adding in this behavior for a test which called multiple methods on a DuckPond object might add up to lots of extra work. Even worse, this work might have to be replicated in multiple tests.

Using DuckPond as-is also means that every call to `haveUltraFun()` will result in a dramatic slowdown in tests. Remember that calls to the disk or network, since they make take an order of magnitude or longer in time than the test would take otherwise, are discouraged in unit testing.

To get around this performance issue, let's create a fake version of the object, which we can use in our tests later. This fake version will be a "stripped-down" version of DuckPond, but will keep the general behavior.

```
public class FakeDuckPond extends Pond {

    private int _funLevel = 0;

    public void haveFun() {
        _funLevel++;
    }

    public void haveUltraFun() {
        // REMOVED DATABASE CALL
        _funLevel += 5 * _funLevel;
    }

    public int getFunLevel() {
        return _funLevel;
    }

}
```

We are now assuming that the `funMultiplier` variable retrieved from the database will always be 5. This will both speed up tests (by removing the database read) and simplify calculations (as well as help us understand what the expected behavior should be). However, unlike with a traditional test double or mock, we don't have to specify what the behavior should be externally. The class itself will determine the (simplified) behavior.

14.5   Setup and Teardown

Oftentimes, there are particular things that you want the tests for a particular class to do before each of the tests start, and after each of the tests end. For example, you may set up a mocked database connection, and want to use it as a precondition for all of the tests, instead of repeating the same line of code to create it in each individual test case. JUnit provides annotations for creating `setUp()` and `tearDown()` methods for cases such as this. Specifically, you can add an `@Before` annotation for any methods you want to have run before each individual test case, and an `@After` annotation for any methods you want to run after. Although you could theoretically name these methods something other than `setUp()` and `tearDown()`, these are common terms that you will see very often.

Here is an example of using `setUp()` and `tearDown()` methods:

```
public class BirdTest {

    DatabaseConnection _dbc = null;

    // Set up a mocked database connection
    @Before
    public void setUp() throws Exception {
        mockedDbc = mock(DatabaseConnection.class);
        _dbc = setupFakeDbConnection(mockedDbc);
    }

    // Tear down our mocked database connection
```

```java
@After
public void tearDown() throws Exception {
    _dbc = null;
}


// Tests that a newly created bird has a default fluffiness
// level of 1
@Test
public void testFluffyBird() {
    Bird b = new Bird(_dbc);
    assertEquals(1, b.fluffinessLevel);
}


// Tests that a newly created bird is pretty
@Test
public void testPrettyBird() {
    Bird b = new Bird(_dbc);
    assertTrue(b.isPretty());
}


}
```

Note that `@Before` and `@After` methods are called before *each* test case, not one time before all of them and one time after all of them. In the above instance, `setUp` will be called twice and `tearDown` will be called twice.

Also note that while there is nothing stopping you from prefacing multiple methods with `@Before` or `@After` annotations, it's usually not necessary and will just make it more difficult to follow the code. If you do make multiple methods with these annotations, they will run in a deterministic order (that is, if you run it again, they will run in the same order). However, since tests should not depend upon each other, this ordering is not specified and is liable to change whenever you update your code and/or JUnit version. Thus, it's generally a good idea to just have one `@Before` and one `@After`, maximum, per test file.

Getting back to setup and teardown procedures specifically, if you have complicated ones, using multiple annotations is usually unnecessary. You can still use a single method, but call out to other methods as helpers, instead of annotating numerous methods.

14.6   Testing System Output

One particular use case that `@After` and `@Before` annotations can help you with is checking for system output. Console output is a very common item to check for, but testing for it in Java is non-intuitive. Although it's possible to just pass in a System object with each method, which you could then mock and stub, this is not idiomatic Java code and will add lots of additional code (and most likely complexity) to your codebase. The best solution that I have seen for checking it involves using the `setOut()` method of `System` to put the output of `System.out` and `System.err` in `ByteArrayOutputStream`.[1]

Here is an example of how to check for specific output from a Java program using this technique:

---

[1]Full disclosure: I saw this on Stack Overflow at http://stackoverflow.com/q/1119385. (Yes, even authors of books go online to look for answers sometimes.)

```java
public class Kangaroo {

    public void hop() {
        System.out.println("Hoppity hop!");
    }

}

public class KangarooTest {

    private ByteArrayOutputStream out = new ByteArrayOutputStream();

    @Before
    public void setUp() {
        System.setOut(new PrintStream(out));
    }

    @After
    public void tearDown() {
        System.setOut(null);
    }

    @Test
    public void testHop() {
        Kangaroo k = new Kangaroo();
        k.hop();
        assertEquals("Hoppity hop!", out.toString());
    }

}
```

14.7   Testing Private Methods

There's quite an argument on whether or not it makes sense to test private methods. It's a great way to start a flame war amongst software developers and testers on your favorite social networking site. I'll provide you with the arguments of both sides, so that you can make a decision yourself, and then I'll let you know my opinion.

Those who argue that private methods should *never* be tested say that any calls from the rest of the program (i.e., the rest of the world from the class's standpoint) will have to come in through the public methods of the class. Those public methods will themselves access private methods; if they don't, then what's the point of having those private methods? By testing only the public interfaces of classes, you're minimizing the number of tests that you have and focusing on the tests and code that matter.

Another reason for not testing private methods is that it inhibits you from refactoring the code later. If you have already written tests for private methods, it is going to be more work to make changes to anything "behind the scenes". In a sense, testing private methods means going against one of the key tenets of object-oriented programming, namely data hiding. The system is going to be less flexible and more difficult to modify going forward.

Those who argue that private methods should *always* be tested point to the fact that private methods are still code, even if they're not called directly from outside the class. Unit testing is supposed to test functionality at the lowest levels possible, which is usually the method or function call. If you're going to start testing higher up the abstraction ladder, then why not just do systems-level testing?

My opinion is that, like most engineering questions, the correct answer depends on what you're trying to do and what the current codebase is like. As a side note, with most technical questions, saying "it depends" is a great way to be right, no matter what. Let's take a look at a few examples.

Imagine that we're adding a service to Rent-A-Cat to automate taking pictures of cats:

```
public class Picture {

    private void setupCamera() {
        // ...
    }

    private void turnOffCamera() {
        // ...
    }

    private Image captureImage() {
        // ...
    }

    public Image takePicture() {
        setupCamera();
        Image i = captureImage();
        turnOffCamera();
        return i;
    }

}
```

This code is relatively simple, and it's easy to see that all of the private methods will be called and tested by the public methods. From the standpoint of a user of this class, it's easy to test that things work correctly—if a valid image is returned, then the method worked.

Now let's imagine in a different part of this service, we have an image transformation library that we also want to test:

```
public class ImageLibrary {

    public Image transform(Image image, int inSize, int outSize, String format,
      boolean color, boolean reduce, boolean dither) {
        if (inSize < outSize && format.equals("jpg") || dither == false) {
            return privateMethod1(image, inSize, outSize);
        } else if (inSize < outSize && format.equals("png") || dither == true) {
            return privateMethod2(image, inSize, outSize);
        } else if (outSize > inSize || (color == false && reduce == false)) {
            return privateMethod3(image, inSize, outSize);
        } else {
            // Imagine lots more if...then...else if statements here
            // You get the idea
```

```
        }
    }

    // Lots of private methods here

}
```

Think of all the complicated tests that would be needed for this one method! Even then, you're not focusing on the actual image transformations. Many of your tests would just be focused on ensuring that the right method was called!

One could argue that this isn't a well-designed piece of code and should be refactored, ideally with the private methods put into, say, an `ImageTransformer` class, where the methods would be public and could easily be unit tested. I wouldn't disagree. However, the fact of the matter is that in the real world, there is often code like this lying around, and the tester is not always in a position to tell management that the company needs to spend a few months burning off technical debt instead of adding new features. If your goal is to test the software, and test it well, you'll probably have to test the occasional private method. For specific information on how to do this in Java, please see the supplemental chapter on *Using Reflection to Test Private Methods in Java* at the end of this book.

14.8 Unit Test Structure

14.8.1 Basic Outline

Unit tests in Java are usually grouped initially by class and further by method; they mirror the structure of the program. Since unit tests are white-box tests which interact closely with the code, this makes finding errors in the codebase based upon the particular failing test case much easier than with integration or manual tests.

14.8.2 What to Test?

Exactly what you test will vary based upon the domain of software you are testing and the amount of time you have for testing, as well as organizational standards and other external factors. Of course, stating this doesn't give you any direction at all, and similar caveats could probably be put in front of every paragraph of this book. There are some heuristics to follow, many of which directly mirror some of the items discussed when developing a test plan.

Ideally, you should look at the method and think of the various success and failure cases, determine the equivalence classes, and think about what some good boundary and interior values might be to test from those equivalence classes. You want to also focus on testing common use cases over use cases which rarely occur, at least at first. If you are writing more safety-critical software, often it makes sense to focus on testing for failure before checking the happy path. Personally, I often work on a base case first, and then think of possible failure cases after that. Oftentimes, I will go back, sometimes with a profiler, and see what code is executed most often and add extra test cases for that. I may try to construct a mental model of what is called often instead of using a profiler. I will definitely think of from where the inputs to the method are coming. If they are from a system that I have no control over (including users, the ultimate example of systems I have no control over) and may be sending unanticipated values, I will definitely spend more time thinking of possible failure cases and checking for edge cases.

You don't want to create a test suite that takes so long to run that people don't run it often, but a well-designed unit test suite with appropriate doubles, mocks, stubs, and the like should run very fast even when there are many tests. I would err on the side of creating too many tests rather than too few, at first. As you determine how many tests are necessary for the particular piece of software you're working on, you can start making trade-offs between the amount of time for development and for testing.

14.8.3   Assert Less, Name Directly

When unit tests fail, they should point you to exactly what went wrong, and where. They should not be large "one size fits all" tests. It is so fast to run a properly-written unit test (rarely taking more than a few tens of milliseconds) that the extra execution time and work involved in writing more tests is absolutely dwarfed by the amount of time that you will save when unit tests tell you exactly what went wrong when they failed. A unit test with lots of assertions shows a lack of thought towards what exactly the unit test was supposed to check for. Consider the following example:

```
public class CatTest {

    @Test
    public void testCatStuff() {
        Cat c = new Cat();
        c.setDefaults();
        assertTrue(c.isAGoodKitty());
        assertEquals(0, c.numKittens());
        assertFalse(c.isUgly());
        assertNull(c.owner());
    }

}
```

When this test fails, what is wrong? It could be that a newly created cat is not a good kitty, as it should be. It could be that there's an error with the number of kittens that a newly created cat has. It could be that the cat was erroneously assigned an owner. You'd have to track down the particular assertion in the test code, because seeing that "cat stuff" has failed does not tell you anything. If the name of the test case failing does not let you know what the failure is and preferably give you a very good pointer to where the failure lies, you are probably testing too much in each individual test case. There are numerous cases where I've gone in and fixed code just based on seeing the name of the test case that failed, without ever looking at the actual test code. This is a common consequence of well-specified, directed tests.

14.8.4   Unit Tests Should Be Independent

Unit tests should not be dependent on run order. That is, Test 2 should not depend on any side effects or result from Test 1. JUnit, and most other unit testing frameworks, will not run individual test cases in a predetermined order. By avoiding dependencies on each other and allowing each test to run independently, failures are localized to a particular test. Now imagine writing the following code:

```
public class Cat {

    private int _length;
```

```
    public Cat(int length) {
        _length = length;
    }

    public int getWhiskersLength() {
        return _length;
    }

    public int growWhiskers() {
        _length++;
        return _length;
    }
}


public class CatTest {

    int _whiskersLength = 5;

    @Test
    public void testWhiskersLength() {
        Cat c = new Cat(5);
        assertEquals(_whiskersLength, c.getWhiskersLength());
    }

    @Test
    public void testGrowWhiskers() {
        Cat c = new Cat(5);
        _whiskersLength = c.growWhiskers();
        assertEquals(6, _whiskersLength);
    }

}
```

If we run these tests with JUnit, which executes test cases in a random order, sometimes the second test would pass, and sometimes it would fail! Why?

Let's assume that the tests are run in the order that they are listed - that is, with testWhiskersLength() executed first. The variable _whiskersLength, which is set to its default value of 5, will be equal to the starting whiskers length in the constructed Cat object. Thus, our assertion that the length of the whiskers is 5 will be correct. When testGrowWhiskers() is called, the whiskers are grown by one unit, and the return value (i.e., the new length of the whiskers) is placed into the _whiskersLength variable, changing it to 6. Since _whiskersLength is equal to 6, the assertion is also correct. Congratulations, all of the tests pass!

Now let's see what happens when the tests are run in the opposite order, with testGrowWhiskers() executed first, then testWhiskersLength(). At the end of the testGrowWhiskers() test, _whiskersLength (which is a class level variable, and thus shared by all methods) is equal to 6. Now testWhiskersLength() is executed, but the new Cat object's whiskers length is 5, which is not equal to _whiskersLength, which is 6. Now we have a failing test - but one that only intermittently fails, depending in which order the test are executed.

We can fix this by ensuring that the tests are not dependent on each other. The easiest and best way to do this is to eliminate any shared data between tests. In this case, it means not depending on the class-level variable `_whiskersLength`. Let's rewrite the tests so that they can be run independently.

```java
public class CatTest {

    @Test
    public void testWhiskersLength() {
        Cat c = new Cat(5);
        assertEquals(5, c.getWhiskersLength());
    }

    @Test
    public void testGrowWhiskers() {
        Cat c = new Cat(5);
        int whiskersLength = c.growWhiskers();
        assertEquals(6, whiskersLength);
    }

}
```

While this example has a relatively simple solution, there may be cases where the dependencies are more difficult to determine or fix. Whenever you find that a test only passes sometimes, you may want to first investigate if there are any "hidden" dependencies betweent tests. These hidden dependencies may be objects or variables shared between methods, static variables on a class, or other external data on which your tests rely.

Note that in JUnit, it *is* possible to specify the order that tests will run in, by using the `@FixMethodOrder` annotation. However, you want to avoid doing that if at all possible. It is all too easy to allow your tests to fall into the trap of depending on each other by ensuring that they always run in the same order.

There is yet another benefit to creating tests which have no dependencies on other tests. Independent tests can be run in parallel, on different cores of a CPU or even on different machines entirely. If test execution depends on running sequentially, then you will not be able to run them in parallel. On a modern multi-core machine, you may find yourself running tests many times more quickly if they can be run independently. While the precise speed-up will depend on the particular tests you are running, what your computer hardware is like, and other factors, you can easily see test execution times reduced by 50% or more.

14.8.5   Try to Make Tests Better Every Time You Touch Them

Oftentimes, you will need to work with legacy code, including code which was poorly written or does not have good test coverage. Although it may be tempting to simply continue working in the same manner that the code was originally written, you should try to do what you can to make the testing of the code better. Keep your code easily testable, and if necessary, build wrappers around code that is difficult to test.

There is more discussion on writing testable code in the chapter *Writing Testable Code* (with a title like that, what else did you expect to find in it?)

14.9   Code Coverage

Code coverage tells you how much of the codebase is actually executed when running the test suite code. Since defining exactly what is meant by "how much of the codebase" can be complex, there are numerous kinds of code coverage. The simplest form of code coverage is method coverage; this measures what percentage of methods have any tests that call into them. For example, imagine a class Turtle with two methods, crawl() and eat():

```
public class Turtle {

    public void crawl() { ... }

    public void eat() { ... }

}
```

If we have a test calling crawl(), but none calling eat(), then we have 50% code coverage (one of two methods was tested). Even if we had a hundred tests calling crawl(), checking out all of the various different ways that a turtle can crawl, but none testing eat(), we still have 50% code coverage. Only once we add at least one test checking eat() will we have 100% code coverage.

A more detailed form of code coverage is statement coverage. This measures what percentage of programming statements were actually executed by at least one test. A programming statement is the smallest "chunk" of code that still makes sense as an individual unit of code; in Java, these are generally the pieces of code separated by semicolons. Some examples of statements include:

1. int j = 7;

2. System.out.println("Bark!");

3. foo--;

Note that "statement" does not mean "a line of code"! For example, in Java, you may have a line such as:

```
doSomething(k); k++;
```

This is actually multiple statements, they just happen to be on the same line.

When developers discuss "code coverage", they usually mean specifically "statement coverage". Compared to method coverage, using statement coverage provides vastly more granularity in knowing what parts of the codebase have actually been tested. For example, let's add some detail to our Turtle class so that we can see what the code is like inside the various methods:

```
public class Turtle {

    CurrentLocation _loc = World.getCurrentLocation();
    GroundType _g = World.getGroundType(_loc);

    public void crawl() {
        if (_g == DIRT) {
            move(SLOWLY);
        } else if (_g == GRASS) {
            eat();
            move(MORE_SLOWLY);
        } else {
            move(EVEN_MORE_SLOWLY);
```

```
        }
    }

    public void eat() {
        System.out.println("Yum yum");
    }

}
```

Using method coverage, having just one test for `eat()` or just one for `crawl()` would show 50% code coverage. This hides the fact that `crawl()` is much more complicated than `eat()` and any single test would miss several different possible outcomes, whereas `eat()` can be tested very well with just one test. It also would not let us know what particular lines were not tested—we would have to examine the test code to determine whether it was testing that the turtle could move on dirt, grass, or whatever else. Statement coverage output can tell us exactly which lines were never executed during a test run, so we know exactly what kinds of tests to add to ensure that we are checking that each line has been tested at least once.

There are other variants of code coverage such as branch coverage, which measures which percentage of conditionals (if statements, case statements, etc.) have been tested. However, these other kinds of code coverage are usually only used for much more specialized testing. Chances are that you will deal with the statement and method coverage much more often.

Having a statement or method covered by tests does not mean that all defects in that unit of code have been found by the test! It's easy to imagine defects slipping through method coverage. In our `Turtle` example, if there was some sort of problem when the turtle was on grass, but our test only checked the case that the turtle was on dirt, we can see how method coverage would say that `crawl()` has been checked but defects can still creep through. At a lower level of abstraction, statement coverage does not check for all variations in the way a particular statement could be executed. Let's consider the following single-method class and its associated test case:

```java
public class Cow {

    public int moo(int mooLevel) {
        int timesToMoo = Math.ceil(100 / mooLevel);
        for (int j=0; j < timesToMoo; j++) {
            System.out.println("moo!");
        }
        return timesToMoo;
    }

}

public class CowTest {

    @Test
    public void mooTest() {
        Cow c = new Cow();
        int mooTimes = c.moo(20);
        assertEquals(5, mooTimes);
    }

}
```

From a code coverage perspective, we have 100% code coverage and 100% method coverage—the only method in the class is called from a test, and every statement in the method is executed. However, calling `moo()` with a `mooLevel` parameter of 0 will cause a `DivideByZeroException` to be thrown. This defect will not be discovered by the test case, despite every statement being executed. Although not foolproof, ensuring that you've checked every equivalence class will help to ameliorate situations like this.

In fact, code coverage metrics can be even more misleading than this example. As long as a statement is *executed* by the test, that code is considered "covered". Nothing verifies that the unit tests actually test anything, though. Consider this case:

```
public class CowTest {

    @Test
    public void mooTest() {
        Cow c = new Cow();
        int mooTimes = c.moo(1);
        assertTrue(true);
    }

}
```

This test results in 100% code coverage of the method, but tells you almost nothing about the code. The only information you can get from this test passing is that calling `c.moo(1)` does not crash the program.

Code coverage is a powerful tool, but like anything else in software development, it is not a silver bullet. It's an excellent way to see what areas of the codebase might need more testing, but it should not assure you that any code that has been covered is guaranteed free of defects. It should not even assure you that a particular piece of code has truly been tested.

Just like your favorite nutritionally-suspect cereals, unit testing should not be your complete breakfast nor your entire test plan. Unit testing is great for checking individual methods and low-level functionality, but it is not good at seeing how everything fits together. It's even worse when trying to determine what the end product will look like; all of the individual methods may work, but together they form something which doesn't meet any of the requirements.

When you are testing, you should remember to perform some manual testing, integration testing, and depending upon your needs, other kinds of testing such as security testing or performance testing. Relying heavily on one particular kind of testing is a recipe for missing important defects.

Chapter 15

Test-Driven Development

Although we have covered how to write unit tests from a broad perspective, the question remains—how do we integrate test writing into the software development process? In the old days, software testing was often an entirely separate process from writing the code, but today, software quality is the job of developers, as well. Conversely, software testing has acquired many aspects of development; it is the rare tester who never has to write any code. Even testers who mostly do manual testing will often write integration scripts or other tools.

Test-Driven Development (TDD) is one methodology for writing quality software with a well-thought-out testing suite. By following the tenets of TDD, developers will know what to test, in what order, and a way of balancing unit testing and coding the application under test. It's not a panacea, of course. In the software world, as Frederick Brooks reminds us, there is no silver bullet. However, by using TDD properly, the werewolf of software development can be tamed a little bit.

15.1 What is TDD?

Test-Driven Development is a software development methodology that comprises several key points:

1. *Writing tests first, before code:* Before you even start thinking of *how* to do something, this forces you to think of *what* is to be done. Since your code has not been written, you can check that the test initially fails (in order to avoid tautological tests which always pass), and have a specific goal that you are reaching toward (getting the test you just wrote to pass).

2. *Writing only code that makes the test pass:* This ensures that you focus on writing relevant code, instead of spending time working on possibly superfluous frameworking or other code. One of the key benefits of TDD is that it allows you to focus, by training you to keep your eye on the one goal of the cycle instead of thinking of all the other possible bits of code that you could be writing.

3. *Writing only tests that test the code:* It's tempting to write tests for the sake of writing them; this will help to keep tests only being written for the functionality being written.

4. *A short turnaround cycle:* TDD emphasizes quick cycles, which work to keep the developer on track and focused on a short, specific goal.

5. *Refactoring early and often:* **Refactoring** is the process of changing code without changing its external functionality. This may include actions as simple as changing a variable name or

adding a comment, all the way to modifying key architectures or algorithms. What differenti-
ates from refactoring from just "writing code" is that refactoring improves the internal quality
of the codebase without having a direct effect on the external quality. While refactoring does
not have an immediate effect on the external quality of the system under test, however, it will
often have an indirect effect. This is because refactoring can make the code easier to read,
understand, maintain, and modify. As the process of development continues, refactoring will
make it easier for developers to continue to do their work.

Here is an example of a poorly-written program. We will refactor it to be easier to read, without
modifying any of its actual functionality.

```java
public class Hours {

    public static void main(String[] args) {
        double chikChirik = 792.34;
        try {
            chikChirik = Double.parseDouble(args[40 / 3 - 13]);
        } catch (Exception ex) {
            System.exit(1 * 1 * 1);
        }
        int kukurigu = 160 % 100;
        int gruhGruh = (2 * 2 * 2 * 2 * 2 * 2) - 4;
        System.out.println((chikChirik * kukurigu * gruhGruh) + " seconds");
    }
}
```

The first thing that we notice is that there are absolutely no comments. This will make it difficult
to read. Also, the use of Bulgarian animal noise onomatopoeias for variable names, while perhaps
interesting from a linguistic standpoint, does not give you much information on what those variables
are supposed to represent (*chik-chirik* is the noise that Bulgarian birds make, *kukurigu* what Bulgarian roosters make, and *gruh-gruh* what Bulgarian pigs make). There is also unnecessary variable
setting and complication. For example, both `kukurigu` and `gruhGruh` variables are set to 60 after
the computations take place. Variable `chikChirik` will never actually be used with its default value
of 792.34; why is it set to this very particular value? All exceptions are caught from the line where
`chikChirik` is set; we should check for very discrete possible failure modes. Several of our variables
are never modified - these should be constants (in Java, `final` variables). Finally, there is most
likely the opportunity to partition some of this computation into separate methods instead of doing
everything in the main method.

All of these are problems that can be fixed without modifying how the program actually behaves.
This is what makes this process *refactoring* instead of fixing defects. The code itself works as
advertised, it just does not do it in a way which will make further development easy. Let's fix some
of these problems and see how the refactored code looks. Software development is a very complicated
process, one which often stretches the minds of even the best programmers, testers, and managers.
Whatever we can do to reduce the cognitive burden on ourselves and future team members will
certainly be appreciated!

```java
public class Hours {

    final static int MINUTES_PER_HOUR = 60;
    final static int SECONDS_PER_MINUTE = 60;

    /**
     * Given a number of hours, return the number of seconds that
```

```
 * would be equivalent to that number of hours.
 */

public static double calculateSeconds(double hours) {
    return hours * MINUTES_PER_HOUR * SECONDS_PER_MINUTE;
}

/**
 * Given a double representing the number of hours as the first
 * argument on the command line, this will print out the number
 * of seconds in that number of hours.
 * For example, 1 hour = 3600.0 seconds.
 * Additional arguments from the command line are ignored.
 */

public static void main(String[] args) {
    double numHours = -1;
    try {
        numHours = Double.parseDouble(args[0]);
    } catch (NumberFormatException nfex) {
        // The argument passed in could not be parsed
        System.exit(1);
    } catch (ArrayIndexOutOfBoundsException oobex) {
        // No argument was passed in
        System.exit(1);
    }
    System.out.println(calculateSeconds(numHours) + " seconds");

}

}
```

This is much easier to read and understand, even though its behavior is exactly the same as the original, unrefactored code. This will also allow us to more easily make modifications. Let's say that we wanted to display an error message instead of silently exiting if an argument could not be read or parsed. With the refactored code, we can see the various failure modes and easily add appropriate error messages based on the problem (e.g., "Argument could not be parsed as a double." or "At least one argument must be passed in."). Perhaps we want to modify our program to calculate French Revolutionary Time, which had 100 seconds per minute and 100 minutes per hour (and 10 hours in a day). It is very simple for me to see the constants indicating values for SECONDS_PER_MINUTE and MINUTES_PER_HOUR and modify them to the appropriate values. It would have been much more difficult with the original code.

Sadly, refactoring is often held off until later in the development process, when it is much more difficult to do. This is especially the case if there has not been much time spent on refactoring earlier, or if the development team has little experience in refactoring code. The difficulties encountered in refactoring then becomes an excuse to continue to avoid doing it. It becomes a self-fulfilling prophecy; avoiding refactoring of code makes it even more difficult to refactor! By refactoring often, it becomes a part of the development process and a habit, instead of something that will be done "if there's enough time" (note: there is never enough time).

15.2   The Red-Green-Refactor Loop

We work within these constraints by using the "red-green-refactor" loop. A single cycle in TDD involves the following three steps:

1. *Red:* TDD is a form of **test-first development** (TFD), so the first thing to do is write a test. The developer writes a failing test for a new piece of functionality or an edge case that should be checked. The newly written test—and only that test—should fail. If the newly written test does not fail, that means that the code has already been written for that functionality. If other tests fail, this means that there is a problem with the test suite—perhaps an intermittent or non-deterministic failure of a test—that should be fixed before moving on. This phase is called "red" because many unit testing frameworks will display failing tests in red. Since red-green colorblindness affects a good portion of the human population, and humans are by far the most likely animal to program, this may not be the best color selection. Regardless, we will follow this standardized naming convention.

2. *Green:* The developer now writes code to make this test pass. This work will focus only on making this test pass, while not causing any other tests to fail. At this point, some "ugly" code is to be expected; the focus is on making it work as opposed to making it pretty. If other tests fail, then the developer has inadvertently caused a regression and should work on fixing that. At the end of this phase, all tests should be passing ("green").

3. *Refactor:* Once all the tests pass, the developer should examine the code that was just written and refactor it. There may be small problems like magic numbers (i.e. "naked" values in a program that are not described or represented by a constant such as `if (mph > 65) { ... }` instead of `if (mph > SPEED_LIMIT) { ... }`) or large problems such as a poorly-chosen algorithm. These can be fixed during this phase, since in the previous phase the focus was simply on getting the results correct. An easy way to remember this is the mnemonic "first make it green, then make it clean". Since there is always a fall-back position of properly functioning (if poorly written) code, the developer can try multiple approaches without worrying about getting to a point where the code doesn't work at all. In the worst case scenario, the code can be reverted back to where it was at the end of the "green" phase and a different path can be chosen for rewriting.

After each red-green-refactor cycle, the developer should think of the next piece of functionality to add, and then loop back. This cycling will continue until the software is done. This is a path of testing, coding, and refactoring that will eventually culminate in a complete product. As a side effect, it will also include a solid test suite that is directly relevant to all the functionality of the program.

This could all be re-written as a very simple algorithm. By doing so, we can see how this helps focus the attention of the person writing the software; there is always a well-defined next step:

1. Write a test for functionality which has not been written yet.

2. Run test suite—only the newly written test should fail. If not, first figure out why other tests are failing and fix that problem.

3. Write enough code to make that test pass, without causing other tests to fail

4. Run test suite—if any test fails, go back to step 3. If all tests pass, continue.

5. Refactor code that you have written, and/or any associated code.

6. Run test suite—if any tests fail, go back to step 5. If all tests pass, continue.

7. If there is any more functionality to add, go to step 1. If there is no more functionality to add, the application is complete!

15.3 Principles of Test-Driven Development

There are several principles to keep in mind when writing in a TDD manner.

- *YAGNI (You Ain't Gonna Need It):* Don't write any code that you don't need in order to make the tests pass! It's always tempting to make a nice abstract system which can handle all sorts of different future variations on whatever it is you're doing now, but you will also make the code more complex. What's worse, you will be making it more complex in ways that may not ever help the system's future development. Avoid complexity until it's absolutely necessary. If there are more edge cases or equivalence classes that need to be dealt with, add more tests first.

- *KISS (Keep It Simple, Stupid):* One of the goals of TDD is to ensure that the codebase is flexible and extensible, and one of the greatest enemies of those two goals is complexity. Complex systems are difficult to understand and thus modify; complex systems tend to be overfit to the specific problem they were developed for, and it's difficult to add new features or functionality. Keep your code simple and your design simple, and consciously avoid adding additional complexity.

- *Fake It 'Til You Make It:* It's okay to use fake methods and objects in your tests, or just use a placeholder such as `return 0;` as the entire body of a method. You can come back later with additional tests and code once they are necessary.

- *Avoid Slow Running Tests:* If you are working with TDD, you are running at least three full test runs each iteration through the red-green-refactor loop. That's a minimum and assuming that your code never causes problems in other tests or has any defects of its own. If running your test suite takes two or three seconds, this is a minor price to pay for the extra quality that TDD provides; if it takes several hours, how long before developers are going to start ignoring the process in order to actually get some work done?

- *Remember That These Are Principles, Not Laws:* It would be counterproductive to entirely ignore what else the software needs to do in the next few iterations of the red-green-refactor loop. Occasionally, a test may be slow but necessary, or actually making a method would be just as simple as adding a fake version of it. Although you should endeavor to follow the principles of TDD, I know of nobody who has never violated one of the principles (although perhaps that speaks more to the type of people with whom I spend time).

15.4 Example: Building FizzBuzz via TDD

In order to understand how TDD works, let's write a simple `FizzBuzz` program using it. Recall that `FizzBuzz` consists of:

1. Printing every number from 1 to 100, with the following exceptions.

2. If the number is evenly divisible by both three and five, then the word "FizzBuzz" should be printed instead of the number.

3. If the number is evenly divisible by three, then the word "Fizz" should be printed instead of the number.

4. If the number is evenly divisible by five, then the word "Buzz" should be printed instead of the number.

First, let's build a "walking skeleton" of the application. Assuming we already have JUnit or a similar testing framework installed, and we aren't deploying it anywhere, all we have to do is generate our initial `FizzBuzz` class. Since we're iterating through a range of values, each of which is entirely decidable based on its value, let's create a class that has a main method and a `fizzbuzzify` method, which will return the correct string for a given value.

Thinking a little ahead, we know that we're going to have to iterate through the numbers 1 through 100. Therefore, there are four cases that we'd like to test for:

1. The number itself should be returned, if the number is not evenly divisible by 3 or 5

2. The string "Fizz" should be returned, if the number is evenly divisible by 3 but not evenly divisible by 5

3. The string "Buzz" should be returned, if the number is evenly divisible by 5, but not evenly divisible by 3

4. The string "FizzBuzz" should be returned, if the number is evenly divisible by both 5 and 3

Our testing is helped by the fact that this is a pure function—its return value is entirely determined by the input parameter. It has no dependence on global values and has no side effects like output, and no other external dependencies. Sending in 2 will always return "2" and do nothing else, sending in 3 will always return "Buzz" and do nothing else, and so on.

```java
public class FizzBuzz {

    private static String fizzbuzzify(int num) {
        return "";
    }

    public static void main(String args[]) {

    }

}
```

Now let's add our first test, using the first case. The first number that is not evenly divisible by 3 or 5 is 1, so let's use 1 as the first value to test for our `fizzbuzzify()` method:

```java
public class FizzBuzzTest {

    @Test
    public void test1Returns1() {
        String returnedVal = FizzBuzz.fizzbuzzify(1);
        assertEquals("1", returnedVal);
    }

}
```

If we run this, it will fail—`fizzbuzzify` returns an empty string, which is not equal to 1, and thus the assertion fails. Well, there's a simple fix for that!

```java
public class FizzBuzz {

    private static String fizzbuzzify(int num) {
        return "1";
    }

    public static void main(String args[]) {
```

```
        }

}
```

When we run the test again, it passes! Let's move on to the next phase and look for refactoring opportunities. In this case, I don't think there are any; sure, there's a magic number (well, technically a magic string consisting of a number), but what can you do, replace it with a constant NUMBER_ONE? That's not any more understandable.

Let's add another test, for 2, which should return a non-fizzy, non-buzzy string, "2":

```java
public class FizzBuzzTest {

    @Test
    public void test1Returns1() {
        String returnedVal = FizzBuzz.fizzbuzzify(1);
        assertEquals("1", returnedVal);
    }

    public void test2Returns2() {
        String returnedVal = FizzBuzz.fizzbuzzify(2);
        assertEquals("2", returnedVal);
    }

}
```

When we run this, as expected, we get one failure; since our fizzbuzzify() method will only ever return 1, it's never going to return 2. We also note that we didn't cause the initial test to fail by adding this test—the only test that fails is the new one, test2Returns2(). Fixing up the code should be pretty simple, right?

```java
public class FizzBuzz {

    private static String fizzbuzzify(int num) {
        if (num == 1) {
            return "1";
        } else {
            return "2";
        }
    }

    public static void main(String args[]) {

    }

}
```

Now all of our tests pass! We are coding geniuses! Go ahead and give yourself a pat on the back!

Of course, this pattern is not going to work going forwards. Let's refactor the code a bit so that it will work with all integers, instead of having to add a new else if for each individual value:

```java
public class FizzBuzz {

    private static String fizzbuzzify(int num) {
```

```
        return String.valueOf(num);
    }

    public static void main(String args[]) {

    }

}
```

Much better! Tests are still passing, so we can move on to the next cycle in the loop. Let's add a test for `fizzbuzzify(3)`, which should return "Fizz":

```
@Test
public void test3ReturnsFizz() {
    String returnedVal = FizzBuzz.fizzbuzzify(3);
    assertEquals("Fizz", returnedVal);
}
```

`fizzbuzzify(3)` will actually return "3", of course, causing our test to fail. However, that can be fixed quickly!

```
private static String fizzbuzzify(int num) {
    if (num == 3) {
        return "Fizz";
    } else {
        return String.valueOf(num);
    }
}
```

Huzzah, our tests pass! This isn't an ideal solution, though—it will only work with 3, and we know that it should be any number that's evenly divisible by 3. A bit of refactoring and we should be able to handle any number divisible by 3:

```
private static String fizzbuzzify(int num) {
    if (num % 3 == 0) {
        return "Fizz";
    } else {
        return String.valueOf(num);
    }
}
```

This also might give us more ideas for additional unit tests later—perhaps we want to check if 6, 9, or 3000 work. For now, though, let's just move on to add "Buzz":

```
@Test
public void test5ReturnsBuzz() {
    String returnedVal = FizzBuzz.fizzbuzzify(5);
    assertEquals("Buzz", returnedVal);
}
```

Once again, the test will fail, so we add an additional else to our conditional:

```
private static String fizzbuzzify(int num) {
    if (num % 3 == 0) {
        return "Fizz";
    } else if (num % 5 == 0) {
        return "Buzz";
```

```
    } else {
        return String.valueOf(num);
    }
}
```

Tests pass now, and there doesn't seem to be any refactoring to do. Let's try one final test for the "FizzBuzz" return value:

```
@Test
public void test15ReturnsFizzBuzz() {
    String returnedVal = FizzBuzz.fizzbuzzify(15);
    assertEquals("FizzBuzz", returnedVal);
}
```

This test fails, since the current method will return "Fizz":

```
private static String fizzbuzzify(int num) {
    if ((num % 3 == 0) && (num % 5 == 0)) {
        return "FizzBuzz";
    } else if (num % 3 == 0) {
        return "Fizz";
    } else if (num % 5 == 0) {
        return "Buzz";
    } else {
        return String.valueOf(num);
    }
}
```

Tests are now passing! We might go further with refactoring—for example, moving num % 3 == 0 and num % 5 == 0 to their own methods—but this shows a simple outline of the TDD process. Oftentimes, steps are bigger in actual development, but a key tenet to keep in mind is to keep the tests relatively specific and targeted at particular output values. Grouping the input and output values into equivalence classes, as discussed earlier, can help you to decide what needs to be tested and what order to test things in.

15.5   Benefits of TDD

One of the biggest benefits of TDD is that it automatically creates a test suite during development. Instead of having to worry about fitting in time to develop a testing framework and writing tests, the mere act of development will create one for you. Testing is, sadly, often relegated to the end of the project (which means that it will be given short shrift or even avoided entirely). Using TDD ensures that you will at least have some sort of test suite even if other testing is curtailed.

When tests are part of the workflow, people remember to do them. You probably don't think "ugh, I need to remember to brush my teeth today" every morning when you wake up; it's just a habit that you do as part of your morning routine. You're more likely to write tests when it's something that you just do all the time and have created a habit around doing. Since more tests are correlated with higher quality code, this is definitely a good thing! When things are done more often, they are also easier to do. Any problems with the test suite will be found quickly, and parts which are problematic and code which is difficult to test will be dealt with sooner.

Yet another benefit is that the tests that you write with TDD are relevant, since new tests must fail first (ensuring that the test is not redundant) and must pass before the cycle of writing a piece of code is considered "complete". You are less likely in this case to write tests which are unnecessary or tautological, or over-test one area and under-test another.

If you are writing tests after the fact, it's easy to fall into the trap of assuming that what the program does is what the program should do. However, remember that tests are supposed to check expected behavior against the observed behavior. If you are "expecting" something that you already "observed", your tests run the risk of being tautological!

TDD forces you to work in small steps. This helps to ensure that you don't go too far off the path working on something. If you wrote four lines of code and introduced a defect, it's much easier to find out where you went wrong than if you find the defect after writing a thousand lines of code. I like to think of writing code as crossing Antarctica with vicious penguins all around, and tests are fortresses against the penguins. You can easily cross the entire continent if you only go a mile or two before setting up another fortress, as there is always a place close by to retreat to if the penguins get that mad gleam in their eye. You can then choose another path, perhaps with fewer penguins, and build a fort there. Crossing the Antarctic without building anti-penguin forts would be a foolhardy maneuver, because any penguin attack might mean re-tracing your steps all the way to your landing craft. Writing large pieces of code without tests similarly prevents you from making solid progress as any defects may cause you to have to scrap much of the code that you have already written.

When you are testing code from the beginning, the code is much more likely to be testable. Not only will you learn how to test the code in this particular application because you are doing it all the time, you are not likely to write code that you can't test. Why would you? Your code needs to pass the test that you've already written, so you are going to make it in a way that will make it testable. Since you are also constantly adding on to the codebase, as opposed to seeing it as one large "version" to be committed as a giant block, your code will also be extensible. You're extending it with each cycle of the red-green-refactor loop!

Using TDD provides 100% test coverage, or at least close to it. Although code coverage is not a perfect metric—there are plenty of defects that can be hidden in code that is entirely covered by tests—it assures you that you are at least checking each line of code once. This is much better than many software projects.

Test-Driven Development provides a structured framework to write software with. Although there are certainly many drawbacks (some of which will be enumerated below) and situations for which it is a suboptimal methodology, it does provide you with a way to move forward. The strict but flexible steps of the red-green-refactor loop provide developers with a list of things to do next. You are constantly adding tests, writing code to make them pass, and refactoring. When you don't have a framework to follow, you may spend lots of time refactoring existing code, or not nearly enough time writing tests, or too much energy writing tests and not writing code. At a bare minimum, you've got to consider how much time and resources you'd like to spend on each section. With TDD, you have ready-made answers, so you don't have to think about it, and your mind is clear to work on other things. There is an excellent book, *The Checklist Manifesto* by Atul Gawande, which explains how having a checklist (even one as simple as red-green-refactor) can help you in a variety of endeavors. Software engineering is no exception.

Finally, and most importantly, developing software using TDD can give you confidence in your codebase. You are walking the tightrope of development with a net; you know that the software you are writing can at least do the things that you ask of it. You have guard rails that let you know when you've caused problems in other parts of the application. You have a seasoned team of developers letting you know what the next steps are. You are not alone.

15.6 Drawbacks of TDD

As mentioned above, there is no silver bullet in software development. Developing software using TDD has many benefits, but it's not always the correct methodology to use. Be aware of the following drawbacks before deciding to use TDD.

Developing in TDD means writing many unit tests. If your team needs to be coerced into testing software in the first place, this focus may drive out other kinds of tests, such as performance testing and systems testing. You need to keep in mind that just because you have written many unit tests for a method which utilizes some functionality, this does not mean that you have thoroughly tested that functionality.

There is no doubt about it—in the short run, writing tests will mean more time spent to get the same amount of features. There are benefits, to be sure, such as improved code quality. However, if one had waited until the night before a project is due for a software class (ahem), TDD would probably not be the way to go. In this case, a bulletproof program which doesn't meet half the requirements for the homework assignment is much worse than a program which does everything it's supposed to do, as long as you don't pass any invalid parameters to it or hit Control-C or breathe too heavily around it. However, for larger projects or projects without such a small deadline, using TDD or a similar methodology will often be faster in the long run. A good analogy is that writing software without tests is like riding a go-kart; it seems really fast, but is actually slow. Writing software with tests is like riding a jet plane; it seems really slow, but is actually very fast.

Traditionally, TDD provides less time up-front for architecture decisions. Due to the short cycle time of the red-green-refactor loop, less time may be spent on design and architecture as opposed to writing code which implements user stories. In many cases, such as simple web applications, this is perfectly valid. Default architectures may be fine and spending too much time thinking about them may be counterproductive. In other cases, especially with new kinds or domains of software, architectural choices may be difficult and consequential, and it makes sense to spend more time at the beginning of the project thinking about them.

Furthermore, architectural design changes made later in development may be difficult to implement. Although the methodology is meant to be flexible, some design decisions would require numerous modifications once code is written. It may be easier to spend more time earlier in the software development life cycle thinking about what is to be done, instead of assuming that you will be able to make changes later.

Certainly for some application domains, test-driven development is the wrong approach. If you are building a prototype of something, and are not sure what the expected behavior should be, but you know that it's going to change rapidly and not be used in production, then TDD is overkill. The ever-growing test suite, which usually acts as a safety net, would become an albatross around your code's neck. If you are trying to figure out the expected behavior as you go along, it makes little sense to use a methodology which presupposes that you know what the expected behavior is. In a different vein, extremely safety-critical applications, such as power systems or avionics controls, will require much more design and forethought than TDD can provide. In this case, TDD may be a little *too* flexible.

Remember that when you write automated tests, you are actually writing code. Sure, the code looks a little different, but you're still adding more and more overhead to your codebase. This is another place for things to go wrong, another place for refactoring, another place to update any time a change is made to the requirements or direction of the project. Although this overhead is often compensated for with an increase in the quality of the application, in some cases it may not be. On especially small projects and scripts, it may be much faster to simply do some manual testing to ensure that it does what it's supposed to do, instead of spending the time on developing an entire framework around the application.

Finally, as an engineer, you often do not start with a greenfield (that is, an entirely new) project. Often, you are modifying or adding features to already-existing software, much of which has been written using different methodologies or paradigms. If you start working on a project which uses a very rigid Waterfall methodology, or code which is not easily testable, trying to use TDD may be more trouble than it's worth. It may also alienate you from team members, or force you to spend too much time to develop your features.

Chapter 16

Writing Testable Code

Although we have been looking at testing from the perspective of a tester, often it can be useful to view it from the perspective of someone writing the code. Just as a tester can make the life of a developer easier by determining defects and the level of quality of a program, the programmer can make life easier for a tester by ensuring that the code they write is easily able to be tested. In today's programming environment, the tester and developer are often the same person, especially when it comes to unit tests. Thus, it makes perfect sense (from a game theory perspective) to make the code as testable as possible.

By writing the code in a testable way, not only will you make it easier to write tests now, but there are a host of other benefits. You will tend to write good, modular code. Future changes will be easier to make, since you will have more tests and can write better tests. The code will be easier to understand, and there will be fewer problems since you're more easily able to test all of the edge cases. Although your goal may be to write testable code, you'll end up writing code that is better in all sorts of other ways.

16.1   What Do We Mean By Testable Code?

In some sense, virtually all code is testable. As long as you can control the inputs and observe the outputs, you can test any piece of software. By **testable code**, we mean code that is easy to test in an automated fashion at multiple levels of abstraction. This means that writing black-box systems tests is simple, that writing unit tests (for classes, methods, or other units of code) is not unreasonably complex, and that more advanced testing such as performance and security testing are possible. Not all testable code is good code—it's possible to write a horrible mess of non-performant spaghetti code which is nevertheless easy to test. However, all good code is testable code. Being able to write tests for a particular piece of code is an integral part of the code being well-written.

Let's imagine that we're testing the following piece of code. It's part of a video game which simulates a bird moving across a landscape. Pressing a button makes the bird fly and updates its height and location on the screen.

```
public class Bird {

    public int _height = 0;

    public int _location = 0;
```

```
public void fly() {
    Random r = new Random();
    _height += r.nextInt(10) + 1;
    _location += r.nextInt(10) + 1;
    Screen.updateWithNewValues(_height, _location);
}

}
```

While this may be a straightforward method, it is going to be very difficult to test via unit test. After all, there are no return values to assert against. The results will have be checked by looking at class-level variables. There's no way to tell a specific "right" answer, since there's dependence on a random number generator which you have no way of overriding. There's no way to check that the Screen was updated without having an actual Screen object available and running. All of these mean that this code will be difficult to test in isolation, and thus very difficult to unit test. Throughout the rest of this chapter, we will look at different strategies to ensure that our code does not end up like this.

16.2   The Basic Strategies for Testable Code

The two key concepts to keep in mind when writing code that is testable at the unit test level are:

1. Ensure code is segmented

2. Ensure that events are repeatable

If a particular method relies on only a few other parts (classes, methods, external programs, etc.) of the system to work—and ideally, if its results are affected only by the values passed in as parameters—then it will be relatively easy to test. However, if it relies on a variety of other parts, then it can get very difficult, very quickly. You not only have to make sure that the part of the system is working, but any parts that it is dependent upon. You may be able to provide test doubles, but if the code is not written with them in mind, it may not be possible. Let's examine some code which is not segmented well, and will be extremely difficult to test:

```
public int getNumGiraffesInZoo() {
    String animalToGet = "Giraffe";
    DatabaseWorker dbw = DatabaseConnectionPool.getWorker();
    NetworkConnection nwc = NetworkConnectionFactory.getConnection();
    dbw.setNetworkConnection(nwc);
    String sql = SqlGenerator.generate("numberQuery", animalToGet);
    int numGiraffes = 0;
    try {
        numGiraffes = (int) dbw.runSql(sql);
    } catch (DatabaseException dbex) {
        numGiraffes = -1;
    }
    return numGiraffes;
}
```

At first glance, this looks easy to test—after all, you just need to assert that the number of giraffes is the number you expect—but this code is not well-segmented. Not only does it depend on the DatabaseWorker, NetworkConnection, DatabaseConnectionPool, NetworkConnectionFactory, and `SqlGenerator` classes to work correctly, along with all of their assorted methods, but there is no way to double them since they are all constructed inside of the method. A problem in any of these will cause your test to fail, and it can be difficult to know why the test failed. Was it in the actual method you are testing, or one of the numerous dependencies?

Let's restructure this so that the method is well-segmented:

```
public int getNumGiraffesInZoo(DatabaseWorker dbw, SqlGenerator sqlg) {
    String animalToGet = "Giraffe";
    int numGiraffes = 0;
    String sql = sqlg.generate("numberQuery", animalToGet);
    try {
        numGiraffes = (int) dbw.runSql(sql);
    } catch (DatabaseException dbex) {
        numGiraffes = -1;
    }
    return numGiraffes;
}
```

While this is still suboptimal, it is at least possible to override all of the dependencies with doubles. There's less concern in the method on items that are unrelated to the method itself (e.g., connecting network connections to the database worker, which probably belongs in the `DatabaseConnectionPool` or the `DatabaseWorker` class itself, certainly not in the `getNumGiraffesInZoo` method). We could go a bit further and move all of the database workings to their own class, wrapping them all up so that only the important parts are visible to this method:

```
public int getNumGiraffesInZoo(AnimalDatabaseWorker adbw) {
    String animalToGet = "Giraffe";
    int numGiraffes = 0;
    try {
        numGiraffes = adbw.getNumAnimals(animalToGet);
    } catch (DatabaseException dbex) {
        numGiraffes = -1;
    }
    return numGiraffes;
}
```

We have now reduced the number of dependencies to that single class `AnimalDatabaseWorker`, and only call one method on it.

The second concept is to ensure that everything you do is repeatable. What you don't want is a test which only works fine sometimes. If there is a failure, you should know about it immediately. If there is not a failure, you do not want to have false alarms.

You can make a test repeatable by ensuring that all of the values that it depends on are able to be replicated. This is one of the (many, many, many) reasons that global variables are, in general, a Bad Idea. Let's consider testing the following method:

```
public int[] sortList() {
    if (_sortingAlgorithm == "MergeSort") {
        return mergeSort(_list);
    } else if (_sortingAlgorithm == "QuickSort") {
        return quickSort(_list);
    } else {
        if (getRandomNumber() % 2 == 0) {
            return bubbleSort(_list);
```

```
    } else {
        return bogoSort(_list);
    }
  }
}
```

What happens when we run this? The execution flow first depends on two variables that were not passed in, so we'd need to add additional checks to make sure that they're the right value before testing if we want to make sure the test is repeatable. Who knows what other code has modified `_list` and `_sortingAlgorithm`? Even if we ensure ahead of time that all the variables are set correctly, how can we test what happens when `_sortingAlgorithm` is set to something other than "MergeSort" or "QuickSort"? The method will call either `bubbleSort()` or `bogoSort()`, and there is no (reasonable) way for us to tell which one will be called ahead of time. If there is an error with `bubbleSort()` but not `bogoSort()`, then the test might randomly fail.

In order to test effectively, code should be segmented, and written in such a way that ensuring that the exact same code with the exact same values can be run multiple times. If this is the case, then the exact output should occur each time, and tests will not randomly fail. Write your code in such a way as to discourage random test failures, not encourage them.

16.3   Provide a Scriptable Interface

While the previous section described how to ensure code is testable from a white-box perspective, creating a program that is easily testable from a black-box, systems-level perspective can be even more difficult. Methods, in general, are meant to be called—there's a built-in interface to do it, and the parameters for each method are generally specified. Entire systems, however, may do many things on their own with only occasional outside influence.

Some interfaces are "automatically" scriptable. If you are writing a web app, for example, you can use a web testing framework such as Selenium or Capybara to access the various pages, click buttons, enter text, and do all of the other things you can do to a web page. Text-based interfaces are also relatively easy to script, since they simply accept text and output it. Output can be redirected to a file or otherwise checked for accuracy.

Programs which do not provide a method of scripting by virtue of their interface, such as native GUI applications, will ideally have some sort of scripting built into them. This can be done via **test hooks**, or "hidden" methods which provide a way to input data or receive information about the program. These are externally accessible, perhaps with a key or other security measure, but usually not publicly advertised.

There are several downsides to adding hooks to your program, or any sort of scriptable interface. It's a security risk, for one thing—if someone discovers how to access the test hooks, they may be able to determine hidden information, overwrite data, or perform other malicious actions (or simply be curious and make a mistake). Adding a scriptable interface will require additional complexity in the program, as well as additional program length and size. The interface may be a drag on performance.

Worse, scripts may give you a false sense of security. Adding a separate way to access user-facing functionality means that you will need to have (at least) two parallel ways to use the system. In some cases, functionality that works perfectly fine via the scriptable interface will not work when accessing it in the "normal" way.

Time spent working on a scripting interface also means less time spent writing other features of the software, or improving its quality. This trade-off may be worthwhile, but it should be considered on a project-by-project basis.

You can test graphical and other non-text interfaces without test hooks, but it will tend to be much more difficult. Writing code to directly interface with something is often the easiest and most direct route. There are programs which allow you to directly manipulate the cursor, take screenshots of the result, and perform other interface interaction which is not scripted. However, these tools are often finicky and require some degree of manual verification.

16.4 Write Tests Up-Front

Ideally, you should be using the TDD paradigm, or something similar. Even if you are not using TDD, you should be writing lots of tests at approximately the same time as you are writing code. You will quickly realize when the code you have written cannot be tested, and you won't continue going down long pathways writing code which you will have trouble testing "later". Note that "later" often means "never".

The longer you go on writing code without writing tests for it, the more likely you are to make code which is difficult to test. Even if you mean to make it testable, you often won't realize that what you wrote will be difficult to test for one reason or another. Actually writing the tests gives you confirmation that you are going down the right path.

16.5 DRYing Up Code

The acronym **DRY** stands for "Don't Repeat Yourself", and it is a key tenet to making your code not only more testable, but better all around. The trivial case of failing to keep code DRY is simply copy-and-pasting, often with a slightly different method name:

```
public int[] sortAllTheNumbers(int[] numsToSort) {
    return quickSort(numsToSort);
}


public int[] sortThemThereNumbers(int[] numsToSort) {
    return quickSort(numsToSort);
}
```

In case you think this is a ludicrous contrived example, I have personally seen—and fixed—code like this in the wild. Although it seems obvious when they're right next to each other, duplicate code loves to hide in little nooks and crannies. When you have a multi-thousand-line class, things like this happen. A programmer needs a method and quickly adds one before searching if another exists, someone writes a "test" version of the method, then forgets that there was an original one, or someone just started copying and pasting from some code they found online. If everything continues to work fine, then there is very little impetus to look for issues like this, let alone fix them. Even if someone does notice it, modifying it may be seen as out-of-scope for whatever they are working on. It would almost certainly require refactoring other code that depends on it. However, not having your code DRY means more tests, more danger when refactoring, and just plain redundancy. Deciding on one method to use instead of having multiple copies will save you time and energy in the long run, as you reduce the ancillary associated costs of extra unit tests and confusion on the part of future maintainers.

What happens when you decide that you are no longer going to use the `quickSort()` method, or decide to support floating-point numbers in addition to integers? You will have to make changes in two (or more... there's practically no limit to how many times code can be copied and pasted) places, which can be easy to forget to do. That's double the room for error, or for doing it slightly differently in one place than the other. Testing for these kind of things can be difficult. Remove duplicate code sooner rather than later.

While the duplicated method above is a simple example, you may have more complex cases of code duplication. Any time you find yourself with repeated code, even if it's in the middle of a statement, it may be a good idea to put it into its own method. Consider the following SQL code which must be called by each of these methods in order to determine how many of a particular kind of breed exists in the database:

```
public int getNumberOfCats(String catBreed) {
    int breedId = DatabaseInterface.execute(
      "SELECT BreedID FROM CatBreeds WHERE BreedName = " + catBreed);
    int numCats = DatabaseInterface.execute(
      "SELECT COUNT(*) FROM Cats WHERE BreedID = " + breedId);
    return numCats;
}


public int getNumberOfPigeons(String pigeonBreed) {
    int breedId = DatabaseInterface.execute(
      "SELECT BreedID FROM PigeonBreeds WHERE BreedName = " + pigeonBreed);
    int numPigeons = DatabaseInterface.execute(
      "SELECT COUNT(*) FROM Pigeons WHERE BreedID = " + breedId);
    return numPigeons;
}
```

While the statements aren't exactly the same, they are similar enough that they are a target for DRYing up. After all, we can always pass in parameters to tweak the behavior to exactly what we want:

```
public int getNumAnimals(String animalType, String breed) {
    int breedId = DatabaseInterface.execute(
      "SELECT BreedID FROM " + animalType + "Breeds WHERE BreedName = " + breed);
    int numAnimals = DatabaseInterface.execute(
      "SELECT COUNT(*) FROM " + animalType + "s WHERE BreedID = " + breedId);
    return numAnimals;
}


public int getNumberOfCats(String catBreed) {
    return getNumAnimals("Cat", catBreed);
}


public int getNumberOfPigeons(String pigeonBreed) {
    return getNumAnimals("Pigeon", pigeonBreed);
}
```

The code is now going to be much more flexible and maintainable. Supporting additional animals will only require ensuring that we add methods that call getNumAnimals() with the appropriate parameters. Directly testing the database, which can be challenging, is now restricted to one particular method. More effort and energy can be focused on testing the more abstracted method instead of spreading out the testing on multiple methods with broader responsibilities.

16.6 Dependency Injection

As we've seen, having dependencies hard-coded into your methods can make them difficult to test. Let's assume you have a class-level reference to a `Duck` object that is created by a `Pond` object. The `Pond` class has a `sayHi()` method which will say "Hi!" to all of the animals in the pond:

```
public class Pond {

    Duck _d = new Duck();

    Otter _o = new Otter();

    public void sayHi() {
        _d.say("Hi!");
        _o.say("Hi!");
    }

}
```

How can you test this? There's no easy way to verify that the duck got the "Hi!" message. **Dependency injection** allows you to avoid this problem. Although this is an excellent term to use to sound knowledgeable about testing, it's actually a very simple concept that you have probably seen in practice already. In a nutshell, dependency injection means passing the dependencies in as parameters to a method, as opposed to having hard-coded references to them. This will make it much easier to pass in test doubles or mocks.

Let's re-write the above `Pond` class allowing for dependency injection:

```
public class Pond {

    Duck _d = null;

    Otter _o = null;

    public Pond(Duck d, Otter o) {
        _d = d;
        _o = o;
    }

    public void sayHi() {
        _d.say("Hi!");
        _o.say("Hi!");
    }

}
```

Note that you are passing in the Duck and the Otter in the constructor, thus moving the responsibility for creating them outside of the Pond class. Because of this, you don't have to send in actual ducks and otters. Instead you can send in mocks, which can then verify that the `say()` method was called with the parameter "Hi!". Dependency injection will allow you to test your methods much more easily than having dependencies automatically created.

16.7   TUFs and TUCs

TUFs are **test-unfriendly features**, whereas TUCs are **test-unfriendly constructs**. TUFs are software features that are by their nature difficult to test. For example, writing to a database requires either some well-thought-out test doubles or dependence on many external factors (database drivers, the database itself, disk usage, etc.) Other test-unfriendly features would be communicating over the network, using a windowing library, or writing to disk. In all of these cases, if you do not provide appropriate doubles, it will be very difficult to test these features. If you do provide doubles, then it only becomes "moderately difficult".

Test-unfriendly constructs are constructs in code where testing is by nature difficult. In Java, this would include private methods (which require the Reflection API to directly access), constructors, or final methods. It can be difficult to override the appropriate methods or provide test doubles easily in many TUCs. This is an additional layer of complexity which, when combined with a test-unfriendly feature, can make your tests convoluted and difficult to reason about.

One method for keeping the complexity of your tests to a reasonable level is to not put TUFs inside of TUCs. Move them to their own methods, or otherwise segment and design the code so that TUCs contain only minimal and easily-tested code.

16.8   Dealing with Legacy Code

Not everybody has had the opportunity to read an excellent book with a chapter on writing testable code. Many existing codebases were written by people who were not familiar with modern software engineering techniques, either through ignorance or because the techniques were not common when the code was written. It would be foolishly optimistic to expect that people writing some FORTRAN IV code in 1966 would be using testing techniques which did not become common until the 1990s. Code that is already existing in production, but which does not follow modern software engineering best practices and often has substandard—or even no—automated test coverage, is known as **legacy code**.

Long story short—working with legacy code is difficult. There is no getting around it. You will be missing many of the benefits of a good testing suite; you may not be able to interact with the original developers if there are issues, ambiguities, or undocumented code; and it may be difficult to understand outdated code written in an older style. However, it is often necessary, especially when you are working for a company which has been writing code for a long time. It wouldn't make sense to rewrite millions of lines of code every time you want to add a new feature to the software suite you are already using.

When you find yourself having to work with legacy code, one of the most important things you can do is create some **pinning tests**. Pinning tests are automated tests, usually unit tests, which check for the existing behavior of the system. Note that the existing behavior is not always the expected, or correct, behavior. The goal of a pinning test is to simply see how the program reacts before you make any changes to it. Oftentimes, those weird, unexpected edge cases are actually used by users of the system. You do not want to unintentionally modify them when adding a feature, unless it is something that you have explicitly set out to do. Making unintentional changes to a program can be dangerous for yourself and for users of the program. Note that this does not mean that you simply ignore the fact that the program is not working correctly. However, fixing it should be seen as a different process than creating the pinning test.

When working with legacy code, you want to be very explicit about the features you are introducing and defects you are fixing. It's very easy to start fixing every error you see, but this can easily get you into trouble. You start forgetting what you came in to fix in the first place, you aren't focused on one thing, and you make changes in massive clumps instead of at the "one step at a time" pace you should be going.

Personally, I like to keep a little text file open which has changes that I would like to make in the future, but are beyond the scope of what I am fixing at the moment. For example, I may be editing a class to add a new method. I note that there are numerous magic numbers in the file, which are not defined anywhere. I may make a note to refactor this class later. This doesn't mean that I won't use appropriate, well-named constants in the method that I have added. However, if I tried to fix everything in the file as I was going along, I may spend three times as long as if I had just done the minimum of what I needed to do. This may not be a good use of my time.

Doing the minimum isn't normally considered a great way to go through life, but oftentimes when writing software it is. You want to make small changes to the codebase, little incremental steps, because large changes are fraught with hard-to-find errors. If you have a 10,000-line code change, and something goes wrong, trying to look through all of that will be a nightmare. However, let's say you make a thousand 10-line code changes. At each point, you can run all of the unit tests and see if the problem manifests itself. Tracking problems down via tiny steps is much easier than tracking it down in one giant commit.

Additionally, doing the minimum can ensure that you are using your time wisely. It may not be worth your time to add documentation to every method in the class you're working on, especially if you don't think it will be modified again anytime in the near future. It's not that it's not a good idea, but perhaps not a good prioritization of your time. Remember that you have a limited amount of time available not just on this Earth, but for completing a project. Spend too much time on the wrong things, and it doesn't get done. While it's an honorable drive to want to fix all of the problems you see in the codebase, the dirty little secret of the software industry is that there is all sorts of ugly code running behind the scenes, and most of the time, it works just fine. Your favorite bank has thousands of GOTO statements in its transfer code. Your favorite three-letter government agency has hundreds of thousands of lines of code that no unit test has ever laid eyes (or mocks or stubs) on. It is okay to cry about the state of the world, but sometimes you just need to let it be.

If possible, you want to start your search for code to modify by looking for **seams**. Seams are locations in code where you can modify *behavior* without modifying *code*. This is probably easiest to see with examples. In this first method, there is no seam—there is no way to modify how the program behaves without modifying some code in the method:

```
public void createDatabaseTable() {
    DatabaseConnection db = new DatabaseConnection(DEFAULT_DB);
    int status = db.executeSql("CREATE TABLE Cats "
        + "(CatID int, Name varchar(255), Breed varChar(255));");
}
```

If you want to change the database this code will update, you will need to modify the constant DEFAULT_DB or otherwise change the line of code. There's no way to pass in a test double for it, or otherwise use a fake database in your test. If you want to add a column, you will need to edit the string that is inside the method. Now let's compare this to a method which is a seam:

```
public int executeSql(DatabaseConnection db, String sqlString) {
    return db.executeSql(sqlString);
}
```

If you want to use a doubled database connection, just pass it in when calling the method. If you want to add a new column, you can just modify the string. You can check for edge or corner cases, like seeing if an exception is thrown or a particular error status is returned, even if the original documentation is missing. Since you can explore these cases without directly modifying any code, it will be infinitely easier to determine that you haven't broken anything when writing your tests. After all, you haven't modified anything! If you had to manually edit the code to observe the behavior, as in the first example, any original results you got from pinning tests would be suspect. Code modification would usually not be as straightforward as the example above. You may have to edit multiple methods, and you would never be entirely sure if the results you see were because that is the way the code executed originally, or if it was a consequence of the edits you made while trying to test it.

Note that having a seam does not mean that the code is good in other ways. After all, being able to pass in arbitrary SQL to be executed is a pretty big security risk if it hasn't been sanitized elsewhere. Writing code with too many seams may be overkill, and will certainly make the codebase larger. Seams are simply where you can start figuring out how the system currently responds to inputs. Finding seams will allow you to easily start writing comprehensive pinning tests, to ensure that you are catching a variety of edge cases.

Perhaps most importantly, it is important from a psychological point of view not to "give in" to the codebase and sink to its level. Just because there are no unit tests for a feature does not mean that it's fine to make some modifications without adding unit tests. If the code for a particular class is uncommented, that shouldn't give you *carte blanche* to not comment the code that you add. As it evolves, code tends to sink towards the lowest common denominator. You need to actively fight that devolution. Write unit tests, fix things up as you find them, and document code and features appropriately.

If you are interested in more details about how to work with legacy code, there are (at least) two great books on the topic. The first is *Refactoring: Improving the Design of Existing Code* by Martin Fowler, and the other is *Working Effectively with Legacy Code* by Michael Feathers. The latter is an especially valuable resource for working with code that does not already have a comprehensive test suite.

One of the things I find so interesting about software engineering is that it is a field which is changing extremely quickly. Many of the techniques that I discuss will probably seem as quaint as GOTO statements and line numbers do at the time of the writing of this book. If this is the case, then please be gentle in your criticism half a century hence.

16.9   Final Thoughts On Writing Testable Code

Software testing is not only about writing the tests, but writing code which will enable the tests to be written easily and well. In today's world of software engineering, writing code and writing tests are not mutually exclusive. Many—I would venture to say "most"—developers write their own unit tests along with their code, and many testers will have to write code to automate their tests or develop testing tools. Even if you do not write code in your role as a tester, you may be asked to review it or to determine how to have more comprehensive automated testing for a software system.

Chapter 17

Pairwise and Combinatorial Testing

Imagine that you're testing a word processor. Specifically, you're testing the ability to add font effects, e.g., bold, italic, superscript, 3-D, etc. Of course, in any word processor worth its salt, these effects can also be combined in one region of text, so that you may have a word which is both bold and italic, or a letter which is both subscripted and in 3-D, or even a sentence which is bold, italic, underlined, 3-D, and superscripted. The number of possible combinations—ranging from absolutely no effects (and thus plain text) all the way to every single effect turned on is 2^n, where n is the number of effects. Thus, if there are 10 different kinds of font effects available, the number of tests that you would have to run to fully test all of the possible combinations of font effects is 2^{10}, or 1,024. This is a non-trivial number of tests to write.

If you want truly complete test coverage, you'll have to test each of these different combinations (e.g., only bold; bold and italic; bold and superscript; bold, superscripted, italic, strikethrough, 3-D; etc.). Imagine if there is an issue that only shows up when a letter is italic, underlined, bold, subscripted, and struck-through. You won't find that defect unless you take the time to go through a comprehensive test of all combinations!

However, it turns out that this situation is rarer than you might think. You may not need to test all of these combinations in order to find a large percentage of the defects in the system. In fact, according to the publication *Practical Combinatorial Testing* by Rick Kuhn, up to 90% of all defects in a software system can be found simply by testing all combinations of two variables. In our example, if you just tested all of the possible pairs (bold and italic, bold and superscript, superscript and 3-D, etc.), you would have found many of the defects in the software but have used only a fraction of the testing time. Of all the software projects that they analyzed, the maximum number of variables that interacted to cause a defect that was found to be six. By keeping this in mind when constructing tests, you can find virtually all of the defects that a comprehensive test approach would find while using orders of magnitude less testing time and resources.

This technique is called **combinatorial testing**. Testing all possible pairs of values is a kind of combinatorial testing, but has its own term, **pairwise testing** or **all-pairs testing**. At the beginning of this book, we discussed how comprehensively testing a non-trivial program was almost impossible. By using the techniques in this chapter, we can reduce the number of tests dramatically (in some cases, by many orders of magnitude), but still find ourselves able to thoroughly test a system.

Let's take a very simple example, a program which has only three variables for a character's formatting: bold, italic, and underline. These can be combined, so that, for example, a character can be just italic; or italic and underlined; or bold, italic and underlined. Since each of these variables is a Boolean (they can only be true or false—you can't have a "half-italic" character), the list of possibilities for a character can be expressed as a **truth table**. A truth table will shows all possible values that a given group of variables may hold.

As an interesting side note, if you think of "false" as 0 and "true" as 1, constructing a truth table is analogous to counting in binary from 0 to the size of the table minus one. In the below instance, we start at "000" (0), then "001" (1), "010" (2), all the way up to "111" (7). This is a useful trick when creating these tables yourself.

```
      BOLD        | ITALIC    | UNDERLINE
   ------------+-----------+------------
1.    false     | false     | false
2.    false     | false     | true
3.    false     | true      | false
4.    false     | true      | true
5.    true      | false     | false
6.    true      | false     | true
7.    true      | true      | false
8.    true      | true      | true
```

In order to exhaustively test the program, we will need to run the eight tests above. Let's assume that our manager is extremely strict, and insists that we only have time to run six tests. How can we reduce the number of tests that we run while still maintaining the highest likelihood of finding defects?

As explained above, checking that all pairs of variables are checked can help us find a large percentage of defects. There are three possible pairs of variables in this example: bold and italic, bold and underline, and italic and underline. How do we know that there are only three possible pairs? For a small number of variables, we can simply check that there are no other possibilities, but as the numbers get larger, we will want to be able to calculate how many are necessary. This will require some mathematical explanation.

17.1   Permutations and Combinations

You may be worried that the title of this book was misleading, and that the "friendly" introduction you were promised is going to be filled with dense mathematical operations. Fear not, however - the math here is relatively easy to understand and the equations are kept to a minimum.

Before we discuss the basis of combinatorial testing, we should understand what a **permutation** is. A permutation is some possible arrangement of a **set** of objects. It will not have any elements removed or added, only their order has changed. One way of thinking about this is shuffling a deck of cards; each time the cards are shuffled, a different permutation is created, as the order has changed but no cards have been added or removed. As a specific numeric example, assume that the array X contains the following values: [1, 12, 4]. The list of possible permutations is:

```
1, 12, 4
1, 4, 12
12, 1, 4
12, 4, 1
4, 1, 12
4, 12, 1
```

The number of possible permutations of a set is equal to the **factorial** of r, or $r!$ (pronounced "r factorial"), or $r * (r - 1) * (r - 2) \ldots * 1$. For example, the factorial of 3 is $3 * 2 * 1 = 6$, and the factorial of 5 is $5 * 4 * 3 * 2 * 1 = 120$.

We may also be interested in how many different ordered subsets it is possible to make using

Assuming that r and n are positive integers, the number of r-permutations of a given set of size n is determined by the following formula:

P(n, r) = n! / ((n - r)!)

It may be helpful to walk through an example and see not only how this is calculated but also how it might be used in a real testing situation. Let us assume that are testing a Turtle Volleyball Game which will match any 2 of 4 turtles with each other. Our turtles' names are Alan, Bob, Charlene, and Darlene. We want to ensure that for any given matchup, the game will work correctly, and for our purposes, the order matters. That is, if Bob is playing Alan, Bob serves first, and thus it will be considered a different game than when Alan plays Bob and Alan serves first.

There are P(4, 2) possible matchups (i.e., 2-permutations). Plugging these values into the equation above, we can see that we will need:

```
P(4, 2)
= 4! / ((4 - 2)!)
= 24 / 2!
= 24 / 2
= 12 matchups
```

1. Alan / Bob

2. Alan / Charlene

3. Alan / Darlene

4. Bob / Alan

5. Bob / Charlenc

6. Bob/ Darlene

7. Charlene / Alan

8. Charlene / Bob

9. Charlene / Darlene

10. Darlene / Alan

11. Darlene / Bob

12. Darlene / Charlene

Remember, since we are looking at permutations, each turtle must be checked against every other turtle.

As you may have already guessed from the name, when we discuss combinatorial testing, we will be interested in checking **combinations** of a set of elements, not permutations. A combination is some *unordered* subset of a set. Using similar nomenclature as with permutations, we can also refer to an **r-combination** of a set to indicate combinations of subsets. Ordinarily, we are interested in combinations of a smaller size than the original set, as an r-combination of a set where r is the same size of the set is just the set itself.

The number of r-combinations of a given set of size n is called the **binomial coefficient**. It is determined by the following formula:

```
C(n, r) = n! / (r! * (n - r)!)
```

For example, the number of possible *3*-combinations of a set consisting of five elements is:

```
C(5, 3)
= 5! / (3! * (5 - 3)!)
= 120 / (6 * 2)
= 10 3-combinations
```

The function `C(n, r)` is often expressed as "n choose r". For example, "10 choose 4" would refer to how many 4-combinations exist in a set of 10 elements (210).

Let us return to our four-turtle Turtle Volleyball game. In this case, however, we don't care which turtle serves first - for the purposes of the game, Alan playing Bob is the same as Bob playing Alan. In order to determine the number of tests necessary to test all of these, we need to determine the number of *2*-combinations of the a 4 element set, or `C(4, 2)`, or 6 tests.

1. Alan / Bob

2. Alan / Charlene

3. Alan / Darlene

4. Bob / Charlene

5. Bob / Darlene

6. Charlene / Darlene

The idea of the factorial becomes clear when viewing the possible results. Note that our first turtle, Alan, must be shown interacting with three other turtles (all of the other turtles). The second turtle, Bob, only needs to interact with two turtles, since we already have a pairing with Bob. When we get to Charlene, we only need to interact with one other turtle, since Charlene has already interacted with Alan and Bob. Finally, Darlene has already interacted with all of the other turtles, so no additional tests need to be added for her.

You will note that fewer tests are necessary for testing all of the possible combinations as opposed to permutations. It turns out that the number of combinations necessary to fully test will grow relatively slowly with the size of n. By taking advantage of the concepts of combinatorials, we will be able to drastically reduce the number of tests we will have to perform in order to have a good understanding of the quality of a particular program.

Permutations and combinations are part of the field known as "discrete mathematics", which has numerous applications to software development as a whole. Most Computer Science majors will take at least one course on discrete mathematics during their undegraduate career.

17.2   Pairwise Testing

Now that we understand the basic concepts of combinatorics, let's put it into use in developing a pairwise testing plan. For each of these pairs, we want to have an entire truth table of the two elements covering all possibilities. For example, to ensure that we test all of the possible combinations of bold and italic, we can make the following truth table:

```
BOLD        | ITALIC
------------+-----------
false       | false
false       | true
true        | false
```

```
true        | true
```

Now we need to ensure that our tests cover every possibility of bold and italic. We can see that Test 1 provides false/false, Test 4 provides false/true, Test 5 provides true/false, and Test 8 provides true/true:

```
      BOLD      | ITALIC    | UNDERLINE
   -----------+-----------+------------
1.  false     | false     | false        <--
2.  false     | false     | true
3.  false     | true      | false
4.  false     | true      | true         <--
5.  true      | false     | false        <--
6.  true      | false     | true
7.  true      | true      | false
8.  true      | true      | true         <--
```

Note that when we test these tests, we're also checking other combinations and pairs at the same time! For example, running Test 1 also gives us the false/false combination for bold/underline, and the false/false combination for italic/underline. We're literally getting multiple tests for the price of one. Feel free to throw that in people's faces when they say that there's no such thing as a free lunch.

The next step is to ensure that the other variable pairs have all their combinations covered, using a similar technique as the one we used for bold and italic. As opposed to randomly selecting any test case which met our criteria as we did in the first selection, we will want to check that we're not already testing that combination in a test that we're already performing. This is to avoid duplicating effort; if Test 1 is already checking for false/false for bold/underline, why add Test 3 as well? Let's check for bold/underline at this point, keeping in mind that we want to use already-existing tests if at all possible. Test 1 gives us the false/false combination; Test 4 gives us false/true; Test 5 gives us true/false, and Test 8 gives us true/true. Wow! All of the combinations were already covered by test cases we were going to do anyway. We've now tested all bold/italic and bold/underline combinations with only four tests!

Finally, we should check the last variable combination, italic/underline. Test 1 gives us false/false and Test 4 gives us true/true. Unfortunately, though, false/true and true/false are not yet covered by any tests that we're already planning on using, so we need to add some more. In fact, since there are two different combinations, and these combinations are mutually exclusive, we will need to add two tests. Let's add Test 2 for false/true and Test 3 for true/false. Our final test plan is the following:

```
      BOLD      | ITALIC    | UNDERLINE
   -----------+-----------+------------
1.  false     | false     | false
2.  false     | false     | true
3.  false     | true      | false
4.  false     | true      | true
5.  true      | false     | false
8.  true      | true      | true
```

We have met our strict manager's demand and reduced the number of tests by 25%. We have used a **covering array** to determine a smaller way to check all 2-way (pairwise) interactions. A covering array is any array representing a combination of tests which will cover all possibilities of n-way interaction (in this case, 2-way interaction). Note that since the original array which covered all possible truth table values also covers all possible combinations of those values, it is technically also a covering array. In general usage, however, the term refers to a smaller version of the array which still contains all of the tests necessary to check the various n-way interactions.

The covering array that we have created is actually not the optimal configuration for testing all combinations, as we used a naïve algorithm and did not check other possibilities. Perhaps by selecting different tests whenever we had a choice, we could have covered the same number of combinations with fewer test cases. Creating these by hand is also extremely time-consuming, especially as the number of interactions and variables go up. For these reasons, combinatorial testing patterns are often created using a software tool. Although the particular algorithms and heuristics used are beyond the scope of this book, these tools will generate these covering arrays quickly and automatically. These combinatorial test generators—such as the free Advanced Combinatorial Testing System from the National Institute of Standards and Technology (NIST)—are invaluable when attempting to generate covering arrays for a non-trivial number of variables.

Using NIST ACTS with the IPOG algorithm, I was able to generate the following optimal covering array. With only four tests, it would literally be impossible to be more efficient, since each pairwise truth table will themselves require four different tests. Even more importantly, we have now exceeded the manager's expectations, cutting the tests down by 50% instead of the 25% that he or she demanded, yet still testing all pairwise interactions:

```
    BOLD        | ITALIC     | UNDERLINE
    ------------+------------+------------
1.  false       | false      | false
4.  false       | true       | true
6.  true        | false      | true
7.  true        | true       | false
```

Let's verify that all possible pairs exist in this test plan.

1. *BOLD/ITALIC* : false/false is handled in test case 1, false/true in test case 4, true/false in test case 6, and true/true in test case 7.

2. *ITALIC/UNDERLINE* : false/false is handled in test case 1, false/true in test case 6, true/false in test case 7, and true/true in test case 4.

3. *BOLD/UNDERLINE* : false/false is handled in test case 1, false/true in test case 4, true/false in test case 7, and true/true in test case 6.

Although this example was done with Boolean variables, any kind of variable can be used as long as it's finite. If it's a variable with infinite possibilities—say, an arbitrary length string—you can map to a certain number of possibilities (e.g., "a", "abcde", and "abcdefghijklmnop"). When doing so, you should first think of the different equivalence classes, if any, and ensure that you have a value from each equivalence class. You should also try to check several different edge cases, especially those which may cause problems when interacting in combination with other variables. Suppose in our previous example that instead of checking a character, we wanted to check a word. We may add different possibilities for the word to be tested. Let's start with "a" (a single character) and "bird", a simple word. Our generated covering array will look similar to the previous one, just using "a" and "bird" as the values for the word variable, instead of true and false as for all of the other variables:

```
    WORD    | BOLD       | ITALIC     | UNDERLINE
    --------+------------+------------+------------
1.  "a"     | true       | false      | false
2.  "a"     | false      | true       | true
3.  "bird"  | true       | true       | false
4.  "bird"  | false      | false      | true
```

```
5.      "bird" | true      | false     | true
6.      "a"    | false     | false     | false
```

Note that we are still checking all pairs. Let's check the word/bold pair to verify that that is the case. In Test 1, we check for the word "a" with bold set to true. In Test 2, we check the word "a" with bold set to false. In Test 3 we check the word "bird" with bold set to true, and in Test 4 we check the word "bird" with bold set to false. What if we're worried that special characters may cause an issue when formatting? We'd want to add a third possibility for the word variable, which is certainly allowed even though all of our possibilities so far have used only two possible values:

```
        WORD   | BOLD      | ITALIC    | UNDERLINE
        -------+-----------+-----------+------------
1.      "a"    | true      | false     | false
2       "a"    | false     | true      | true
3       "bird" | true      | true      | false
4       "bird" | false     | false     | true
5       "!@#$" | true      | true      | true
6       "!@#$" | false     | false     | false
```

As a side note, notice that we are now testing even more pairwise combinations and yet there are still only six tests. This is merely a foreshadowing of how much time can be saved with combinatorial testing.

17.3 n-Way Interactions

Although many errors will be found by ensuring that all pairwise interactions are tested, often we would like to go even further and check for errors in three-way, four-way, or even more interactions. The same theory holds for doing this: tests should be generated that cover the entire truth table for each 3-way variable interaction. Just like we checked that all four true/false value combinations were tested for each two-way interaction in the first example, we will check that all eight value combinations for each three-way interaction are tested.

Let's expand the number of formatting variables in our system, adding SUPERSCRIPT and STRIKETHROUGH as possibilities. In order to exhaustively test this, we will need 2^5, or 32, tests. Generating a covering array for all pairwise interactions creates a six-case test plan. Once again, notice how we are testing even more variables than in the last case, but we are using the same number of tests. In this case, we are running only 18.75% of the tests we would need for exhaustive testing, yet we are still testing all pairwise interactions:

```
        BOLD     | ITALIC    | UNDERLINE | SUPERSCRIPT | STRIKETHROUGH
        ---------+-----------+-----------+-------------+--------------
1.      true     | true      | false     | false       | false
2.      true     | false     | true      | true        | true
3.      false    | true      | true      | false       | true
4.      false    | false     | false     | true        | false
5.      false    | true      | false     | true        | true
6.      false    | false     | true      | false       | false
```

Checking for every possible three-way interaction is going to involve more tests. If you think about it, this is logically necessary. Since there are eight possible combinations for each three-way interaction, it would be impossible to cover any combination using only six tests:

```
        BOLD     | ITALIC    | UNDERLINE | SUPERSCRIPT | STRIKETHROUGH
        ---------+-----------+-----------+-------------+--------------
```

1.	true		true		true		true		true
2.	true		true		false		false		false
3.	true		false		true		false		true
4.	true		false		false		true		false
5.	false		true		true		false		false
6.	false		true		false		true		true
7.	false		false		true		true		false
8.	false		false		false		false		true
9.	false		false		true		true		true
10.	true		true		false		false		true
11.	true		true		true		true		false
12.	false		false		false		false		false

Let's examine a given three-way interaction, bold/italic/underline, and double-check that we are testing all of the possibilities. False/false/false is covered by Test 12; false/false/true is covered by Test 9; false/true/false is covered by Test 6; false/true/true is covered by Test 5; true/false/false is covered by Test 4; true/false/true is covered by Test 3; true/true/false is covered by Test 10; and true/true/true is covered by Test 1. Note that there are eight possible combinations and ten tests, so there is some repetition (for example, true/true/true is covered by both Tests 1 and 11).

The number of interactions can be tuned upwards as high as you would like, although if you are planning on testing n-way interactions where n is the number of variables you have, you are just doing exhaustive testing. According to empirical studies done by NIST, the maximum number of interactions that caused an error was six, so checking for more than that would be over-testing in many situations.

17.4   Working with Larger Variable Sets

Combinatorial testing seems to work well with relatively small data sets, saving us large percentages of time by reducing the number of tests necessary. However, going from 32 to 12 tests is not that impressive; after all, 32 tests could probably still be run in a reasonable amount of time. How well does combinatorial testing work for larger numbers of variables or possible values?

The answer is, incredibly well. Instead of five Boolean variables, let's assume that we have fifty. In order to exhaustively test all possible combinations, you'd need to run 2^50 (1,125,899,906,842,624) tests. That's over a quintillion tests—you could do a test per second for the rest of your life and not make a dent. However, if you're content with just checking each 2-way interaction, you can reduce that to 14 tests! That's a savings in tests that is really incomprehensible using percentages; you're talking many, many orders of magnitude. What once looked to be daunting is now easily attainable. Increasing the number of interactions does not increase the amount of tests that greatly, either: testing all three-way interactions requires forty tests, and testing all four-way interactions only requires one hundred tests. Even better, NIST ACTS was able to generate these test plans, even on my underpowered laptop, in less than a few seconds.

You can see that not only does the number of tests you need grow sublinearly; the more variables you have, the higher percentage of time you will be saving by using combinatorial testing. In the beginning of this book, we talked about how exhaustive testing was, for many programs, essentially impossible. Using combinatorial testing is one way to ameliorate that problem. With only a small percentage of the effort needed for exhaustive testing, we can find the vast majority of defects that would have been caught by it.

Chapter 18

Stochastic and Property-Based Testing

The term "stochastic" comes from the Greek *stokhastikos*, which is a form of *stokhazesthai*, which means "aim at" or "guess". It's a good etymology for **stochastic testing**, which uses random processes that can be analyzed using statistics, but not exactly predicted. At first blush, it may seem ridiculous to use randomness in software testing; after all, isn't the fundamental concept of testing to determine what the observed behavior is and if it is equal to the expected behavior? If you don't know what the input is, how would you know what the expected output is?

The answer is that there are expected behaviors and properties you expect from a system, no matter what the input. For example, no matter what code is passed to a compiler, you will expect it not to crash. It may generate an error message saying that the code is unparseable. It may make an executable. That executable may run, or it may not. You do expect the system not to have a segmentation fault. Thus, you can still run tests where the expected behavior for any input is "does not crash the system".

By providing a method for the system to use random data as an input, you also reduce the cost of testing. No longer do you have to imagine lots of specific test cases and then painstakingly program all of them in or write them down as test cases. Instead, you just tie together some sort of random number generator and some way to generate data based on it, and your computer can do all the work of generating test cases. Even though the random number generator may not be as good as a dedicated testing professional in coming up with edge cases, varying equivalence classes, etc., it will often find many problems simply by the sheer number of tests it can generate and how quickly it can do it.

Stochastic testing is also referred to as **monkey testing**, by analogy with a monkey banging on computer keys. However, "stochastic testing" sounds much more impressive if you are talking to your manager, or writing a book on software testing.

18.1 Infinite Monkeys and Infinite Typewriters

There is an old parable about monkeys and typewriters, which normally would not seem like two things that go together well. The parable states that given a million monkeys and infinite amount of time, the monkeys will eventually write the works of Shakespeare (the monkeys in this scenario are immortal). Stochastic testing follows a similar principle—given a large enough set of random input (a million monkeys banging on keys) and a large enough period of time, defects will be found. In this analogy, our tester is William Shakespeare (don't let the comparison go to your head). The tester could certainly write the works of Shakespeare in less time than the million monkeys. However, monkeys (like the computer's random number generator) are much cheaper than re-animating Zombie William Shakespeare. Even if the random number generator isn't as good a writer of tests as you (or Shakespeare), by sheer dint of numbers, it's bound to hit on numerous interesting edge cases and perhaps find defects.

Since you—or more precisely, the stochastic testing system—may not know exactly what the expected behavior should be for a given input, you need to check for properties of the system. At the unit testing level, where you are checking individual methods, this is called **property-based testing**.

18.2   Property-Based Testing

Let's say once again that we are testing our sorting function, `billSort`. As you'll recall, it's meant to be twenty times faster than any other sorting algorithm. However, there are questions about its correctness, so you have been tasked to test that it works in all cases. What kind of input values would you test it with? Assume the method signature looks like this:

```
public int[] billSort(int[] arrToSort) {
    ...
}
```

We'd definitely want to pass in a wide variety of values that hit different base, edge, and corner cases. Single-element arrays. Zero-element arrays. Arrays with negative integers. Arrays that are already sorted. Arrays that are sorted the opposite way as the sort works (ascending versus descending, or vice versa). Very long arrays. Arrays that contain multiple values, and arrays that consist of the same value repeated over and over again. This doesn't even take into account the fact that Java is a statically typed language, so we don't have to worry about what happens when an array contains strings, or references to other arrays, or complex numbers, or a variety of other kinds of things. If this sort were implemented in a dynamically typed language such as Ruby, we'd really have a lot to worry about. Just considering the Java method above, though, let's think about some of the different inputs and their respective expected output values for this method:

```
[] => []
[1] => [1]
[1, 2, 3, 4, 5] => [1, 2, 3, 4, 5]
[5, 4, 3, 2, 1] => [1, 2, 3, 4, 5]
[0, 0, 0, 0] => [0, 0, 0, 0]
[9, 3, 1, 2] => [1, 2, 3, 9]
[-9, 9, -4, 4] => [-9, -4, 4, 9]
[3, 3, 3, 2, 1, 1, 1] => [1, 1, 1, 2, 3, 3, 3]
[-1, -2, -3] => [-3, -2, -1]
[1000000, 10000, 100, 10, 1] => [1, 10, 100, 10000, 1000000]
```

Even without any additional wrinkles, there's an absolutely huge number of possible combinations of numbers to test. That was just a taste. There's even a huge number of equivalence cases to test, ignoring the fact there could be a problem with, say, a specific number; maybe only sorts with the number 5 don't work, for example. Writing tests for all of these various kinds of input would be extremely tedious and error-prone. How can we avoid having to write such a large number of tests?

18.2.1 Climbing the Abstraction Ladder

Why not hop up a rung on the abstraction ladder and instead of thinking about the specific values that you want as input and output, you think about the *properties* you'd expect of your input and output? That way, you don't have to consider each individual test. You can let the computer know that you expect all of the output to have certain properties, and what kind of values you expect as input, and let the computer write and execute the tests for you.

For example, what kinds of properties did all of the correct output values of the `billSort` method have, in relationship to the input values? There are quite a few. These properties should hold for all sorted lists. Thus, they are called **invariants**.

Some invariants for a sort function would be:

1. The output array has the same number of elements as the input array

2. Every value in the output array corresponds to one in the input array

3. The value of each successive element in the output array is greater than or equal to the previous value

4. No element not in the input array is found in the output array

5. The function is **idempotent**; that is, no matter how many times the function is is called, the same output should always be returned. If I run the sort method on a list, and then run the sort again on the output of that first sort, the second sort call should produce the same output array as just running it once. Note that it would be harder to test the opposite of an idempotent function (a **non-idempotent** function), since in that case, the output may or may not be changed (for example, assume a function which increments a value and returns that value modulo 6; any time you call that function some factor of six times, it will return the same value).

6. The function is pure; running it two times on the same input array should always produce the same output array. Any time I call sort on the list `[3, 2, 1]`, it will return `[1, 2, 3]`. It does not matter if the moon is waxing gibbous or waning crescent, or what the value of any global variables are, it will always return the same value if given the same input array.

Now that we have some of the properties we expect from *any* output of the `billSort` method, we can let the computer do the grunt work of thinking up random arrays of data, passing them in to our method, and then checking that whatever output array is produced meets all of the properties that we set. If an output array does not meet one of the invariants, we can then report the error to the tester. Producing output that does not meet the specified invariant is called **falsifying the invariant**.

There are multiple libraries for Java which perform property-based testing but no standard. Property-based testing is much more popular in the functional programming world, with programs like QuickCheck for Haskell being more used than standard unit tests. In fact, the concept of automated property-based testing of this sort comes from the functional world and from the Haskell community in particular. For more information, see the paper *QuickCheck: A Lightweight Tool for Random Testing of Haskell Programs* by Koen Claessen and John Hughes.

18.3 Smart, Dumb, Evil, and Chaos Monkeys

As mentioned above, stochastic testing is often called monkey testing. What is not as well known is that there are different kinds of monkeys doing our testing work for us.

Let's imagine a simple program which accepts a string argument from the user, and attempts to read that string as an arithmetic expression and display its result. For example, "5 + 6" would display "11" and "5 - (2 * 1) + 10" would display "13". If the program cannot parse the string because it is not a valid arithmetic expression (e.g., "$%--0"), then the program will print "ERROR".

Dumb monkey testing is sending in just any old input you can think of (or, as it happens more often, that your input generation program creates). "Mfdsjbkfd", "1 + 2", and "(*@()" all seem like good inputs to the dumb monkey. There is no rhyme or reason, just lots of different randomized input. This can be helpful for catching edge cases, but it is not very focused. Remember that the world of possible values is absolutely huge. The chances of finding a specific defect might be minimal when using dumb monkey testing. By chance, we happened to find at least one valid arithmetic expression, but what are the odds of that occurring on a regular basis? The vast majority of randomly generated inputs will cause the same behavior: simply printing ERROR. The chance of it catching well-known and easy-to-test-for errors such as integer overflow or underflow, or floating-point rounding issues, is minuscule.

As a more real-life example, let us assume that you have a defect where arbitrary JavaScript code can be executed by entering it into a text box on your web application. However, if the JavaScript code is not syntactically correct, nothing bad happens. Think of how long it would take for a dumb monkey to randomly generate a valid JavaScript string that would take advantage of this obvious vulnerability! It may be years. Even then, it may be some JavaScript code which does not cause any problems, or even any noticeable output, such as a comment or logging a message to the console. Meanwhile, even a novice tester is going to try to enter some JavaScript on any text box they can find.

Dumb monkey testing has some very obvious drawbacks, chief among them that without direction, most inputs are invalid and uninteresting. However, implementing it can be done very quickly, and a large number of tests can be performed very quickly.

Smart monkey testing involves using input which a user might conceivably enter, as opposed to being strictly random. For example, suppose you are testing a calculator program, which accepts a string of numbers and arithmetic operators and displays a result. It is rational to assume that an ordinary user is much more likely to enter the following input:

```
> 1 + 2
3
> 4 + + 6
ERROR
> 4 + 6
10
```

than:

```
> jiwh0t34h803h8t32h8t3h8t23
ERROR
> aaaaaaaaaaaaa
ERROR
> 084_==wjw2933
ERROR
```

While this assumption may not hold when it comes to toddlers, in general it is most likely true. Thus, in order to focus our testing resources on finding defects which are more likely to occur, we can use smart monkey testing to act as a user. Since the smart monkey test is automated, however, it will be able to operate much more quickly and on many more possible inputs than manual testing by an actual user.

Creating a smart monkey test can be difficult, because not only do you have to first understand what users would likely do with the application, but then also develop a model and a generator for it. However, the smart monkey is much more likely to discover a defect in the system under test.

Evil monkey testing simulates a malicious user who is actively trying to hurt your system. This can be through sending very long strings, potential injection attacks, malformed data, unsupported characters, or other inputs which are designed to cause havoc in your system. In today's networked world, systems are almost always under attack if they are connected to the Internet for more than a few milliseconds. It is much better to have an evil monkey under our control determine that the system is vulnerable than let some actual malicious user figure it out!

Let us assume that we are storing all of the entered data for our arithmetic program in a database. An evil monkey test may check to see if it can cause the program to somehow overwrite or modify that data by passing in a malicious SQL command, or some characters which may be interpreted as nulls, or an extremely long string to try to overflow a buffer.

```
> '); DELETE FROM entries; --"
ERROR
> \000\000\000
ERROR
> Well, Prince, so Genoa and Lucca are now just family estates of the Buonapartes...
ERROR
```

For that final line, you may assume that the entire text of *War and Peace* by Leo Tolstoy was actually entered by the evil monkey. I considered adding the whole thing in to inflate the word count of my book, but decided against it to help reduce the weight of the printed version. These are only a few examples of how evil monkey testing might look for defects in a system. For more examples of testing the security of systems, see the chapter in this book entitled *Security Testing*.

Perhaps the best-named kind of monkey is the **Chaos Monkey**. Chaos Monkey is a tool developed by Netflix which randomly shuts down servers that their system is running on, in order to simulate random outages. For any large system, servers will go down on a regular basis, and at any given time some percentage of systems will be unavailable. Chaos monkey testing ensures that the system as a whole will be able to operate effectively even when individual machines are not responding.

You do not have to use the official Chaos Monkey tool to do this kind of testing, however. Think of all the things that can go wrong with a multiple-server system, and simulate them. What happens when the network topography changes? Does the system stay active when somebody pulls out some power or networking cables? What happens if latency is increased to several seconds? A distributed system is ripe for problems. Testing that it can handle them now will allow you to prepare for when they happen in reality. After all, the best way to avoid a problem is to induce it repeatedly; soon, you will have automated procedures to ameliorate it or ensure that it doesn't happen.

18.4   Mutation Testing

Yet another usage of randomness in testing will allow us to test our tests! In **mutation testing**, we modify the code itself in random ways (keeping a copy of the original code to which we will eventually revert back, of course). We are thus **seeding** the system under test with defects. Seeding is deliberately adding defects to a system in order to determine whether or not our testing process is capable of catching them. This can provide us a general idea of the quality of our tests. For example, if ten different defects are deliberately added to a system, and the quality assurance team catches all ten of them, then their other assessments of quality are more likely to be accurate. If the quality assurance team catches only one or none of the ten seeded defects, then we would be justified in thinking that there are many *actual* defects which are not being caught. This would certainly call into question any guarantees that the team has made regarding the quality of the system uder test.

After each random modification of code, the test suite, or the subset of it associated with the code that was modified, is then run. If our test suite has full coverage of the code that was modified, at least one test should fail. If none fail, there is a very good chance that our test coverage is incomplete. There exists the possibility that the mutation was completely benign; say, it modified the default value of a variable which gets immediately overwritten. Another possibility is that the modification made a change that would never be seen in practice, such as

Let's work through an example of mutation testing. Assume we have a method which calculates what kind of animal something might be based on the length of its neck.

```
public class Guess {
    public static String animalType(int neckLength) {
        String toReturn = "UNKNOWN";
        if (neckLength < 10) {
            toReturn = "Rhinoceros";
        } else if (neckLength < 20) {
            toReturn = "Hippopotamus";
        } else {
            toReturn = "Giraffe";
        }
        return toReturn;
    }
}
```

Our test cases check one value from each of the equivalence classes.

```
@Test
public void animalTypeRhinoceros() {
    assertEquals("Rhinoceros", Guess.animalType(5));
}

@Test
public void animalTypeHippopotamus() {
    assertEquals("Hippopotamus", Guess.animalType(15));
}

@Test
public void animalTypeGiraffe() {
    assertEquals("Giraffe", Guess.animalType(25));
}
```

Now, if you recall from our chapter on unit testing, this is not providing very good coverage. Of course, it's also not the worst case of unit testing a method that I have seen. Mutation testing can give us a better idea of the overall quality of our tests than a simple code coverage metric. Let's see a few mutations which will cause a failure, showing us first the strengths of the unit tests and how they can be made to fail.

```
public class Guess {
    public static String animalType(int neckLength) {
        String toReturn = "UNKNOWN";
        // Value was changed from 10 to 1
        if (neckLength < 1) {
```

```
            toReturn = "Rhinoceros";
        } else if (neckLength < 20) {
            toReturn = "Hippopotamus";
        } else {
            toReturn = "Giraffe";
        }
        return toReturn;
    }
}
```

In this case, we modified the conditional checking to see if `neckLength < 10` to `neckLength < 1`. This will rightly cause the test `animalTypeRhinoceros` to fail, since our mutated version of the method will return "Hippopotamus" for a `neckLength` argument of 5.

```
public class Guess {
    public static String animalType(int neckLength) {
        String toReturn = "UNKNOWN";
        // Less-than sign changed to greater-than sign
        if (neckLength > 10) {
            toReturn = "Rhinoceros";
        } else if (neckLength < 20) {
            toReturn = "Hippopotamus";
        } else {
            toReturn = "Giraffe";
        }
        return toReturn;
    }
}
```

In this case, *all* of the unit tests fail: the first will show that what should be a "Rhinoceros" is listed as a "Giraffe", and both of the other tests will return that the animal is a "Rhinoceros". Good job, unit tests!

The more interesting cases which can help our codebase is when mutations do *not* cause the tests to fail. This generally means that our tests are not providing as much coverage of the method as we think. Various errors in the method could slip through the test suite, now or in the future. Remember, the failure of a unit test to catch a mutation does not mean there is a problem with the code now. The code could have been implemented perfectly correctly. It is a failure of the *unit tests* to catch a possible issue. We will just have no way of knowing, from a testing perspective, if the method fails under certain circumstances.

Let's take a look at an example of a mutation which will not cause any unit tests to fail, but has an impact on the execution of the code.

```
public class Guess {
    public static String animalType(int neckLength) {
        String toReturn = "UNKNOWN";
        // Value was changed from 10 to 8
        if (neckLength < 8) {
            toReturn = "Rhinoceros";
        } else if (neckLength < 20) {
            toReturn = "Hippopotamus";
        } else {
            toReturn = "Giraffe";
```

```
        }
        return toReturn;
    }
}
```

In this case, all of our unit tests will pass: an animal with a neck length of 5 will be seen as a rhinoceros, one with a neck length of 15 will be seen as a hippopotamus, and one with a neck length of 25 will be seen as a giraffe. Sadly, though, the functionality of our method has definitely changed! If somebody calls this mutated method with a `neckLength` argument of 9, that animal will be seen as a hippopotamus when it should be seen as a rhinoceros. This shows us the importance of checking for boundary values between equivalence classes. If we had checked for all of the boundaries, then one of our unit tests would have failed whenever these values were changed.

As we mentioned, some mutations may not cause any tests to fail, but are generally benign. This often means that the code that it modified is superfluous, or that the code is implemented improperly but it does not matter during normal execution.

```
public class Guess {
    public static String animalType(int neckLength) {
        // String value changed from "UNKNOWN" to "AMBER"
        String toReturn = "AMBER";
        if (neckLength > 10) {
            toReturn = "Rhinoceros";
        } else if (neckLength < 20) {
            toReturn = "Hippopotamus";
        } else {
            toReturn = "Giraffe";
        }
        return toReturn;
    }
}
```

This will not cause any failures in our unit tests, since the "UNKNOWN" value was just a placeholder and never actually used for anything. It does tell us that perhaps we don't need to set a default value here, or that there is a better way to implement the method. For example, this is a slightly more efficient way to implement the same method:

```
public class Guess {
    public static String animalType(int neckLength) {
        // Default value is now a giraffe, no need for final else
        String toReturn = "Giraffe";
        if (neckLength > 10) {
            toReturn = "Rhinoceros";
        } else if (neckLength < 20) {
            toReturn = "Hippopotamus";
        }
        return toReturn;
    }
}
```

However, this could also be a code spell that we forgot to implement some functionality. Perhaps we meant to return that default value if an animal with a negative-length neck was passed in, but never got around to actually coding that!

```
public class Guess {
```

```java
public static String animalType(int neckLength) {
    String toReturn = "UNKNOWN";

    // If invalid neckLength value passed in, return default
    if (neckLength < 0) {
        return toReturn;
    }

    if (neckLength < 10) {
        toReturn = "Rhinoceros";
    } else if (neckLength < 20) {
        toReturn = "Hippopotamus";
    } else {
        toReturn = "Giraffe";
    }
    return toReturn;
}
}
```

Mutation testing is a valuable way to determine how well your tests are testing your code. It is very easy for a tester to miss an equivalence class, or a boundary value, or a failure mode. When a mutation which cannot be caught by your tests shows up, though, you can see not only that there is a hole in your testing strategy, but also see how a coding mistake would cause it.

Chapter 19

Performance Testing

What, exactly, is performance testing? Before we can define "performance testing", we first need to define "performance". I assume that at this point in the book, everybody understands what "testing" means.

Most technically savvy people will have a gut feeling for what performance means—systems that are "fast", that "don't take up much memory", etc. The more you try to define it, though, the more slippery the definition becomes. Faster, compared to what? What if a system uses lots of RAM, and a competing system uses less RAM but more hard drive space? If System A returns a response in three seconds, and System B returns a response in five seconds, which is more performant? The answer may seem obvious, unless the queries to which the systems are responding are themselves different. Performance is one of those concepts that is hard to pin down, because it will mean different things for different systems.

Imagine a video game where you play a software tester fighting evil Bugs. You can use the arrow keys to move and the space key to shoot your insecticide gun. Whenever you press the space key, you will expect your avatar on-screen to shoot the insecticide within, say, 200 milliseconds—anything more and you'll feel like the video game is "lagging" behind your keypresses. Now imagine a second system, a weather forecasting supercomputing cluster, with the ability to run millions of calculations in parallel. However, as weather forecasting requires a large number of calculations, it takes half an hour after hitting the "run" command for the system to return what the weather forecast is for tomorrow. Until that time, the screen just says "Calculating..." The supercomputer has several orders of magnitude longer response time than the video game, but does this mean the supercomputer is less performant than your video game console? On the particular **performance indicator** of response time, one could argue so, but the response time metric was very different for the results of the weather forecaster.

How do you determine which system has better performance? The short answer is, you can't! The systems are trying to do different—and basically incomparable—actions. How you measure performance will be based upon the kind of system you are testing. That does not mean, however, that there are no rules or heuristics. In this chapter, we'll go over some different kinds of performance and how one would go about testing them. It is not an exhaustive list, though. The system you are testing may have unique performance aspects which no book of finite length (which this book most assuredly is) could reasonably contain.

19.1   Categories of Performance Indicators

As mentioned above, defining performance for a particular system means determining which performance indicators the user or customer cares about. Although there are a large number of possible performance indicators, there are two main categories: service-oriented and efficiency-oriented.

A **service-oriented indicator** measures how well a system is providing a service to a particular user. These are measured from the user's perspective and quantify aspects of the system the user would directly care about. Some examples of service-oriented indicators would be average page load time, response time, or what percentage of the time the system is available.

There are two main subcategories of service-oriented indicators. The first is availability—how available is the system to the user? This could mean anything from what percentage of the time can the system be accessed to how available different features are to the users at different times. The second main category is response time—how long does it take for the system to respond to the user's input or return a result?

An **efficiency-oriented indicator** measures how efficiently a system makes use of available computational resources. You can think of these as being measured "from the program's point of view", or at least from the computer's point of view. Examples of efficiency-oriented indicators would be what percentage of CPU operations are being used for performing some functionality, how much disk space is being used, or how many concurrent users the system can handle on a particular server. Although the last may seem like it may be a service-oriented indicator, the fact that it's from the system level—how many users can the system handle, rather than how does it appear to a specific user—means that it's an efficiency-oriented indicator. Whenever you are measuring from the perspective of the system, as opposed to something *directly* experienced by the user, you are testing an efficiency-oriented indicator.

Just like service-oriented indicators, there are two main subcategories in efficiency-oriented testing. **Throughput** measures how many events can the system handle in a given amount of time, such as how many users can log in at the same time, or how many packets can a system route in 30 seconds. **Utilization** measures what percentage or absolute amount of computing resources are used to perform a given task. For example, how much disk space does a database take to store a specified table? How much RAM is necessary when sorting it?

Service-oriented indicators are similar to black-box testing in that they measure the system from an external perspective, without determining the cause of the problem precisely. As blunt instruments, they are broadly effective in finding where one should look more closely for problems. Efficiency-oriented indicators are similar to white-box testing in that they require knowledge of the system as well as general technical knowledge. Oftentimes, you can use service-oriented indicators to determine general areas where performance might be an issue to users, and then use efficiency-oriented indicators to nail down exactly what is causing the problem. Long response times from the perspective of the user may result from physical RAM being used up and much of the information needing to be swapped in from disk. Service-oriented testing would catch the former, but efficiency-oriented testing would be able to figure out the latter.

19.2   Testing Performance: Thresholds and Targets

In order to determine whether or not a performance test has "passed", you need **performance targets**, or specific quantitative values that the performance indicators are supposed to reach. For example, you may have an efficiency-oriented performance target that the installer for the software under test should be less than ten megabytes (it seems like a "Hello, world" program takes up over ten megabytes nowadays, but let's leave that complaint to the side for now). You may have a service-oriented indicator that the system should respond within 500 milliseconds under normal load. By quantifying a target, you can write a test and determine whether or not the system has met the target.

Targets, though, are the ideal. Oftentimes, a particular performance indicator for a system may not reach its target, or may not be able to. **Performance thresholds** indicate the point where a performance indicator reaches an absolutely minimal acceptable performance. For example, while the target for response time may be 500 milliseconds, systems engineers may have determined that the system would be releasable with a response time of 3000 milliseconds. It would not be great if it only met that mark, but if it takes any longer, the system would probably not be releasable.

A system whose performance indicators merely meet the threshold should not be considered as "passing" that particular performance metric. There is still work to do! You can see that the standard "pass"/"fail" metric often used for functional testing is often not really appropriate for performance metrics. There are shades of gray, and they are often able to be manipulated. What kind of hardware are you running the tests on? What operating system? What other processes are running? Which web browser are you using to access the site? By changing these, the same system may show very different results on a performance test.

19.3 Key Performance Indicators

Particular performance indicators may be more or less important. Going back to our weather forecasting supercomputer, there was definitely a response time requirement; it was supposed to return results within half an hour. Although response time may be important - if a hurricane is coming, users want that result after thirty minutes exactly so that you can start evacuating residents. In other cases, such as when testing with archived data, response time may be off by double the amount of time or more, and it wouldn't make much difference. Some performance indicators might be very important (in this example, response time when running at highest priority) and others might not be important at all (response time when testing on archived data).

Although there are a very large number of potential performance indicators for a system, there will always be a subset of them that you are most interested in. A video game may require very fast response time and high availability, but very little need for minimizing disk space, CPU, or RAM usage. A long-term daemon process running in the background will have very different requirements— minimal RAM and CPU usage are very important, but response time is really not important at all. Only rarely will a user or another process interact with it, and when it does, it will be via signals and a near real-time response is not expected.

By selecting the most important performance indicators—referred to as **key performance indicators** or **KPIs**—you can focus on testing the aspects of performance most important to the users. This will then allow developers to tune the system to meet the needs of the users, instead of wasting time on parts of the system which the users will not tend to care about or which are already sufficiently performant. Depending on the level of specificity of the requirements, it may be possible to determine what the KPIs are while designing the system. In many cases, you will have to determine them via user testing, researching similar applications in the domain, or using your testing knowledge to estimate them.

Selecting key performance indicators should be done before testing begins; you should not test a bunch of indicators, then turn around and note which ones were important. You should determine which ones are most important ahead of time, when designing the test plan for the system. If you are following a more lightweight development process, with less significant upfront design, you should at least determine whether or not a particular performance indicator is a KPI before running the appropriate test. This forces you to keep in mind which aspects of the system's performance are important and which are not before coming up with results. If you try to pick out the KPIs afterwards, you may be tempted (even if subconsciously) to simply select the indicators that met their targets. Leave that kind of thinking to advertisers.

19.4   Testing Service-Oriented Indicators: Response Time

The easiest way to measure response time, of course, is to simply follow this algorithm:

1. Do something

2. Click "start" button on stopwatch

3. Wait for response

4. When response is seen, click "stop" button on stopwatch

5. Write down how long it took

While this may be the easiest way to measure response time, it is far from the best. There are a plethora of problems with this approach. First, it is impossible to measure sub-second times; human response time is simply too variable and not fast enough. You can't measure anything internal to the system if your only interface to the system is what you see. It's very time-consuming, thus making it difficult to collect large datasets. It's subject to human error (ever spend an entire day timing things? At some point, you're bound to forget to click the "start" button, or accidentally click the "reset" button before you've written down the time). It's an absolutely fantastic way to destroy tester morale (ever spend an entire day timing things? At some point, you're bound to remember to go look for another job). Because of all these issues (and more), performance testing is often done with the aid of tools.

Although testing in general is becoming increasingly automated, performance testing in particular tends to depend heavily on automated tests. There can be quite a bit of variation in performance indicators from run to run, due to other variables over which you may have little control. Examples of these variables include other processes running on a server, how much physical RAM was already being used, garbage collection runs, and virtual machine startup times, among others. Often the only way to get a truly valid result is running a performance test for numerous iterations and statistically analyzing it (obtaining the mean, median, and maximum response times, for example). The only way to gain a reasonable number of samples in a reasonable amount of time is to automate the process.

19.4.1   What is Time?

Although this may sound like a philosophical question, it actually has very direct ramifications when testing response times. To a computer, there are actually several different ways of measuring time. To a performance tester, how you report and measure time will depend upon what factors you are most interested in for the specific performance test.

The first kind of time, and probably the easiest to understand, is **real time**. This is the kind of time measured by the clock on the wall, and is thus also referred to as **wall clock time**. (And you thought technical terms would be difficult to learn.) This is analogous to stopwatch time—how long does it take, from the user's perspective, for a program to do something? Thus, this is usually the kind of time that users will care most about. However, it does not tell the whole story.

Real time takes into account *everything* that needs to be done by the system to perform the given task. If this means reading data in from the disk, or over the network, that counts towards the real time total—no matter how slow the disk or bandwidth-restricted the network. If this means that it's running on a system which is running lots of other processes concurrently, meaning that it only got a chance to use 5% of the CPU's time, then that counts towards the real time. Real time is often not a great metric to track because it takes into account many things that are entirely out of the hands of the developers of the system.

User time, by contrast, measures specifically how much time was spent executing user code. This does not count any time spent waiting for input, reading from the disk, idling while another process has control of the processor, or even executing system calls. It is very focused on that section of the system which developers have direct control over. After all, you can easily change the sorting algorithm you use in your code, but if you need to get the resolution of the clock running on a system, the only way to do that is through a system call whose code you have no control over (unless you want to, for example, fork Linux).

The time spent in system calls—where code is being executed, but the code that is being executed is in the kernel and not in your program—is known as **system time**. While developers do not have direct control over system time since they did not write the kernel code, they do have indirect control since it is possible to reduce the number of system calls the program makes, change the ordering in which they are made, call different functions altogether, or use other techniques to minimize system time.

By adding together user time and system time, you get **total time**—the amount of time spent executing code either in user space or kernel space. This is a good measurement of how much time your code is actually spending for its execution. It avoids calculating time that other processes were being executed on the processor or the system was waiting for input and allows focus simply on how long the code was being executed. However, focusing on system time may blind you to issues related to these external factors. For example, if you are testing database software, then much of your time will be spent reading from, and writing to, a disk. It would be foolish to discount all of this time even if the developers have no direct control over it, it should be taken into account.

Depending on what you're measuring and how much control you have over the test environment, tracking user, total, or real time might be the optimal indicator. System time rarely is, unless you are testing a new kernel or operating system or deeply care about the split for arcane reasons. Keep in mind that while developers have the most control over user time, indirect control over total time, and only minimal control over real time in most instances, users usually only care about real time! If a user of your system finds it slow, they will not accept that you can't control how fast disk reads are as an excuse. From a testing perspective, you should generally focus on measuring real time, avoiding as many extraneous factors, such as other programs running concurrently, as possible. However, for certain processes which are CPU-bound or tend to operate in the background, focusing on total or user time may be more appropriate.

On most Unix-like systems (e.g. Linux or OS X), you can very easily get these values to benchmark a program. Simply run `time <command>`, and after the command is finished executing, the real, user, and system times will be displayed (total time is easily calculated by adding user and system time):

```
$ time wc -w * | tail -n 1
   66156 total

real    0m0.028s
user    0m0.009s
sys     0m0.014s
```

$

There are various timing programs available for Windows machines, such as `timeit.exe` which comes with the Windows Server 2003 Resource Kit, but there is no almost universally-installed command such as `time` available.

19.4.2   What Events Should Be Timed?

This will depend on what your performance indicator is. If you have a specific indicator, either spelled out in the requirements or agreed to by the team, then measuring is a straightforward process. However, if you need to determine this on your own, then your first step should be to figure out which events are important to the user of the system, where slow response times would cause hardship or annoyance.

If you are testing a system which is running on a server, some events you might want to think of checking for response time are:

1. Page load time (for web servers)
2. Download time
3. Connection response time
4. Time for data to appear on-screen on client
5. Time between connection and readiness for user input

For local programs, some events you may want to check for response time are:

1. Total execution time
2. Time from start of execution until ready for input
3. Time between input and response
4. Time between input and confirmation of input (e.g., a "loading" indicator)

Additionally, you may have some more specific response times to check for based on the program you are using. For example, imagine a program which allows students to register for classes. There may be one performance indicator for how long it takes to list all classes in a department and a separate performance indicator for how long it takes to enroll in a selected course. Not all response times are created equal, and some may be key performance indicators while others are not. For example, since students probably list courses much more often than enroll in them, listing all courses may be a KPI, whereas enrolling is measured but does not have any specific threshold or target.

Just because a particular indicator does not have a target or threshold does not mean it cannot be measured. Oftentimes, especially if the performance indicator measurement is automated, it makes sense to just gather response times for many different events and store them. These can be analyzed in an exploratory manner to see if there are any oddities or problems. For example, even if enrollment time was not listed as a performance indicator, but we notice that it takes five minutes on average for a student to enroll in a class, it may be worthwhile to take a look for a chance to lower that time. Not all performance requirements will be specified clearly before development, so it is often up to the tester to bring problems to the attention of the team even if the tester wasn't specifically looking for those issues.

Determining what kind of target time is acceptable for response time can be difficult. However, there are some rough guidelines. These were taken from *Usability Engineering* by Jakob Neilsen.

- *< 100 ms:* Response time required to feel that system is instantaneous

- *< 1 s:* Response time required for flow of thought to not be interrupted

- *< 10 s:* Response time required for user to stay focused on application (and not go see what's happening on the Internet)

Although these are rough guidelines for targets, they are not laws in and of themselves, and good response times will depend on a whole host of factors (what kind of network the system is running over, what kind of calculations the system is running, etc.) There is empirical evidence, based on studies from Google, that people will choose websites, even if not consciously, based on less than 250 ms difference in load times. Any load time over 400 milliseconds for a web page causes a drop-off in visitors, and this time has been decreasing steadily. Users are becoming less patient as time goes on.

As a final note, it is possible for response time to be too fast! Think of a scroll box that scrolls so fast that the user can't control it, or a screen which changes so quickly that it disorients the reader. A performance indicator for response time might include an upper bound and a lower bound in some instances.

19.5 Testing Service-Oriented Indicators: Availability

Availability, often referred to as uptime, refers to the percentage of the time that a user can access the system when they expect to be able to do so. Thus, any time that a system spends being down reduces availability—whether due to maintenance, an uncaught exception crashing a process, or a hard drive blowing up.

Many cloud service providers provide a **service level agreement** (SLA) which specifies the level of availability that they provide. This is often specified in the **n nines** format, which specifies "how many nines" of reliability they provide. These "nines" refer to 99% (2 nines), 99.9% (3 nines), 99.99% (4 nines), etc. At the time of this writing, for example, Amazon S3 promises to have 3 nines' availability (available 99.9% of time, meaning downtime of less than around 45 minutes per month). For certain systems, such as autonomous vehicles and space probes, uptime requirements might be much higher.

How do we determine what an appropriate level of availability is for a system under test? If it is a key performance indicator, it will probably be specified as a requirement. If not, however, it may be necessary to discuss with systems engineers to determine the proper level of availability for your system. Note that increasing the level of availability one "level" of nines gets more and more difficult and will require larger amounts of engineering and design. For example, going from 1 nine (90% availability, or less than approximately 40 days of downtime per year) to 2 nines (99%, or less than approximately four days of downtime per year) availability may involve simply adding some backup software and a daemon which can reboot processes when they fail. Going one step further, to 99.9% availability (downtime of less than 9 hours per year) may require additional servers as backup and a redesign of the system to be more distributed. Going further on, you may need to do formal verification of your software, buy hot-swappable hard drives, etc. For example, if you are attempting to have 6 nines' reliability, that's approximately 30 seconds of downtime per year. Everything that can go wrong—power outages, network disconnects, meteor strikes, etc.—will have to be dealt with automatically. At those levels of availability, no human in the loop would be fast enough to prevent a level of downtime which would ruin your performance target.

This doesn't really answer the question, because there is no one answer. The level of availability will depend on the domain of the software you're testing and the particular business or other needs of the user. Even large web services have noticeable amounts of downtime during which you won't be able to check mail or see what inane, easily refuted stories your friends are posting on social media.

Some systems—such as avionics or spacecraft control software—are continuously available for years or even decades at a stretch, with no downtime. Others, such as research software, may be down more often than they are up. As a tester, though, you can ask several question to determine what an acceptable level of availability would be:

1. *What is the downside if the system is not available?* For research software, an experiment may be delayed. For a website, it could mean that a business loses money. For avionics software, it could mean a plane crash.

2. *How much effort is the team willing and able to put into availability?* If the team has no internal impetus to work on increasing availability, and no money or resources are available to work on it, it may not be worthwhile to spend much time testing it.

3. *How does a focus on availability hamper other aspects of the software?* Every minute you spend testing availability means less time testing other aspects of the system. In some systems, your availability tests may help to uncover other defects. In others, it may be a pure drain on other testing of the system.

By asking these questions, you can, in tandem with developers and other stakeholders of the system, determine what a good level of availability is. Remember that target *and* threshold levels can be set! Most users would of course say that they would prefer that a system be available 100% of the time, and there's no issue with having that as a target. However, by probing more deeply—e.g., would you be willing to pay three times as much for a system that's available 99.999% of the time, as opposed to 99.9% of the time?—you can often determine a good threshold value for this performance indicator.

Once we have determined what the target and threshold levels for availability are, how do we test them? A simple answer might be to just run the system for a year, determine what amount of time the system was up and running, and divide by the total time to get the percentage of uptime per year. Boom, we have our results! This, of course, assumes that the business is perfectly fine waiting for a year to get results, and that no further development will take place during that time. After all, if different code was deployed, that would ruin the experiment! There are not many systems where this would be a reasonable way to determine availability. Just like we determined with using a stopwatch for response time testing, the simple solution is not feasible to use in practice.

Instead, one can model the system to be tested. A simple model may involve running the system for one day, noting how many failures occur and calculating how much time it would take to fix them. Divide this time by the time in a day, and you theoretically have how much availability the system will have over any length of time. If the system experiences two problems eleven hours and fifty minutes apart, for instance, each of which caused it to not be available for ten minutes, then you can add up 2 * 10 = 20 minutes, divide it by 24 hours (1440 minutes), and you had an availability that day of 20 / 1440, or 98.6% uptime—not quite two nines.

In fact, this is the general idea behind the standard model of availability. Once you calculate the **mean time between failures** (often abbreviated as **MTBF**) and the **mean time to repair** (**MTTR**) for those failures, you can just use the following equation as a rough estimate of system availability:

```
(MTBF / (MTBF + MTTR)) * 100%
```

In our example above, the mean time between failures is 710 minutes, and the mean time to repair is 10 minutes. Thus, MTBF + MTTR is 720 minutes.

```
(710 / (710 + 10)) * 100% = 98.61% availability
```

This simple model fails to take into account that components tend not to fail at the same rate throughout time. Although you will be able to see some of the random failures that a system will inevitably hit, and probably more than a fair share of problems resulting from the first time that code is executed in a real environment, this error rate will probably not reflect a longer-term rate of error in the system. Along with the "ramp-up failures" and "random failures", you also have to take into account that hardware will wear out. A second factor is that things which you know are likely to happen, but did not during the day of test, will certainly occur if the system is running for any reasonable length of time—for example, power outages or cooling system failures. Just because you didn't see them that day does not mean that they will never happen, just as you rolling a die once and getting a 4 does not mean that you can assume that you will never get a 6. Finally, there may be what Donald Rumsfeld famously called "unknown unknowns"—situations that you and the system designers never took into consideration or even imagined happening. According to astronomer Phil Plait, your chances of dying via meteor strike are approximately 1 in 700,000—slightly less than your chances of dying in a firework accident and slightly more than your chances of dying in a terrorist attack. Can you assume that the data center where your site is hosted will survive indefinitely and not be struck by a meteor? The longer the system is running, the higher the chances that these small-probability events will occur, and these will be difficult to catch using the naïve model of simply multiplying one day's worth of results by the number of days in a year.

Systems tend to follow what is called the **bathtub curve**. This means that many failures tend to happen at the beginning, when the system is just starting up, then the number of failures decreases, then finally starts to increase again as components wear out, libraries stop being updated, external APIs stop being supported, etc. When plotted out, the curve looks like a side view of a bathtub. There's a high amount of downtime and errors at first, then a drastic drop-off in downtime and error rate as the obvious problems manifest themselves and are fixed, then a long period of relatively low amount of downtime, then a slope upwards as the system gets older and things start to go wrong. Including the bathtub curve in your model planning can be helpful, although it's only a rough guide. You should assume that the system will have more downtime at the beginning as your team sees and fixes defects that were only observable once the system started running "for real".

For your particular system, you may want to determine how much more complicated you want to make the model, how much time you want to spend gathering data, and how many external factors such as outside APIs being down or other problems you would like to take into consideration. Remember that in performance testing in general, it is rarely a good idea to use one data point to generalize. If you are going to use a "day" as the basis for your calculations, don't use just one day's worth of testing to determine the mean time to failure and mean time to repair. Remember to factor in at least some room for things that you didn't think of that will go wrong—remember Murphy's Law. All that being said, the basic concept of (MTBF / (MTBF + MTTR)) should provide a nice starting point for any given system to determine its level of availability.

Now that you know what you're looking for and how you're going to deal with the results, it's time to generate those numbers. This can be done by **load testing**. In load testing, a system is set up and monitored while events are processed. The kind of events will depend on the system under test—for a web server, for example, it might be page loads, or for a router, it would be packets routed. By using different kinds of load tests based on realistic assumptions, one can determine the MTBF and MTTR, and thus the availability that users can expect to see.

A **baseline test** runs the system with few or no events to process, just to check that the system can in fact handle running for a given period of time. This is often not a realistic scenario—a system which never does much is not likely to be developed in the first place—but provides a "baseline" which future tests can compare results against. The opposite of a baseline test is a **stress test**, in which the system is "stressed" by having it process a large number of events in small time frame. Stress tests are not typically run for extended periods of time, but are useful for modeling those periods when the system is under heavy stress. Examples of those times would be a DDoS attack for a website, or the beginning of the Fall semester for a class registration system.

A **stability test**, sometimes also called a **soak test**, is often the single most realistic load test that is run. During this kind of load test, a constant but small-to-medium number of events are processed over a long period of time, in order to determine that the system is in fact stable when doing realistic work.

If at all possible, determine what real-world usage is like, so that you can model your system appropriately. It's not at all uncommon to combine various load tests together to come up with single MTBF and MTTR values. For example, you may be able to determine that the system under test spends 10% of its time in a "stress state" and 90% of its time in a "stability state". If the MTBF is 10 minutes during a stress state, and 12 hours during a stability state, with a MTTR of 5 minutes in each case, you can create a more nuanced calculation:

```
MTBF(stress) = 10
MTBF(stable) = 720
MTTR = 5
MTBF = (0.1 * MTBF(stress)) + (0.9 * MTBF(stable)) = 649
(MTBF / (MTBF + MTTR)) * 100
(649 / (649 + 5)) * 100 = 99.23% availability
```

This is just an example, and it could certainly be further enhanced (and any state of the system that reaches such high levels of unavailability during stress states probably should be looked at further) . Some systems do have spikes of usage, where others do not. Some systems will handle lots of small events, others will handle a smaller number of harder-to-process events. If you are able to gather real-world data and metrics about the usage of your system, you will be able to model its behavior better, and thus produce better availability numbers. The more realistic the data, the more realistic the model you will be able to create. Even with the most realistic of data, however, be prepared to be wrong—there are so many things that can go wrong with a complex system, it is impossible to take all of them into account in any model.

19.6   Testing Efficiency-Oriented Indicators: Throughput

If you'll recall from earlier, efficiency-oriented indicators take a view of the system from the perspective of the system and how efficiently it makes use of the computation resources available to it. One measure of efficiency is the amount of **throughput**, or number of events that can be processed in a given amount of time on a specified hardware setup. Examples would include how many web pages a web server could serve in one minute, or how many SQL queries a database server could perform in one minute. This may seem similar to response time, or at least its inverse, but it isn't quite so simple. While response time was measuring the response time from the point of view of a particular user of the system, throughput is how performant the system as a whole is in responding to a number of users. If I am simply using a web server, I don't care about how fast other users get their data. If I am an administrator of a web site using a particular server, then I certainly do care!

Just as we did when testing availability, we can use load testing to determine the throughput of the system. Instead of determining if the system is up however, we can specifically check for what sustained rate of events can occur before some predetermined lower threshold on performance is reached. For example, in our web server example, how many pages per minute can the web server serve before the average response time dips below 3 seconds? For a web-based course registration system, how many students can view courses at the same time before the database request queue is saturated? The exact parameters of what counts as "below the performance threshold" will vary by system, but it is commonly average or maximum response time. We are using a service-oriented indicator as part of testing an efficiency-oriented indicator! This goes to show that different aspects of performance are often intertwined; poor throughput could be the cause of slow response time, or poor utilization of resources could directly lead to a lack of availability.

Determining the values for the lowest threshold will be heavily dependent on the KPIs for this particular system. Once again, these should be determined before testing starts, so as not to cherry-pick the results. Once they are determined, you should ramp up the number of events until the system can no longer perform within the determined performance threshold.

Remember to track the level of events and the equivalent throughput, and if possible, relevant utilization measures (see next section for more on measuring utilization). This will allow you to see if there are any patterns in the throughput levels, thus allowing you to extrapolate further than the data points you have collected. For example, assume that you see that response time is always approximately 500 milliseconds up to 100 events per second, but at 150 events per second, response time slows to 800 milliseconds. At 200 events per second, response time increases to 2500 milliseconds. We can see some superlinear growth starting at approximately the 100 events per second mark, and developers will then have more information to start tracking down bottlenecks. Is that the point where data starts being swapped to disk? Do we have 100 threads, and this is the point where the thread pool runs dry? Although you may not have these answers up front, having an idea of the growth, and especially a general area where throughput starts to slow down, will make improving the performance much easier. Just as we discussed regarding filing defects, being more specific is almost always better than being less specific!

Throughput levels are very sensitive to what kind of hardware you are running the software on, so even more than with other tests, you will need to ensure that you are running on the same kind of hardware from run to run to ensure valid results. You may also want to determine throughput using the same software on different hardware configurations, which may also help to track down the cause of any slowdowns. For example, a system which has extremely reduced throughput when run on a system with slightly less RAM than another may indicate a memory bottleneck.

19.7 Testing Efficiency-Oriented Indicators: Utilization

Testing **utilization** means determining what amount of computing resources—on an absolute or relative basis—a particular system uses when performing some functionality. "Computing resources" is a very broad term, covering anything that a program could be "using" on a machine. Common examples include:

1. CPU

2. Disk usage

3. RAM

4. Network usage

While these are some of the most common resources measured, there are also very specific ones which can be measured. The number of disk bytes read? Standby cache normal priority bytes? Number of C3 transitions on your CPU in the last second? All of these (along with literally thousands of others) can be tested right out of the box on your Windows machine by using a tool called `perfmon`. For other operating systems, there are equivalent tools, such as Activity Monitor for OS X or `sar` for Linux. However, these very specific measurements are usually only needed after discovering a problem with the more generalized measurements enumerated above.

Often, you only need a "finger in the wind" estimate of resource usage, or to see which process is using the most resources. This can be done by using tools that are freely available on various operating systems: Windows systems have Task Manager, while OS X and Linux systems use `top`. Each of these programs will enable you to see which programs you have running that are using the most CPU or memory. I'll skip over the particulars of running them; you can use `man top` to get the Unix manual entry for `top`, or look up the appropriate Microsoft documentation for Task Manager.

Both of these tools are similar in showing snapshots of resource usage at a particular moment in time. They'll let you see if there is a particular spike in CPU usage when you perform some action, or how the memory usage of a process will vary as time goes on. For a Java program, for example, you will often see the telltale sign of a garbage-collected program, as memory usage drifts up, then suddenly comes back down, in a "sawtooth" pattern.

While service-oriented indicators can often give a warning that something is wrong with the system, using a tool such as `top` will allow you to drill down just a bit further, determining, say, that slow response times (a service-oriented indicator) seem to be the result of the CPU going to 99% usage every time a response is requested. However, looking at resource utilization this way is a very blunt instrument. Modern CPUs are complex, modern software is complex, modern memory is complex, and together, they mean that trying to understand the resource utilization of a system is complex. Instructions can be pipelined or threads can be running on different cores, there are different levels of cache and different kinds of memory usage, software may operate differently and use resources in different ways on different systems. More importantly, once you've determined that the problem is extreme CPU usage or too much memory being used, how do you put that in terms of a defect that a developer can address?

The answer is that you get more specific via a **profiler** (also known as a **profiling tool**). A profiler, such as JProfiler or VisualVM for Java programs, will allow you to not only see that the process is using lots of CPU, but how much CPU each particular method is using. It's much easier for a developer to track down an issue when they know in what method the problem is likely to be! Instead of simply letting you know that a system is taking up 100 megabytes of memory, you can see which objects have been instantiated, and which classes they are instantiations of. While this will help you narrow in on the problem, trying to determine whether or not there *is* a problem in the first place by using a profiler might be overkill. It is very easy to become overwhelmed with data if you do not have a specific target.

If you determine that the problem is with network usage, you can use a **packet analyzer** such as Wireshark to inspect individual packets or run statistical analyses. This will allow you to see specifically which packets are being sent or received and may be causing a bottleneck, or if there is superfluous data being sent out which may be a cause of performance degradation. For example, while timestamps may be necessary to send out on a regular basis, is the inclusion of the timezone of the originating system really necessary? Could timestamps simply always be in UTC and adjusted locally according to the settings of each receiving system?

19.8   General Tips and Advice When Performance Testing

1. Use a tool for any non-trivial performance measurement. Relying on humans to execute many performance tests will lead to mistakes due to human error, as well as increasing the possibility of demoralized testers.

2. Compare apples to apples; keep variables the same between runs of the same test! Don't run the first version of the software on a laptop and the second version on a supercomputer and proclaim a massive increase in speed.

3. Be mindful of startup and/or shutdown costs. If a system needs to start up a VM (e.g., a JVM for all Java processes), then you may need a way to standardize that across all runs, ignore the first result since it will include startup times, or otherwise take it into consideration.

4. Be mindful of caching. If a system is caching results, you may see very different performance measurements the first time running a test versus the second and third times.

5. Have control over the testing system. You want to make sure that others are not logged in to the system, that settings are the same between runs, that no additional software has been installed, etc. Remember that performance testing is like running a science experiment—if you can't reduce extraneous variables, you won't be able to trust it.

6. Have good input data. If you can, try to test with real, or at least possibly real, data. Many times the kind of performance that you see on a system will depend upon data. If you used a bubble sort, but all of your test data was in order, you may not notice the bad performance that comes with normally unordered data, since bubble sort is $O(n)$ for already-sorted data but $O(n^2)$ in the average case.

7. Don't trust a single test run. Although you endeavor to remove all extraneous variables from your performance test, there will always be elements you can't control, from how the memory is allocated to which order threads are run. While these may or may not have a significant impact on the performance of your system, they are always there. The only way to minimize their impact is to run the test multiple times and hopefully smooth out the data by taking the mean result or otherwise analyzing it statistically.

8. Keep track of your test runs, and store the data. This will allow you to determine when problems first started appearing, problems which you may not have noticed at first glance. It will also let you determine trends. For example, you may notice that with each successive version of the software you test, memory usage is going up while CPU usage is going down.

9. Finally, consider how much performance testing is necessary and that you have to do. If your system only executes overnight, does response time actually matter that much? If the system does take up too much CPU, is that something that will be prioritized to fix? Just like with any other kind of testing, time spent looking for problems in one place inevitably means less time to look for problems of other kinds. Be sure that you are using your time, limited as it is, wisely.

Chapter 20

Security Testing

When computers were first starting to become a thing (that's a technical term), security was not a key driver behind developing software for them. Systems were rarely networked, so in order to tamper with the system or view its data, you would have to physically get to the computer. Even in the 1950s, people knew how to secure physical locations (locks and security guards are pretty useful in the real world). In the rare instances that computers were networked or publicly accessible, there were few users, and they tended to be grad students, developers, or other authorized users. Supposing somebody was able to break into a system, it was usually not a big deal. Richard Stallman, the founder of the Free Software Foundation, argued against having passwords in the operating system ITS. If you wanted to crash a system running ITS, all any user had to do was type KILL SYSTEM. In other words, people generally trusted each other to do the right thing. If you're interested in reading about this Golden Age of Computing, I recommend *Hackers: Heroes of the Computer Revolution* by Steven Levy.

The title of that book is a good place for a quick tangent. The term "hacker", although often used to mean "one who maliciously breaks into computer systems", is actually of a much older vintage. It meant one who did something clever, new, or interesting. Despite the world's insistence on the term "hacker", I will be using the term "cracker" to mean a person who breaks into systems which they are not authorized to access.

Anyways, humanity being what it is, the idyllic state of affairs where computer users mostly trusted each other was not meant to last. Although there were few networked computers in the 1960s, there was a huge, networked system that reached a huge percentage of the population—the phone system. People known as "phone phreaks" would explore the phone system, figuring out how to make devices that would allow for free incoming calls or fool pay phones into thinking that coins were dropped into them. While the primary goal of most of these phone phreaks was simply understanding the labyrinthine complexity of the phone system, telephone security personnel and police saw it is as an early form of "digital trespassing".

As the world became more and more networked, stories of software security failures became commonplace. Among these were movies such as *WarGames*, which included an artificial intelligence in charge of the United States' nuclear arsenal being fooled by a teenage computer whiz, and books such as *The Cuckoo's Egg*, which detailed the true story of a former astronomer tracking down a West German computer cracker. Real-life events, such as the Morris Worm, which shut down a large portion of the Internet in 1988, also helped to mark the introduction of security as a risk that programmers needed to concern themselves with. The concept of **information security** was born. Software started to include features which would prevent unauthorized access or modification of data.

Today, breaking computer security is a big business, with many crackers infiltrating systems in order to blackmail companies, steal credit card information, or shut down websites which they find objectionable. Likewise, protecting systems from unauthorized access, and helping to find weak points in a system before the "bad guys" do, is also a big business.

20.1   Challenges in Security Testing

Security testing differs from other kinds of software testing in that there is an intelligent adversary—indeed, many adversaries, although not all of them are really "intelligent"—also looking for defects. You can think of malicious crackers trying to break into your system as just a variant of a tester—they are constantly testing for weak points in your software that they can use to gain access or steal data. When you're unit testing, you don't need to worry that the system will change from under you or *try* to cause your tests to fail, but this is definitely the case in security testing.

In some ways, you have it much harder than your adversaries. The common—some would say cliché—metaphor is that of defending a castle. If the enemy finds one unlocked and undefended door, they will have the run of the castle. You, on the other hand, need to ensure that you have defended every single entrance. Similarly, you will have to check for all of the weak points in your software, while they only need to find one. It doesn't matter if you are protected from a SQL injection attack if the attacker is easily able to find passwords from an insecure storage vulnerability.

Although there's still a *mythos* involving computer security where those trying to break into computers are just curious kids (although this is still the case sometimes!), many attacks are done for some sort of financial remuneration. People sell botnet time to the highest bidder to send spam. They develop and sell exploits to "offensive hacking" groups or unnamed government agencies. They break into a retailer's credit card database not to see if it can be done, but because they want to buy things with credit cards (or sell them on the black market and get money that way). There is a huge market for security information and for "secret" data.

Security testing requires you to think like your adversary. In order to test a system effectively, you will need to stop thinking like the upstanding person I'm sure you are. Instead, you will need to think like someone who will do sneaky things to get into the system and approach it in a way that ordinary users would not. After all, if there were vulnerabilities which could be found by routine use of the software, they have probably already been discovered and fixed. The most dangerous defects tend to be the ones that use the system in ways that normal people generally don't even conceive. Again, this is very different from standard functional testing, where the most dangerous defects are the ones that ordinary users will hit into the most! If your text editor fails whenever you hit the E key, for example, that's a major defect with huge impact, basically making the text editor useless. This assumes, of course, that you are not Georges Perec writing *La Disparition*—an obscure corner case. If it only fails whenever the user types "`%&#@@!_!<Ctrl-R><Ctrl-Q>`", well, that defect may not even be worth fixing. The only people who will try it are the ones reading this book and wondering if it's really a defect in some text editor (I'll never tell). However, if the same defects allowed access to a bank account, the reverse might be true. The fact that E causes the failure means that it will be caught readily; perhaps only a dedicated attacker will figure out to type "`%&#@@!_!<Ctrl-R><Ctrl-Q>`" and it flies under the radar for months as more accounts are mysteriously depleted.

Security failures can be catastrophic and tend to have worse impacts than similar functional failures. Assuming a good backup strategy and other simple safety procedures, most functional or non-functional defects will not cause much havoc. Not all defects are trivial, of course; there are numerous examples of software defects causing problems up to and including loss of life (for a famous case, see *An Investigation of the Therac-25 Accidents* by N. Leveson and C.S. Turner, which details how a software race condition caused massive overdoses of radiation for several patients). However, the vast majority of defects do not have an impact quite so dire. The impact of security-related defects, however, can be multiplied by the attacker. If there is a race condition that makes brakes temporarily inoperable on a car, this is bad. However, if the vulnerability allowing this can be exploited at will by an attacker, it can be timed to make it much, much worse—after all, if your brakes fail when parked or when going very slowly, then the only damage may be some adrenaline and a scuffed fender. If they are disabled deliberately and maliciously, the attacker may wait until you're going down a steep grade, where the damage is likely to be much more serious. If your software accidentally allows a bank account to be credited an extra thousand dollars under certain, but nondeterministic, circumstances, it may not be a big issue at all—eventually the bank notices the extra money in the account and removes it. If somebody can deliberately trigger it, they're going to go to the ATM as soon as possible and start dispensing cash, which is a much more difficult problem to fix.

Finally, just because you have found every single vulnerability in your system's code and fixed them until the system is entirely bulletproof, all of your hard work can be undone by somebody calling one of your users, saying that they're the Allegheny County Password Police, and would they mind confirming their password. This happens more often than you might think—read *Ghost in the Wires* by Kevin Mitnick for some great stories about successfully using similar techniques. People are often confounded by technology and information security, or simply aren't paying that much attention to what somebody's asking them. As Georgia Weidman, author of *Penetration Testing*, says, "Users are a vulnerability that can never be patched."

20.2   Basic Concepts in Computer Security

Although we've already used some of them, it's time to make some formal definitions of security-related terms so that we can discuss them in more detail.

The key element of security is the **InfoSec Triad**, also called the **CIA Triad**. This consists of the following three attributes of a system: **confidentiality**, **integrity**, and **availability**. Confidentiality means that no unauthorized users may read any data. This could be data on the entire system (for example, the root user on a Unix system has access to everything stored on it), or a specific piece of data (an engineer may be authorized to view the source code for a system, but not employee payroll information; a financial auditor may be able to view the latter but not the former). Integrity means that no unauthorized users can write data; for example, anybody is free to look at the source code for Rails (a Ruby web framework), but only a select few are allowed to directly write to it (although you may submit a pull request asking those people to merge your changes). Given these definitions, it would be extremely simple to create a secure system—after creating the system, smash it with a sledgehammer, encase it in concrete, and drop it to the bottom of the Marianas Trench. No unauthorized users will be reading or writing any data from it now!

Of course, no authorized users would be able to use it, either, and few customers would be willing to pay for a system that nobody can access. In order to prevent such a trivial but non-useful solution for creating secure systems, the final element of the InfoSec Triad is necessary: availability. That is, the system must be available to authorized users to read and write data. A system which has all the elements of the InfoSec Triad under all circumstances is considered secure. In practice, for most software there will often be particular circumstances where one or more of the elements is not met.

Attacks on the security of a system can be either **active attacks** or **passive attacks**. Active attacks actually change the system under attack somehow, such as by adding an additional program that runs in the background, changing users' passwords, or modifying data stored on the system. Passive attacks do not cause any changes to the system. Examples of passive attacks would be eavesdropping on network traffic or monitoring an area for unsecured wireless networks. While active attacks often cause more damage, they are also much easier to spot, whereas passive attacks can be very difficult to observe.

There are several kinds of attacks, both passive and active, possible on elements of the InfoSec Triad. An **interruption** attack is an attack on availability. It reduces or eliminates the availability of a given system. Perhaps the simplest version of this attack would be somebody sneaking into a building and unplugging all servers from the network. More advanced attacks would include sending so many unauthorized requests that authorized ones cannot get through (referred to as a **denial of service** attack) or changing all users' passwords.

An **interception** attack is an attack on confidentiality. It enables an unauthorized user to read data which they are not authorized to read, even if they are not able to actually change any data. Just because they cannot directly change any data does not mean this is a lesser form of attack. Think of how much harm could befall you if an attacker gained access to your credit card number, social security number, and other identifying information. The simplest version of an interception attack would be peering over somebody's shoulder when they are typing in their password. There are much more technically challenging ones such as **keylogging** programs and hardware, which store and/or transmit any keypresses you make, or **packet sniffing**, where a packet analyzer inspects any packets going over your network looking for passwords or other interesting data.

There are two related kinds of attacks on integrity: **modification** attacks which modify already-existing data, and **fabrication** attacks which add additional data to the system. A modification attack might change the current gift card balance in an account on an e-commerce site, whereas a fabrication attack might add an entirely fictitious user to an account.

If a system has a way that one of the attacks can be utilized against it, that system has a **vulnerability**. For example, let's assume that a system is set up with a default administrative user, DEFAULT, with password DEFAULT. If nobody ever discovers this vulnerability (although this is unlikely for a system with even a nominal number of users), then there's never any actual damage done to the system. However, if a user discovers and uses it, this is an **exploit** of the vulnerability. An exploit is a technique or mechanism which is used to compromise one of the elements of the InfoSec Triad of a system. This can range from knowing that there is a default password to complex pieces of software which interact with the system in known ways to cause the undesired behavior.

There is a wide variety of these tools, which are known as **malware**. Malware is any software which is deliberately designed to have an undesired effect on a computer system, generally unbeknownst to the authorized user of the system. An incomplete list of the kinds of malware includes:

1. **Bacteria**: A program which consumes an excess amount of system resources, perhaps taking up all file descriptors or disk space.

2. **Fork bomb**: A special kind of **bacteria** which continually forks itself, causing all CPU resources to be used up creating more copies of the fork bomb.

3. **Logic bomb**: Code within a program which executes an unauthorized function, such as deleting all data on the first day of the month.

4. **Trapdoor**: A program or piece of a program which provides secret access to a system or application.

5. **Trojan Horse**: A piece of software which pretends to be another in order to trick users into installing and executing it. For example, a Trojan Horse may state that it contains different funny mouse cursors, but after installing it, it deletes everything on your hard drive.

6. **Virus**: A computer program, often small, that replicates itself with human intervention. This

intervention could be something such as clicking on a link or running a program sent to you as an attachment.

7. **Worm**: A computer program, often small, that replicates itself without human intervention. For example, once installed on a machine, it may have that machine try to break into other machines and copy the code of the worm over to others.

8. **Zombie**: A computer with software installed which allows unauthorized users access to it to perform unauthorized functionality. For example, a system might have a mailer program built in which will allow other users to send spam from your machine, so that the actual senders cannot be tracked.

9. **Bot network**: A collection of zombies controlled by a master.

10. **Spyware**: Software which surreptitiously monitors the actions of the user of the system. For example, software may report back daily what all of the keystrokes of the user were.

11. **DoS Tools**: Tools which enable denial of service attacks.

12. **Ransomware**: Software which performs an unwanted action (e.g., encrypting your hard drive) and asks for money or other compensation in order to undo it. This money usually goes to the creators or users of the software, not the software itself (until artificial intelligences become more advanced).

Malware may belong to more than one variety. For example, a program could propagate like a computer worm, and once resident on a computer, report back the activities of the user, thus making it spyware. Another possibility is that a program is offered for download which states that it will "clean your registry" but will actually make your computer a zombie and under the control of a bot network.

It is not necessary for malware to be involved for there to be an attack on a system. Just as there are automated tests and manual tests, there are automated attacks and manual attacks. If I can guess the password of a user or send in a string to a text box which causes the system to crash, I am attacking the system without any kind of program. While nowadays many of these vulnerabilities are found and exploited with software tools, good ol'-fashioned manual exploitation is still used on a regular basis.

20.3 Common Attacks and How to Test Against Them

20.3.1 Injection

In an **injection attack**, the attacker is attempting to get your computer to run some arbitrary code of their choosing. One of the most common types of injection attacks is a **SQL injection attack**, since many programmers, especially new ones, do not **sanitize** their database inputs. Sanitization involves ensuring that input from a user will not be directly executed, by "cleaning it up" so that it can't run. As an example, imagine some code that accepts a string from the user asking for their name, searches in the database for any users with that name, and returns the unique ID (uid) for the first user with that name:

```
public int findUidByName(String name) {

    Result dbResult = DatabaseConnection.executeSQL(
      "SELECT uid FROM users WHERE name = '" + name + "';");
    if (dbResult == null) {
       return NO_RESULTS_CODE;
```

```
    } else {
        return dbResult.get("uid");
    }
}
```

This is a relatively simple method, but contains a glaring security flaw—there is nothing preventing the user from sending in other SQL commands instead of a name. These SQL commands will be executed by the machine uncomplainingly, even if the commands say to delete the database. Imagine that the user passes in the value "`a'; DROP TABLE Users;`" as their name. The following SQL will be executed:

```
SELECT uid FROM users WHERE name = 'a'; DROP TABLE Users;
```

You can try this out on your local database if you don't believe me, but that will delete the `users` table when it's executed. This is probably not something you want anyone who can search for a user in your application to be able to do! There are numerous other kinds of injection attacks, for example by mis-using `eval()` in JavaScript code, or adding "`OR 1=1`" to a SQL query to show all rows instead of the one that the code would ordinarily be looking for. The common denominator in injection attacks is that they all execute code that the designers and administrators of the system do not want to have executed.

As mentioned, this can be avoided by sanitizing input in various ways. For example, semicolons, tick marks, and spaces may not be allowed in a user name. A check could be added so that if any of those characters exist in the name parameter, then the `NO_RESULTS_CODE` would be returned before any SQL could be executed. This technique is a simple blacklist, and there are more in-depth ways of preventing injection attacks, but they are beyond the scope of this book.

How does one test that injection attacks are not possible? The most straightforward way is to find all places where user input is accepted and ensure that sending in code will not result in it being executed. This will often be a form of grey-box testing, as it wouldn't be very helpful to check that, say, COBOL code could be executed on a Java-only system. White-box testing, including unit testing, will also be helpful to ensure that methods that receive user input ensure that it is sanitized before passing it on, or that methods which access the database can never be called with code that can exploit a vulnerability. Static analysis tools also exist which can check the codebase statically to help guard against possible injection attacks.

Stochastic testing—especially "evil monkey" testing, which passes in executable code—can be helpful for large systems which request and process input in many different ways and in different places. By passing in large amounts of random data, you may find kinds of data which cause the system to perform oddly or crash. These out-of-the-ordinary events may help point you to which specific parts of the system are vulnerable to injection attacks. For example, if a particular parameter is parsed with an `eval()` at some point, your randomized testing may pass in some invalid code, causing the system under test to crash. Closer examination of the code which handles that kind of data will allow you to determine that code injection is possible there.

20.3.2   Buffer Overruns

What happens when you try to put ten pounds of data in a five-pound bag? A **buffer overrun**, that's what. In many programming languages, you have to allocate a finite amount of space for data to be put into. In Java, for example, if you wanted to store five integers in an array, you could do something like this:

```
int[] _fiveInts = new int[5];
```

Now let's say that you have a method that accepts a string of integers, separated by commas (e.g. 7,4,29,3,2), and then puts each of the integers into the _fiveInts array:

```
public void putDataIntoFiveInts(String data) {
    int[] intData = data.split(",");
    for (int j=0; j < intData.length; j++) {
        _fiveInts[j] = intData[j];
    }
}
```

This works fine if 7,4,29,3,2 is passed in to the method. However, if 1,2,3,4,5,6,7 is passed in, then an ArrayIndexOutOfBounds exception will be thrown when trying to write the sixth piece of data to _fiveInts. This may cause the program to crash if the exception is not properly handled. In some languages, such as C, no exception is thrown, because there is no **bounds checking** (checking at run-time that data is not being written outside the bounds of an array). The system will keep on merrily writing data past the end of the array, which may overwrite executable code or other system data. If this data is carefully crafted, it may even allow the attacker to get shell access to the system.

This can be tested for by passing in very large amounts of data to all places where input can be expected into the system. The amount of data to be passed in will vary, and can often be determined by checking the code (thus making grey- or white-box testing very effective when checking for this particular kind of vulnerability). Static analysis tools can also help determine where buffer overruns are possible. Finally, using a language that has built-in bounds checking, like Java, can help mitigate the problem. It is usually better for a program to stop running due to a missed exception bubbling up than code or data being overwritten.

20.3.3 Security Misconfiguration

Although your system may operate in a bulletproof way if it's set up correctly, not everybody is going to be as rigid as you are when setting up their version of the system. People leave default passwords set, or give everybody read/write access because it's easier that way, or don't turn on two-factor authentication because they hate having a program text them every time they log in. For complex programs, people may miss the one checkbox that encrypts data, or enables HTTPS, or requires users to log in before modifying data.

In order to avoid these, you want to have a sensible set of defaults for your software, and ensure that users understand the weak points of the application that they have set up. They should also be able to easily determine how to remedy these weak points that they have created. If the only way to properly set up the system is to thoroughly read through the 500-page instruction manual and set some obscure command line switches, then virtually every system you ship will be configured improperly.

How do you test for them, though? Often, you will have to do some form of **user testing**. User testing involves having a user perform some task, often with minimal—or no—guidance from the development team or their representatives. While this is usually done in order to determine the best user interface for a system, it can also be done to figure out how typical users configure the system and what parts of the system they do not configure properly. After seeing that users often forget to change default passwords, for example, perhaps developers add a red warning to all administrative pages warning them that the default password has not yet been changed. Further user testing can verify that this causes the desired change in behavior.

20.3.4   Insecure Storage

Even if the code running your system is secure itself—free from all known exploits, all input sanitized, formally verified to not contain any buffer overflows—this is of little consolation if its data is not stored properly! Examples of insecure storage would be writing sensitive data to log files, allowing users direct access to a database, or storing private keys in your code which is stored in a publicly available repository.

Note that this can be more tricky to verify than simply checking the log files or searching for passwords hard-coded into your program. For example, under normal circumstances, only boring debug data may be sent to a log file, and so you think that, even though the log file is publicly accessible, it is not a large security risk. However, if an error occurs when processing a credit card, an exception is thrown which includes debug data. In this debug data is the credit card information that the system was attempting to process. Under these circumstances, if this exception is written to the log file, the fact that the log file is publicly accessible is a very big problem.

Testing for insecure storage can be as straightforward as attempting to access data directly on the database or on the filesystem. However, it can get more complex in larger systems. In general, you want to follow the **principle of least privilege**, which means limiting users to the minimal amount of access that they need to do their job. Developers do not require access to personnel records; likewise, the head of Human Resources does not need to have access to the source code for a system. Checking for insecure storage can also involve automated checks, which may run before code check-in, that verify that no private keys, passwords, or similar secrets are checked into the repository.

20.3.5   Social Engineering

This is it, the king of attacks, the most common way of exploiting systems everywhere—going through "the vulnerability that can never be patched", people. **Social engineering** involves manipulating people (often authorized users of a system) to underhandedly cause them to perform actions that put the security of a system at risk. Some examples would be telling a user of a system that they are from the IT department and need to know their password for "routine maintenance", or an email that has a forged "from" field asking the user to run the Unix command `chmod -R 777 *` in their home directory so that testing can commence.

While these may seem ridiculous to many readers of this text (and if they are not, then remind me to put you in touch with a certain deposed nobleman looking to give away some of his millions), social engineering is used to access many systems. One common method is **phishing**—trying to get personal or other sensitive information via email or other communications. These are usually sent to a wide variety of email addresses, hoping that somebody responds and will fall for their shenanigans.

Phishing attacks often seem very poorly prepared, with broken English and technical inaccuracies, but this is actually a part of the plan! There are usually multiple steps after the initial contact phase in order to achieve the primary goal of the phishing expedition. Let's say that the target received an email stating that their email account was compromised and they have to click here to verify their password (if you're not reading this online, links don't work as well on dead-tree books, but don't worry, you're not missing much). If the user clicks the malicious link, they will be taken to a page created by the attackers (and which may not look exactly like the actual, legitimate account information page) that allows them to steal the user's password. Ideally, the user won't check with their IT department afterwards about the email; the attackers want time to use the email for whatever malicious people do with stolen email accounts. In other words, they want people who are not very conscientious or technically literate, who overlook minor issues, who are trusting of whatever they see in front of them. These are the same people who would overlook the poor grammar and inaccuracy of the original email. People who are less trusting might be even more work for the attackers, as they may deliberately enter false data or even work on trying to track them down. The poorly constructed email is actually a screening mechanism.

A much more dangerous variant of phishing is **spear phishing**, in which the user is specifically targeted. In this case, the attacker goes out of their way to ensure that the user will not be suspicious of the email. Relevant details will be carefully crafted: any other users mentioned in the email will be verified, grammar will be excellent (or at least appropriate), the user's actual name will be used, its headers will be forged to look like it came from the targeted user's boss, etc. Spear phishing attacks are much more difficult and time-consuming to set up than a traditional phishing attack, but they also tend to be more effective; think of them as precision-guided munitions compared to the carpet bombing of a regular phishing attack. Even experienced users may have difficulty determining that the email is not legitimate.

Testing that social engineering will not work on a system is difficult. After all, there is no technical aspect to check; the programmed aspects of the system would work correctly, and by authorized users, but authorized users who are actually doing the bidding of an unauthorized user. While we have discussed the difficulty of testing impure functions, which may rely on global variables or other external mutable state, people are the ultimate unpredictable external state. A person who may never fall for a phishing email may be tricked by somebody calling them; someone who would normally never fall for anything may have had a rough night the evening before and isn't thinking clearly; someone else may be overwhelmed with other work and click on a malicious link in an email.

Ensuring that user accounts follow the principle of least privilege will limit the extent of any damage that can be done by an attacker acting through the authorized user. For example, an ordinary user of our Rent-A-Cat system should never have access to the payroll system for employees. This will help to compartmentalize the attack to only the data and functionality to which the social engineering victim has access. Checking if there is any way for a user to access data (read or write access) that they don't need to will help to find possible areas where this access can be compromised.

Running tests on people can be helpful, as well! Some companies send fake phishing emails and see how many of their people click on suspicious links. Those who do click on the links are sent to a page warning them that this could have caused unauthorized access to the system, and those employees will (hopefully) be less likely to do so when they receive an actual phishing email.

20.4   Penetration Testing

While I've gone over various ways in which the security of a system can be compromised, often the best way to test a system is to think like an attacker. **Penetration testing** has a user, often external to the development team, attempt to gain unauthorized access to a system using any means at their disposal (tempered by the limits of the contract, e.g. "no deleting data"). This follows the "set a thief to catch a thief" theory—those who are acting like the people who are trying to break into your system will be the most effective at finding any holes in your security systems.

During a penetration test, a person will act as though they were a cracker trying to get in to your system. They may gather data to determine which operating systems or programming languages you use and scan your networks, try common passwords, or use other tactics and techniques specific to the system that you're running. These are often external consultants or at least personnel unrelated to the team developing it, so as to avoid preset theories of how the system is "supposed" to work. The entire *modus operandi* of people trying to break into systems is that they manipulate systems to do things that they are not "supposed" to do.

A penetration tester will then develop a report of what the weak points of the system are, as well as the ramifications of those weak points. For example, they may find a SQL injection vulnerability for one particular subsystem which allows access to a particular database. While this may sound like technical gobbledygook to a manager, explaining the ramifications—that all of the payroll data for the company is available to anybody with an Internet connection—is much clearer (and scarier).

20.5   General Guidelines

Before developing a testing plan for security, you should try to determine how much testing will be necessary. This will depend on the domain in which you are operating, but mostly on what the risks are if an opponent is able to compromise the system. Remember that time and resources spent on security testing are time and resources that are not spent elsewhere. If you are running a system which controls nuclear weapons launch codes, it makes sense to spend a large percentage of the time testing the system on security testing; if you are running a startup for renting cats, less time and fewer resources are probably necessary.

If you are operating in a regulated field, ensure that you are following all of the standards for that field. For example, in the United States, if you are storing medical data, you should be familiar with HIPAA; if you are dealing with student data, you should read up on FERPA. Although these are not the be-all, end-all of security for a system, they are additional parameters you should know about while determining its security.

Determine what are the most important aspects of the system to guard against. Attacks which may cause data to be overwritten will in most cases be more damaging than those that allow read access to data. Certain aspects of the system may be more damaging if they are compromised. If there is an employee-run wiki which is mostly full of in-jokes and Dungeons and Dragons schedules, this is less important than bank account information. This doesn't mean that the employee wiki should be ignored, but there should definitely be more emphasis put on the bank account data.

Remember the Pareto Principle, as well. By performing a broad check, spending not much time on each individual component, you may be able to find many more defects, and more easily-found defects, than spending months and months on one particular part. These will often also be the first vulnerabilities looked for by potential attackers. Even if a very difficult-to-exploit vulnerability exists on a given system, most attackers will be deterred if many of the common attacks are ineffective.

The most effective security testing is that which gets done. If you can, argue for the security tests that you not only believe will be best for the system, but also have a chance to get done and to continue to get done. In today's networked world, security is becoming more and more of an ongoing practice, as anybody who has gotten a pop-up asking them to upgrade their software is aware. You should develop a plan which will allow ongoing security maintenance and verification as long as the system is potentially exploitable.

Chapter 21

Interacting with Stakeholders

Through much of this book, we have spoken of testing as if in a vacuum. You write the tests, the software either passes or fails (or you realize you wrote the test incorrectly), you file a defect report, and eventually the problem is fixed. There is another aspect to testing that you will experience working on projects—the human element. Managers may disagree with you on what the testing priorities are. Developers may argue that the "defect" you found is actually expected behavior. Fellow testers may get into shouting matches with you over subtleties in a requirements specification.

Conflict is inevitable on any team, and in fact, it's probably a positive overall. If everybody on your team agrees about everything all of the time, beware: You are probably working on a pretty trivial project, and your job is likely to be replaced by a small shell script in the near future. Resolving conflicts, although it can be difficult, is the key to successfully preparing a product for launch. Conflicts, as long as they are conducted professionally and productively, are often the fuel that allows a team to perform better as time goes on.

As a software tester, you will have specific challenges when interacting with other members of the development team. After all, the whole job of a tester is to find problems with software. They're professional critics, constantly looking for all the weak points of a system in order to make it better. If this is not done with a gentle touch, it can often be mistaken for being a jerk. Nobody likes to hear about the problems or shortcomings of the software they wrote, and managers don't like hearing that a product won't be ready. As a professional fault-finder, it also becomes very easy to sink into a morass of unjustified pessimism about a product. In this chapter, we'll discuss how to deal with these problems and successfully interact with all the people necessary to bring a project to completion.

21.1   Who and What are Stakeholders?

A **stakeholder** is any person who has a direct interest in the product. The specific kind of interest may vary based on the person and their role. For example, the customer of a product—that is, the person who pays for it—will have a vested interest in paying as little as possible for the product. Upper management and marketers have the exact opposite goal—they want customers to pay as much for it as possible, within epsilon of the price where people would choose a competitor. Developers may have an interest in seeing the product written correctly, or using a language or framework that they prefer. Quality assurance personnel may care about the quality of a product; assessors may care that the product meets all of its legal requirements; the list goes on and on.

Note that stakeholders have a *direct* interest in the product. In the philosophical sense, many others will have an interest in the product, or at least will be impacted by it. For example, the owners of the coffee shop next door will hope that developers start working late and thus start buying more of that sweet, sweet caffeine that comes with their coffee, thus improving their bottom line. The spouses of the testers may want there to be fewer defects so that the testers can spend more time with their family. However, these are not direct interests in the product, and it could be argued that any human being is somehow impacted by the project (the Prime Minister of Luxembourg may hope to have your nation's GDP go up in order to improve their position in trade negotiations, and a successful launch of your product will help that goal!) Although it can be a fuzzy boundary, if a person is not directly familiar with your product, they are in all likelihood not a stakeholder.

As mentioned above, different stakeholders will care about different aspects of the software. When discussing the product with someone who is in a different stakeholder group than yourself, keep in mind what *they* are thinking about when they think about the product. Put yourself in their shoes; does an ordinary user of your system care if the application was written in Haskell, Ruby, or Java? Does upper management in a Fortune 500 company care about the beautiful symmetry of the icons? Does a developer care about the latest quarterly earnings report? Perhaps, in a few cases, or there may be some general curiosity or indirect interest. After all, if quarterly earnings are negative too many times, there may not be a company to pay the developer's salary, or an ordinary user may also really care about type safety in the programming languages of the applications that they use. However, in general, people spend enough time worrying about the aspects of the system that they care about that they have very little time for worrying about the rest of it.

The following is a non-exhaustive list of groups of stakeholders and a high-level view of what they are likely to care about. Depending on the domain in which you are working, there are bound to be additional classifications, or some of these may be combined, but this should give you a general idea.

- *Customers:* These are the people who will pay for the software. They will focus on receiving a working system for a low price, and care about cost and the return on investment of purchasing it.

- *Users:* These are the people who will use the software. Note that these are sometimes the same as customers, but sometimes not—for example, when a school purchases class registration software, the school is the customer, but students are the users. They will care about the usability of the system and if it allows them to easily accomplish their goals.

- *Project Management:* These are the people who manage the specific project, ensuring that it is developed at an appropriate rate and released on time and on budget. They will care about scheduling (from a resource, time, and scope perspective) and software quality.

- *Upper Management:* Usually higher up in the management chain, to the point where they will often not be very familiar with a project itself. They will care about the financials of the project, such as whether or not it is likely to make a profit.

- *Developers:* The people who write the software. They will care about the tools that they use, how well the program works from a technological standpoint, and how well it solves the problem and meets the requirements.

- *Testers / Quality Assurance:* The people who test the software and determine the quality of the system. They will focus on finding defects on the software and care about releasing a quality product.

- *Support Personnel:* The people who keep the software running, such as field engineers, help desk personnel, and deployment personnel. They will care about uptime and quality of the system, and its ease of use on behalf of customers.

- *Assessors:* These people focus on the assessing the legality of a system, ensuring that it meets all the demands made of it by laws for the domain in which it is operating. They will care about meeting the legal or other documented requirements.

This is only a rough guide to some of the kinds of stakeholders you will interact with as a software tester. Remember that these are drawn with very broad strokes! People are individuals, not faceless members of groups, no matter what your friend who has read too many philosophy books has to say. Although you can use this information to get a general idea of what individual stakeholders are interested in, nothing will take the place of having real interactions, and more importantly, *asking* what is important to them.

21.2 Reporting and Communicating

When communicating with a stakeholder who has a different focus from you, you should take care to understand the language of that person and what they care about. You should care enough to talk about the things they care about in their language. Try to put yourself in their shoes before talking to them—first, ask yourself if they care about what you want to talk with them about. If not, try to think if there is any deeper reason you want to discuss it with them. In some cases, it is still essential—your manager may not care about a harassment claim, but it's still your duty to report it. In other cases, though, it won't be necessary, and for someone who has quite a bit on their plate (as most workers do today), it's taking away valuable time that could be used for doing other things. Second, if they do care about the topic, try to put it in terms that they understand and can conceptualize. Don't view a conversation as a way to prove your intellect. Use it as a way to provide valuable information in a form that the other person can use, and receive valuable information that you can likewise use.

One of the key chasms in communication is between technical and non-technical personnel. If you're reading this book, and I tell you that since you've got a O(n^2) sorting algorithm, you're going to see an exponential increase in RAM usage with larger data sets, you're going to have a pretty good idea of what I mean. You may even know how to fix it (by quickly searching for "efficient sorting algorithms", of course). However, this sentence is basically Greek to non-technical personnel (except for fluent speakers of Greek, for whom it is some other language that they don't know). However, this is the way developers, testers, and other technical personnel talk, because it's how you end up thinking when you deal with it all day, every day. Remember, though, that other people may spend the majority of their day dealing with accounting, or sales, or marketing, or a million other things, and simply do not have the same frame of reference as you do when it comes to the system you are working on.

If you are communicating with those who are not technical or do not have the domain knowledge of the software under test, remember to explain things as a consequence they care about. Upper management does not directly care about which sorting algorithm the program uses, but they do care if it means that only small businesses will be able to use the software because it does not handle the data sets of larger businesses. This has a direct impact that they can understand. When you are discussing a defect with a developer, you can be more technical and explain the situation in more detail.

When you're in school, the teachers tend to have more knowledge than you on whatever topic you're learning. That's why they are teachers. In the real world, though, your managers will often have much less knowledge than you on the specific system or part of the system you are working on. This can be a shock—isn't the whole point of having bosses to have someone who understands something better than their subordinates?

Not at all. The point of a manager is to manage. This means more time spent on estimating, more time dealing with personnel issues, more time dealing with budget issues, etc. This leaves precious little time for writing code or sometimes even interacting with the system at all. Even if the manager does remain technical, they are now overseeing a larger part of the system, or even the entire system, and thus will not be able to keep up with as many specifics as you have on the particular part of the system you're working on. Imagine someone working at the Department of Motor Vehicles, who focuses on renewing driver's licenses—let's call them Redli. Redli is going to have driver's license renewals down cold. A person transferring from out-of-state? Someone has the wrong form of identification? A new driver who has an old license which was suspended, but a governor's pardon has lifted the felony from their record, thus allowing them to drive again? Redli knows all of the regulations and laws around all of them, knows exactly how to enter them into the system, and does it quickly and efficiently.

Now let's imagine Guvvy, the governor who gave out that pardon. Guvvy is, technically speaking, Redli's boss (more like a great-great-great-great-great-grand-boss). If you put Guvvy in Redli's place tomorrow, all hell will break loose. Being the executive in charge of the entire state, Guvvy had to have a high-level knowledge of not only the Department of Motor Vehicles, but also environmental regulations, business conditions, the budget of the government, and lots of other things besides. There is no way Guvvy is going to know the specifics of driver's license renewal and how to take somebody's picture, thus leading to a long line of angry motorists at the local DMV office.

This example was extended *ad absurdum*, but the point remains. As an individual contributor, you will be focusing on a very small part of a larger project, but you will often have very detailed knowledge of it. Managers will have a broader view of a project or projects, but will have less knowledge on the specifics of it. The further up the chain you go, the more this is true; your immediate supervisor will have a good idea of what you do on a day-to-day basis, but the CEO of the company may not even know that you—or your project—exists.

If Redli has a chance to talk to Guvvy about some problems with the driver's license renewal process, a bad idea would be to start with technical details of regulation 437-A, subsection 4, paragraph C, and its definition of "resident". Redli should talk about it in terms that Guvvy understands—things that annoy voters and would make them more likely to vote for AntiGuvvy (who is, of course, the opponent in the upcoming gubernatorial election). Guvvy is going to be more receptive to knowing that the law doesn't handle people who own houses in two different states than going into detail about the legalese. This is impactful for politicians because annoyed voters are less likely to vote for the incumbent (note to political science majors—I am dramatically oversimplifying to make a point, so please do not send me angry letters about gubernatorial election theory).

Similarly, when discussing the system or problems that you are having with your boss, put it into terms that they can understand. Remember that they often have a broader view of the system than you do, and things that you consider very important may not be as important to them. In fact, they may not even be aware of problems that you consider obvious. Providing an open flow of information can be very helpful in both directions, allowing you as a tester to understand the system more holistically and channel your energy and time appropriately. It can also give your supervisors knowledge of the nitty-gritty of the data, defects, and concerns you are finding in your testing.

21.3   The Red-Yellow-Green Template

One of the best ways I have found to communicate status to managers higher up on the totem pole is the red-yellow-green template. This is not my invention, or even unique to the software industry, but has been proven useful in many different fields. It allows you to provide a very high-level overview of status while still providing hooks to go deeper into detail if necessary. Remember that managers will often not have the same granularity of knowledge of the system that you as a tester will have, and so putting it into simpler terms will allow the system to be intellectually manageable.

If you're familiar with US traffic lights, you know that they consist of three lights: green meaning "go", yellow meaning "slow down", and red meaning "stop". The standard OS X Windows manager uses a similar convention: green for "maximize", yellow for "minimize", and red for "close". In each case, green means there is nothing stopping you (drive quickly, maximum window size), yellow means that there are some impediments to progress (the light is about to change to red, the window is minimized), and red means that there are some more serious impediments (traffic is coming from the orthogonal direction, the window is closed).

Using this metaphor, we can divide the system into subsystems or aspects, and mark each one with a red, yellow, or green status. A green status indicates that there are no issues—that particular subsystem is working fine and/or is on track to being completed on target and on budget. A yellow status indicates that there a few issues, but they are relatively minor and fixable, although that subsystem may have reduced quality or functionality, or additional resources may be necessary to complete it on time. A red status indicates a major problem or problems, where that particular subsystem will need substantial help in order to be released on time, if it is even possible to do so. Putting these into colors allows the eye, which has been trained on these particular colors for years (not to mention "trained" by evolution for millions of years), to quickly ascertain a high-level view of the quality of a system. Partitioning status into the broad categories of "red-yellow-green" means that you are not going to get a very granular view of the status, but the benefit is that it forces you to put the status into very simple terms. People tend to deal better with a limited number of options for status.

Dividing the system into subsystems is often already done at this point—for example, you can divide them up based on how you've already developed test plans, or how different work has been assigned to members of the team. You can adjust it based on what will work best for reporting, however, and whatever makes logical sense. Remember when interacting with other stakeholders, especially when you are crossing the technical/non-technical divide, that you should take into consideration what they care about, and reduce the focus on what you care about. Let's assume that your project manager has divided the system up into Subsystems A, B, and C. You have developed your test plans into Subsystems A, B, C, and D, because you feel that D makes more sense as its own subsystem instead of as a part of C. In most cases, this means that your best course of action when reporting to the project manager is to group your D and C statuses together into Subsystem C.

Along with each subsystem and its status, there should be a short notes section going into detail about *why* that specific status was chosen. This section is usually only a few sentences, but provides insight into what possible problems could crop up. It also allows for knowledgeable questions to be asked, and does not rely solely on the producer of the status for determining it. Another stakeholder may see what seems like a minor problem to the tester, but actually has major import for delivering the system.

Let's walk through some examples to see how we can use the red-yellow-green template to quickly display status to a manager. These two examples both involve a system which accepts customer information via an API, stores it in a database, and then emails weekly reports to the marketing department:

```
-----------------------------------------------------------------------
Subsystem    Status    Notes
----------   ----------   --------------------------------------------------
Database     Green     Test plan passed with no defects. Performance meets or
                       exceeds all KPIs.
```

Input API	Green	Latest version passed all tests, including all edge cases, without any defects.
Report Generation	Yellow	Several arithmetic errors found on latest test run. May need one additional developer to complete all functionality on schedule, but likely to be on target as-is.
Email	Green	Two minor design defects found, but due to be fixed by tomorrow.

In this first instance, we have a system which is going well. There are no known major problems, and no worries about major schedule slippage or scope reduction. At a glance, we can see a sea of green, with only one small island of yellow. Importantly, it's possible to see why these subsystems have the status they do. If a stakeholder wanted to know more detail about the design defects in the emails, they can ask more questions, or if they want to know what edge cases were checked in the input API, they can do so.

Now let's look at another version of the system which is perhaps not going as well:

Subsystem	Status	Notes
Database	Red	Database cannot store more than one customer's information at a time and randomly deletes data every Thursday.
Input API	Yellow	System takes several minutes to process each (one kilobyte) request.
Report Generation	Red	All reports just say "LOL" hundreds of times, and the developer in charge of this seems to have fled to Belarus.
Email	Red	As far as the testing team can determine, there is no email functionality at this time, and no developers scheduled to work on it.

This is not a project that I would like to be managing. Our nice, green sea has been replaced with a hellish landscape of red. Even the one yellow subsystem, the Input API, is probably going to require some additional work before it's ready to be released. Note that this yellow status is very different from the yellow status in the previous example. These statuses are very broad; having a few known arithmetic errors is an issue which we can probably deal with by making a few simple code changes. Having a performance issue of the magnitude described here may be very difficult to fix, but the program is still releasable with it, just very slow. Remember that statuses are subjective and how you categorize subsystems will vary based on the domain of the system you are working on. For example, a program which crashes once per year of normal use may be acceptable for a video game, but it would be unacceptable for avionics software.

Overall, though, the goal of using this template is to report the status of a system under test to others. It is not meant for an in-depth review or to stand in for a test report, but merely a way to summarize how a system is operating. Managers and other stakeholders will appreciate having a way to see the status of the system as a whole before diving down into the technical details.

21.4 Status Reports

Although useful for providing the status of a system, the red-yellow-green template is less useful when describing the status of a tester. In many places of employment, a daily status report is common. I found these very useful when dealing with a geographically distributed team, especially if there is little communication during the day (for example, because parts of the team are in different time zones). Many agile development shops will have daily stand-ups to discuss status, and so an additional email is superfluous. In workplaces that do not have these or similar meetings, I have found that a quick email at the end of the day will allow managers to understand what all of their employees are doing. It also allows managers to know if there are any problems, and to provide a check to ensure that their employees are working efficiently and on the correct problems.

21.4.1 Example: Daily Status Report For A Software Tester

DAILY STATUS: 7 AUG 2015

- Finished running Test Plan "Database Subsystem Regression"—recorded as Test Run 471, no new defects

- Wrote script to convert old tab-delimited test data to new comma-delimited format—available in /scripts directory on server

- Started writing Test Plan "Graphical Symbology Display"—need to get latest version of symbology standard

BLOCKERS: Need to find latest version of symbology standards before finishing test plan

---

These should not take very long to write; a few sentences should suffice, and bullet points allow for a good overall summary instead of focusing on developing a narrative. This simple email allows the manager to know what the tester is working on (writing a new test plan), what additional resources are available (a script for reformatting data, which may be helpful for other team members), and where the tester may need additional resources (the latest version of the symbology standard).

Armed with this information, a manager can ask the team members to refocus efforts, or report up to their own manager that there are problems. They may be able to help with any problems that the tester is experiencing; perhaps they have a copy of the symbology standard the tester can borrow. Finally, the team can be run more effectively when knowledge is shared in such a manner. If the entire team can run the script that the tester has developed, they may save hours of time that would have been spent updating the test data files manually.

21.5 A Note on Managing Expectations

As a new member of the team, often there is an urge to promise more than you can deliver. Although it seems like this is the way to win hearts and minds, it can actually be very problematic. Software projects almost inevitably run late, and it's fiendishly difficult to accurately estimate how long anything is going to take while developing software. A project manager is going to be more upset that you promised them something and did not deliver than if you promise a little and deliver quite a bit. Additionally, the fact that you will have less stress when trying to meet a less ambitious goal may make it easier to actually accomplish more, since you're less likely to make a mistake.

You want to manage expectations. People will tend to assume that if you don't mention something, then everything is going well with it. This is a dangerous assumption, but it is also human nature, and going against human nature is a sure-fire way to be disappointed (for examples, see every single project to make a utopian society in the history of Mankind). Thus, you want to communicate early and communicate often. If there are problems, don't wait until the last minute to let other stakeholders know, hoping against hope that you'll be able to best them through your heroic efforts. Software development is not an epic fairy tale, where a noble hero can defeat the evil hordes of defects through sheer willpower and a wise-cracking sidekick.

A professor once said to me, "if you're ever in doubt over whether or not to communicate something, do it." More information is almost always better than less, especially about problems. Software development is going to have problems, and testing specifically is always going to uncover defects (if it didn't, I would have been out of a job long ago). If you have appropriate avenues for communicating these found defects, as well as issues and needs for resources, other stakeholders will appreciate being kept in the loop.

This does not mean that you should spread the news of everything that happens to you far and wide. Upper management doesn't need to know about every defect you find, and the software developers don't need to know where you went for lunch. Use the proper channels of communication, which will vary based on the team you are working with. A daily status report to your immediate manager is usually very useful, because it will provide a secondary view at what might be considered important to other stakeholders. For example, you may have found what you think is a minor defect, and include it only as a bullet point in your daily status, but your manager realizes that it could have far-reaching ramifications and announces it to the larger team.

21.6 A Note on Meetings

Very few people really enjoy meetings, outside of those who are probably busy taking courses in business school instead of reading a book about software testing. However, they are often essential to determining the best path forward, and ensuring that the input of all relevant stakeholders is heard. They often can actually be the most efficient way to get consensus on an issue, as well.

This does not mean that your presence is required at all meetings. If you find yourself not getting any useful information, or not giving out much information—or at least not enough to justify the time you spend on it—you should consider not going to that meeting any more. Although it may seem presumptuous to say that you don't think that you belong in a meeting, remember that any time you spend in a meeting is time that you are not spending doing something else. A good manager will thank you for bringing it to their attention, because it means that you are thinking of your job strategically, and not just doing what is asked of you.

21.7 Clarifying Requirements

One of the most common and important conversations you will have as a tester is clarifying requirements. Writing down what a software system needs to do is very difficult. It's almost impossible to do for a non-trivial system without introducing some ambiguity. Testers will often come across these areas of ambiguity because they are constantly pushing the envelope of what a system is capable of, trying edge cases and corner cases with abandon. After discovering one of these undefined or under-defined areas, they will need to come to a decision on what is the expected behavior.

If possible, take a moment to step back and think about how the requirement works in tandem with all of the other requirements. Did you miss something? Does this requirement make more sense in light of what other requirements are saying? Is there a logical conclusion that can be made of how the system should act when considered holistically as opposed to focusing on the exact terminology of this particular requirement?

If you still have questions or think you have found some ambiguity, you should discuss the problem with the relevant stakeholders. These stakeholders will vary based on the domain of the software you're working on and the kind of team you're working with. In many large companies, systems engineers are in charge of requirements definitions and can help you understand what they were trying to convey. If it is a design issue, perhaps the UI/UX designers can help you. If you are working on a startup or a very small team, you may even ask users directly what they think the software should do under those circumstances.

When seeking to clarify requirements, keep in mind that your job as a tester is to objectively test that the system meets the requirements, not to make them! That means that in general, you should assume that other stakeholders have a better idea of what the expected behavior of a system should be. This does not mean that you should ignore your thoughts on the matter, or stand idly by while people let you know that "of *course* the calculator subsystem should crash if anybody enters a number greater than 24." You should respectfully disagree and tell people your opinions and what you've discovered from a technical perspective. This is part of being a professional. However, other stakeholders are also professionals in their particular roles. Those whose goals focus on *generating* requirements instead of *testing* them will often be a more authoritative source for answers.

Finally, if you cannot reason out the best solution, and other stakeholders don't know, you may need to make your own assumption as to the expected behavior. This is definitely not the preferred solution, but often it is the only possible one. If nobody has thought about a particular edge case, but you have determined that it needs to be tested, you need to come up with some sort of expected behavior. Make sure that your assumption is internally and externally consistent with the other requirements of the system, and that it makes sense, at least to you, as reasonable behavior. When you do this, you should be cognizant of the fact that your assumption may be wrong. At a bare minimum, mark down what assumptions you made, as part of the test plan or otherwise appropriately documented. You may want to let other stakeholders know what the assumptions you made were and why you chose them.

Remember that translating from a requirements specification to an actual working system is not an objective, straightforward process. If it were, we would have no need of technical personnel; we'd merely need to talk about the system that is necessary and a compiler would create it for us. However, English (or any other natural language) is not nearly specific enough to describe a system in as much detail as a computer needs. Even if it were, the human mind may not be able to comprehend a listing of the thousands, if not millions, of requirements such a system would entail. Communicating with others will continue to be an essential part of testing software.

21.8   Ethical Obligations

As a tester of software, you have obligations to ensure that you are doing your job in an ethical and upright manner. One may argue that one's job is simply that - a job - and that the benchmark for success is simply to do exactly what is expected of you by your superiors. However, I would say that the position of tester is a profession. A profession has obligations outside of the particular company for which the person is doing work. For example, no (reputable) psychiatrist would violate patient confidentiality in order to make their job easier. A lawyer should not bill hours that they didn't work, even if it would make their firm more money.

Similarly, a tester should stand up when the situation demands it. If you have determined that the software is storing personal information in an insecure manner, but your manager has ordered you to ignore it so that the software can be released earlier, what should you do? If you think that the team is spending too much time adding new features and not enough time fixing defects, is that something that you should bring up to your manager? Suppose the software itself is doing something underhanded, such as spying on users or sending unsolicited commercial email to millions of email addresses. Should you continue to work at the company, or on the software? Should you report it to the media or appropriate law enforcement personnel? Of course, you may have to pay for toeing the moral line, with additional work, loss of trust from your peers or leaders, or even the loss of your job. While it's easy to read and discuss ethical dilemmas from a textbook, it's an entirely different matter when your child may not eat unless you do continue doing something morally dubious.

This is a tough line to walk, and there are no easy answers. If you wait until you have determined that there are absolutely no defects in the software being produced which might cause an issue, then the software will never be released. If you act solely as a dispassionate observer, drily noting in a footnote that the product could easily cause loss of life, then you are not acting in an ethical manner - even if you followed the letter of the rules.

What you cannot do is ignore the ethical quandaries which come with being a software tester. Aside from facing mundane software development ethical issues - such as entering time correctly, not falsifying test reports, etc. - you will, in all likelihood, encounter these less tractable issues. I recommend you at least think about what your code of ethics is before you encounter such situations in reality.

21.9 Respect

You may have noticed that this subject is full of caveats. There's a reason for that—dealing with people is hard and full of ambiguity. In comparison, dealing with software can be a walk in the park. Part of being a professional is learning to deal with these difficulties and ambiguities with grace and aplomb, and it's very difficult to put together step by step instructions or a template for that.

Much of this chapter can be summarized by the phrase, "be respectful". Remember that other stakeholders are going to care about different aspects of the system, or they may have a different view of the best path forward. They may not understand everything that you do, and you may not understand anything that they do. They may not have the same technical background or domain knowledge as you, leading to very different views of the same data.

It takes more than one kind of stakeholder to see a program to completion, and there are bound to be disagreements. You are unlikely to change anybody's mind by treating them disrespectfully or condescendingly, and small bits of bad interaction may poison the entire well. Keep in mind that you are looking at the problem from a very specific point of view, and you don't always have all of the answers. If you treat people respectfully and listen dispassionately to what stakeholders have to say, you may even change your mind. Even if you don't, ensuring peaceful dialogue amongst team members—especially those with whom you disagree—will go a long way towards successfully releasing a software product.

Chapter 22

Conclusion

Tens of thousands of words later, hopefully you've learned a little bit about testing software. You would have to be trying pretty hard not to have learned something in the time you've been reading this. However, you've only just scratched the surface! Many topics have only received the most cursory of outlines when they deserve so much more. It would be easy to fill up an entire book on performance testing (to which I only dedicated a chapter), penetration testing (to which I devoted a section), or formal verification (to which I only alluded a couple times). Testing software in any specific domain is going to come with its own set of challenges. If you become involved in testing any non-trivial application, you could probably write a reasonably-sized book on the corner cases specific to it.

As I mentioned in the introduction, this book was meant to be a whirlwind tour of the topic. Nobody thinks that they understand Paris after staying there for a day and seeing nothing but the Eiffel Tower. I encourage you to research further in topics that interest you, and to keep abreast of developments in software testing. Just like any field in software, best practices are constantly changing and being updated, and we are figuring out better ways to do things, better understanding of theory, and developing better tools.

Ensuring the quality of software is a noble undertaking, and there are many different ways to go about doing it. I hope that your appetite for software quality has been whetted and that you go on to help produce software as free from unknown defects as is humanly possible. I will grant you that that is a strange and specific wish, but what can I say? I'm a strange and specific kind of guy.

Chapter 23

Testing Templates

This is a reference for various templates used in the book.

23.1 Test Case Template

IDENTIFIER: *A unique identifier for this test case, which ideally will also serve as a simple way to remember what the test case is testing.* Example: VALID-PARAMETER-MESSAGE.

TEST CASE: *A short description of what the test case does.*

PRECONDITIONS: *Any conditions which must be true before the test case is executed.*

INPUT VALUES: *Any input values to be passed in as part of the execution steps.*

EXECUTION STEPS: *The steps the tester should take to run the test.*

OUTPUT VALUES: *Any specific output values expected after the execution steps.*

POSTCONDITIONS: *Any conditions which must hold true after the execution steps have been completed. If these conditions are not met, the test fails.*

23.2 Defect Reporting Template

SUMMARY: *A short (one sentence or less) summary of what the defect is.*

DESCRIPTION: *A more in-depth (can be a paragraph or more) description of the defect.*

REPRODUCTION STEPS: *The specific steps to reproduce the defect.*

EXPECTED BEHAVIOR: *What is expected to occur after the reproduction steps have been executed.*

OBSERVED BEHAVIOR: *What actually happened after the reproduction steps were executed.*

IMPACT: *How this specifically impacts a user of the software.*

SEVERITY: *How severe this problem is, from TRIVIAL to BLOCKER.*

WORKAROUND: *How to avoid triggering this defect, if known or possible.*

NOTES: *Any other notes that may be useful in fixing or tracking down this defect, such as system configuration, thread dumps, or logging files.*

23.3   Red-Yellow-Green Template

The system should be divided into a reasonable number, usually between three and ten, subsystems or areas of functionality. Each subsystem or area should then be given a "color rating" of red, yellow, or green, as well as a short description (a few sentences, maximum) of why that rating was given.

RED: *This aspect of the system has major problems, and should not be released in this state. Substantial additional help in the form of resources, scope reduction, or schedule increase will be necessary in order to get it ready for release.*

YELLOW: *There are a few problems with this aspect of the system, some of them substantial. Some additional help may be necessary to get it to a reasonable level of quality.*

GREEN: *There are no major problems with this aspect of the system, and no additional help is necessary to see it to completion.*

23.4   Daily Status Report

This is a template for reporting your daily status to a manager or other supervisor.

DATE

- *What you worked on today, and its status. This can be several different bullet points.*
- *What you plan on working on tomorrow. This can also be several bullet points.*

BLOCKERS: *Anything that is preventing you from getting work done, be that resources, time, or knowledge.*

Chapter 24

Using Reflection to Test Private Methods in Java

In Java, there's no way to directly call private methods from a unit test, although this is definitely not the case in other languages (such as with Ruby's `.send(:method_name)` method, which bypasses the concept of "private" entirely). However, using the reflection library, we can "reflect" what the structure of the class is at runtime. The reflection library is built into the Java language, so you don't need to install anything else to use it.

Let's give an example—if you've never worked with reflection before, it can be a bit strange. Say we want to write a class which tells the user what methods are available in that class. Without reflection, this is impossible in Java; how can you know what other methods exist without hard-coding them into a String or something along those lines? It's actually relatively simple to do using reflection:

```java
import java.lang.reflect.Method;

public class ReflectionFun {

    public void printQuack() {
        System.out.println("Quack!");
    }

    public static void main(String[] args) {
        Method[] methods = ReflectionFun.class.getMethods();

        // Get all methods from class and any from superclasses callable
        // on this class.
        System.out.println("All methods:");
        for (Method method : methods){
            System.out.println(method.getName());
        }
    }

}
```

When we run this program, we get the following output:

```
All methods:
```

```
main
printQuack
wait
wait
wait
equals
toString
hashCode
getClass
notify
notifyAll
```

We can then do things like check to see if a method exists before calling it, or let the programmer know what methods exist. If you've ever used a language like Ruby, where you can quickly check what methods are available on an object, you can see how useful this can be. If you're new to a codebase, and you know that you want to do something related to quacking, but you're not sure if the method you want to call is named `displayQuack()`, or `quackify()`, or `quackAlot()`, or whatever, you can do a quick method listing and see that the method you are looking for is `printQuack()`.

You may have noticed that there are many more methods here than are listed in the `ReflectionFun` class. This is because the `getMethods()` method returns a list of *all* methods callable on an object (that is, public methods, we will see how to get private methods soon). Since all objects in Java descend from the `Object` class, any of the public methods on the `Object` class will also appear here.

You'll also note that there are three different `wait` methods listed. This is simply because Java considers methods with the same name but different argument lists as different methods. Reviewing the Java API, we can see that the following three methods exist:

```
public void wait();
public void wait(long timeout);
public void wait(long timeout, int nanos);
```

Reviewing the code above, you can see that the `methods[]` array actually contains methods as objects! This may not seem strange in a functional language, but if you are only used to straightforward Java programming, it may seem a bit weird. If the concept of a method or function existing as a first-class object seems strange to you, my first recommendation is to learn Haskell or another functional programming language until it seems like second nature. If you don't particularly have the time for that, just think of them as functions that you can pick up and carry around, then do something with them at a later date, instead of having them only be in one place.

Now that we have this list of methods, we can actually invoke them by name, by passing in the name of the method to which we'd like to have a reference to the `getMethod()` method:

```
import java.lang.reflect.InvocationTargetException;
import java.lang.reflect.Method;

public class ReflectionFun {

    public void printQuack() {
        System.out.println("Quack!");
    }

    public static void main(String[] args) {
        try {
            System.out.println("Call public method (printQuack):");
```

```
        Method method = ReflectionFun.class.getMethod("printQuack");
        ReflectionFun rf = new ReflectionFun();
        Object returnValue = method.invoke(rf);
    } catch (NoSuchMethodException|IllegalAccessException|InvocationTargetException ex) {
        System.err.println("Failure!");
    }
}

}
```

This displays:

```
Call public method (printQuack):
Quack!
```

Using this, you could add a way to manually test and call methods, by having the user enter a string and trying to call a method by that name on the object. We now have run-time control of what methods to call. This is very useful for metaprogramming and programmer interfaces such as REPLs (read-eval-print-loop systems, which let you enter some code, see the results, and repeat). Now that you understand reflection, it only takes some minor tweaks to our existing code for us to be able to easily access and test private methods.

You can't use the getMethod() or getMethods() methods, as they only return publicly available methods. Instead, you need to use either the getDeclaredMethod() or getDeclaredMethods() methods. These have two key differences from the getMethod()-style methods listed above:

1. They only return methods declared in that specific class. They will not return methods defined in superclasses.

2. They return public, private, and protected methods.

Therefore, if we wanted a list of *all* methods defined on ReflectionFun, we could use the getDeclaredMethods() method. Just for fun, let's also add a private printQuock() method to go along with our public printQuack() method (my definition of "fun" may be slightly different than yours):

```
import java.lang.reflect.Method;

public class ReflectionFun {

    public void printQuack() {
        System.out.println("Quack!");
    }

    private void printQuock() {
        System.out.println("Quock!");
    }

    public static void main(String[] args) {
        System.out.println("Declared methods:");
        Method[] methods = ReflectionFun.class.getDeclaredMethods();
        for(Method method : methods){
            System.out.println(method.getName());
        }
    }
```

```
}
```

The output of this program is:

```
Declared methods:
main
printQuack
printQuock
```

We once again have a list of Method objects, and we can now invoke them. There's only one small snag—we first need to set that method to "accessible" before calling it, using the `setAccessible()` method. It accepts a Boolean parameter to determine whether or not the method should be accessible outside the class:

```
import java.lang.reflect.InvocationTargetException;
import java.lang.reflect.Method;

public class ReflectionFun {

    public void printQuack() {
        System.out.println("Quack!");
    }

    private void printQuock() {
        System.out.println("Quock!");
    }

    public static void main(String[] args) {
        try {
            System.out.println("Call private method (printQuock):");
            ReflectionFun rf = new ReflectionFun();
            Method method2 = ReflectionFun.class.getDeclaredMethod("printQuock");
            method2.setAccessible(true);
            Object returnValue = method2.invoke(rf);
        } catch (NoSuchMethodException|IllegalAccessException|InvocationTargetException ex) {
            System.err.println("Failure!");
        }
    }

}
```

This will output:

```
Call private method (printQuock):
Quock!
```

We can combine this with the other unit testing we've learned earlier in the chapter to write a unit test for a private method:

```
public class LaboonStuff {
    private int laboonify(int x) { return x; }
}

@Test
public void testPrivateLaboonify() {
```

```
    try {
        Method method = LaboonStuff.class.getDeclaredMethod("laboonify");
        method.setAccessible(true);
        LaboonStuff ls = new LaboonStuff();
        Object returnValue = method.invoke(ls, 4);
        int foo = ((Integer) returnValue).intValue();
        assertEquals(4, foo);
    } catch (NoSuchMethodException|IllegalAccessException|InvocationTargetException ex) {
        // The method does not exist
        fail();
    }
}
```

It is plain to see that testing even simple private methods can include quite a bit of boilerplate code. In many cases, you will probably want to wrap the private method access code in a separate helper method.

Chapter 25

Further Reading

This section contains a selection of books on various topics which you may find interesting, or if you would like to dig deeper into a particular topic covered in this book. This was, after all, only an introduction to the world of software quality; it was meant to have very broad coverage of a variety of fields. If you're interested in a specific one, I highly recommend you dig deeper.

Exploratory Testing

Hendrickson, Elisabeth. *Explore It! Reduce Risk and Increase Confidence with Exploratory Testing.* Dallas, TX: The Pragmatic Bookshelf, 2013.

General Testing

Crispin, Lisa and Janet Gregory. *Agile Testing: A Practical Guide for Testers and Agile Teams.* Boston: Addison-Wesley, 2009.

Jorgensen, Paul C. *Software Testing: A Craftsman's Approach.* Boca Raton: CRC Press, 2014.

McCaffrey, James. *Software Testing: Fundamental Principles and Essential Knowledge.* 2009.

Whittaker, James. *How To Break Software.* New York: Pearson, 2002.

Whittaker, James, Jason Arbon and Jeff Carollo. *How Google Tests Software.* New York: Pearson, 2012.

Integration Testing

Duvall, Paul, Stephen M. Matyas III and Andrew Glover. *Continuous Integration: Improving Software Quality and Reducing Risk.* Boston: Addison-Wesley, 2007.

Narratives and History

Kidder, Tracy. *The Soul of a New Machine.* Boston: Little, Brown and Company, 2000.

Levy, Steven. *Hackers: Heroes of the Computer Revolution.* New York: Penguin Books, 2000.

Mitnick, Kevin. *Ghost in the Wires: My Adventures as the World's Most Wanted Hacker.* Boston: Little, Brown and Company, 2011.

Stoll, Clifford. *The Cuckoo's Egg: Tracking a Spy Through the Maze of Computer Espionage.* New York: Doubleday, 2012.

Zachary, G. Pascal. *Showstopper! The Breakneck Race to Create Windows NT and the Next Generation at Microsoft.* New York: Open Road Media, 2014.

Performance Testing

Molyneaux, Ian. *The Art of Application Performance Testing: Help for Programmers and Quality Assurance.* Sebastopol, CA: O'Reilly and Associates, Inc., 2009.

Risks of Software

Neumann, Peter G. *Computer-Related Risks.* New York: ACM Press, 1995.

Security Testing

Garfinkel, Simson, Gene Spafford and Alan Schwartz. *Practical Unix and Internet Security.* Sebastopol, CA: O'Reilly and Associates, Inc., 2003.

Mitnick, Kevin and William L. Simon. *The Art of Deception: Controlling the Human Element of Security.* Hoboken, NJ: John Wiley & Sons, 2007.

Weidman, Georgia. *Penetration Testing: A Hands-On Introduction to Hacking.* San Francisco: No Starch Press, 2014.

Quality-Focused Software Engineering

Brooks, Frederick P. *The Mythical Man-Month: Essays on Software Engineering, 2nd Edition.* Boston: Addison-Wesley, 1995.

Feathers, Michael C. *Working Effectively with Legacy Code.* Upper Saddle River, NJ: Prentice Hall, 2004.

Fowler, Martin. *Refactoring: Improving the Design of Existing Code.* Addison-Wesley, 1999.

Hunt, Andrew, and David Thomas. *The Pragmatic Programmer: From Journeyman to Master.* Boston: Addison-Wesley, 1999.

Martin, Robert C. *Clean Code: A Handbook of Agile Software Craftsmanship.* Upper Saddle River, NJ: Prentice Hall, 2008.

McConnell, Steve. *Code Complete: A Practical Handbook of Software Construction, Second Edition.* Seattle: Microsoft Press, 2003.

Stakeholder Interaction

Stone, Douglas, Bruce Patton and Sheila Heen. *Difficult Conversations: How To Discuss What Matters Most.* New York: Penguin Books, 2010.

Test-Driven Development

Beck, Kent. *Test-Driven Development: By Example.* Boston: Addison-Wesley, 2003.

Chelimsky, David and Aslak Hellsoy. *The RSpec Book: Behaviour-Driven Development with RSpec, Cucumber, and Friends.* Dallas, TX: The Pragmatic Bookshelf, 2010.

Freeman, Steve and Nat Pryce. *Growing Object-Oriented Software, Guided by Tests.* Boston: Addison-Wesley, 2009.

Usability Testing

Krug, Steve. *Don't Make Me Think: A Common Sense Approach to Web Usability.* Berkeley, CA: New Riders Publishers, 2006.

Web Testing

Rappin, Noel. *Rails 4 Test Prescriptions: Build a Healthy Codebase.* Dallas, TX: The Pragmatic Bookshelf, 2014.

Chapter 26

Glossary of Terms

9's: See **n nines**.

Acceptance testing: Testing by an end user, customer, or other independent personnel to verify that the system can be accepted for use.

Accessibility error: An error resulting from a user employing a non-standard input or output device, where the system is not usable for those who do not access the system using "standard" devices.

Active attack: In **security testing**, an attack on a system which causes some changes to the system, such as adding a program or modifying data in a database.

Ad hoc testing: A (sometimes considered pejorative) term for **exploratory testing**.

All-pairs testing: Another term for **pairwise testing**.

Alpha testing: "Real-world" testing by a small group of test engineers or some other small group of technically proficient personnel. Often succeeded by beta testing.

Application under test: The system which the tester is testing.

Assertion: In a unit test, a statement which states that a certain condition must hold. If the condition does not hold, the test is considered to have failed. For example, `assertEquals(2, Math.sqrt(4));`.

Availability: In **performance testing**, what percentage of the time the system is available to the user (not in a failure mode, unresponsive, etc.) In **security testing**, one of the elements of the **InfoSec Triad**, an attribute that refers to the ability of authorized users to access a system.

Bacteria: A kind of **malware** which consumes an excess amount of system resources, perhaps taking up all file descriptors or disk space.

Bad data error: An error resulting from the system receiving malformed, corrupt, or otherwise invalid data.

Base case: A test case for the basic expected functionality of a system, or an interior value in an equivalence class. For example, when testing a calculator, a base case might be a user adding 2 and 2 together.

Baseline test: A kind of **load test** where a bare minimum amount of events, perhaps even none, are processed, to provide a "baseline" to show what minimal load on the system looks like.

Bathtub curve: A generalized function of failure rates, which start out high (as poor components fail soon after being implemented), stay low throughout much of the life of the system, then start increasing as the system nears it end of life. So named because it looks like the outline of a bathtub as viewed from the side.

Beta testing: "Real-world" testing by a subset of the actual user base prior to release of the system. Often preceded by alpha testing.

Binomial coefficient: The number of **r-combinations** of a given **set** of size n. It is determined by the formula `C(n, r) = n! / (r! * (n - r)!)`.

Black-box testing: Testing the code as a user would, with no knowledge of the codebase. Most manual tests are black-box tests.

Blocked: A status for a test case in a test run. It indicates that the test case cannot be executed at this time, for reasons outside the tester's control. For example, the functionality it tests is not yet at a testable state, perhaps because it has not yet been developed.

Blocker: A defect of the highest severity, where the system cannot reasonably be released without fixing it or providing a **workaround**.

Bot network: A collection of **zombies** controlled by a master.

Boundary value: A value which is "on the boundary" between equivalence classes. For example, a system that has two equivalence classes, between 0 and 19, and 20 or higher, would have boundary values at 19 and 20.

Bounds checking: Run-time checking that data is not being written outside of a properly allocated array.

Branch coverage: What percentage of branches in the code are tested, usually by unit tests.

Brownfield development: Writing software which must interact with already-existing software in production, thus limiting potential design, solutions, architecture, etc.

Buffer overrun: A **vulnerability** where more data can be written than has been allocated for it. This can cause system crashes or unauthorized access.

Bug: Another term for **defect**.

Chaos Monkey: A **stochastic testing** tool developed by Netflix which tests distributed systems by shutting off random servers in the system.

choose: When used in combinatorics, a way of expressing the **binomial coefficient** of a set of size n and r-combinations of size r. For example, "5 choose 3" means the number of 3-combinations possible in a set of 5 elements.

CIA Triad: Another term for the **InfoSec Triad**.

Code coverage: How much of the codebase is actually tested, usually via unit tests. Although there are different kinds of code coverage, the majority of the time that non-specialists use it, they are referring to **statement coverage**.

Combination: A selection of elements from a **set**, in which order does not matter.

Combinatorial testing: Testing in such a way so as to ensure that various combinations of variables will work as expected.

Complete (requirements): The property of having the requirements specify the entirety of the system.

Confidentiality: An attribute of a system, that only authorized users may read data. An element of the **InfoSec Triad**.

Configuration error: An error resulting from a misconfiguration of the system, as opposed to an error in the code which comprises the system itself.

Consistent (requirements): The property of having requirements which can all be followed without a paradox (e.g., "the system shall display the message 'Hello' upon startup" and "the system shall not display any message upon startup" are not consistent).

Corner case: A test case for functionality of a system which is unlikely to occur, or is beyond the realm where a user will likely reproduce it. By analogy with **edge case** (a corner is where multiple edges intersect).

Covering array: An array which covers all possible combinations of variable values.

Cracker: An unauthorized person attempting to access and/or modify a system or data using underhanded techniques.

Critical: A defect of the second-highest level of severity, which severely impacts how a user could use the system.

DDos: See **Distributed Denial of Service**.

Defect: A flaw in a system which causes it to behave in an unexpected or incorrect manner, or does not meet the requirements of the system. Much of software testing is involved in finding defects in a system.

Denial of Service: A method of attacking **availability** by sending so many unauthorized packets or other events to a computing resource that no authorized users have access to it.

Dependency injection: Passing dependencies of a method in as parameters, as opposed to having them be hard-coded. This helps with testing as they can easily be replaced with test doubles or fakes.

Deterministic: Something for which the causal behaviors are entirely known and reproducible.

Disk I/O Error: An error resulting from a fault in reading or writing to long-term local storage (usually, but not always, a disk).

Display error: An error where the correct value was computed, but it was not displayed correctly.

Distributed Denial of Service: A **denial of service** attack which consists of many different sources of the unauthorized packets, so as to increase the number of events the system must process as well as help disguise the ultimate source. Often abbreviated as **DDos**.

Distributed system error: An error arising as a consequence of the system being distributed, as opposed to running entirely on one computer.

Dogfood, eating your own: Another term for **dogfooding**.

Dogfooding: Using your own software while developing it. For example, running the operating system that you are developing on your own computer.

DoS: An acronym for **denial of service**.

DoS tools: Tools which enable denial of service attacks.

DRY: Don't Repeat Yourself. A tenet of writing good, testable code which states that code should not be repeated, for example by having two different methods which do the same thing, or copy/pasting code from one part of the codebase to another instead of making it into a callable method.

Dumb monkey: A **stochastic testing** method in which random data is sent in to a system.

Dynamic testing: Testing the system by executing it. Examples would be unit testing or black-box testing.

Edge case: A test case for functionality of a system which can be expected to happen, but will be rare and may require special work to handle appropriately from a development point of view. For example, when testing a calculator, an edge case might be ensuring that trying to divide by zero provides a correct error message.

Efficiency-oriented indicator: A performance metric related to the efficiency of use of the computational resources available to the system.

Enhancement: A requested modification or additional functionality which was not originally specified in the requirements.

Equivalence class: A group of input values which provide the same, or similar type, of output.

Equivalence class partitioning: Separating a specific functionality into distinct equivalence classes based on input values.

Error: A status for a test case in a test run. It indicates that there is an issue with the test case itself, and the test cannot be run. For example, the preconditions indicate an impossible condition.

Error of assumption: An error resulting from a developer or other person making an incorrect assumption about how the system should work.

Evil monkey: A **stochastic testing** method whereby malicious code or data is sent in to a system. Simulates an attacker trying to gain access or cause damage to a system.

Execution steps: The actual steps that the test will execute after ensuring that all preconditions hold.

Exhaustive testing: Testing every single possibility of input, environment, and other relevant factors for a given system under test. For example, if testing a int max(int a, int b) Java method which returns the greater of the two values a and b, ensuring that it worked for every single combination of values a (MININT..MAXINT) and b (MININT..MAXINT), or 18,446,744,073,709,551,616 test cases. Exhaustive testing is often not feasible in practice.

expect: A program which allows you to automate interactions with command-line programs.

Expected behavior: What the system is expected to do under certain circumstances. For example, after typing in "2 + 2 =" on a calculator, the expected behavior is that the system will display "4" on the screen.

Explicit boundary value: A **boundary value** explicitly called out by the system requirements. For example, requirements for an automated thermometer may state the system will turn on the DANGER light when the registered temperature is 102 degrees or over. The explicit boundary values would be 101 and 102. Contrast with **implicit boundary value**.

Exploit: A program or piece of data which takes advantage of a vulnerability. A vulnerability is "strictly theoretical" until somebody develops a way to exploit it.

Exploratory testing: An informal style of testing, where the goal is often both to learn about the system by testing it as well as find defects.

External quality: The quality of the system from a user's perspective - that is, does it meet the requirements, perform as expected, produce correct results, etc.

Externally consistent (requirements): The property of having the system be consistent with requirements of other systems or of the universe. For example, having a system which mandates that the system will be able to communicate with a base on Pluto instantaneously would require faster-than-light communication, and would thus be inconsistent with the laws of this universe.

Fabrication: In **security testing**, an attack on **integrity**, which deliberately adds data, such as an attack which allows a user to create an entirely new bank account.

Factorial: A mathematical function which calculates the result of an integer n multiplied by n - 1, n - 2, etc. all the way until 1. For example, 5! = 5 * 4 * 3 * 2 * 1, or 120.

Failed: A status for a test case in a test run. It indicates that, while the test itself was executed without error, the system has not met at least one postcondition or expected output value, or some other unexpected behavior has taken place. In other words, the observed behavior was not the expected behavior.

Failure case: A kind of test where the expected behavior of the system is to fail in a certain way. For example, sending in a negative number to a square root function which does not support complex numbers may be expected to throw an exception. Compare to **success case**.

Fake: A kind of **test double** in which the behavior of the double is handled by the object itself, as opposed to being referenced by stub methods. These act as simpler, faster versions of the actual object, in order to make tests run faster or reduce dependencies.

Falsifying the invariant: Showing an example where an **invariant** does not hold, such as an invariant for arithmetic method that adding two positive integers should always result in a number greater than one of the numbers, and showing that $1 + 1 = 0$.

Feasible: In regard to requirements, possible to test with a realistic timeframe and allocation of resources.

Field testing: Testing that a system works while actually operating with real users.

Fishing: Catching marine animals for food or enjoyment. Has nothing to do with **security testing**. If you think it did, you are probably thinking of **phishing**.

Floating-point error: An error caused by a floating-point number being rounded or being inaccurate due to the incomplete mapping between actual decimal numbers and floating-point values.

Fork bomb: A special kind of **bacteria** which continually forks itself, causing all CPU resources to be used up creating more copies of the fork bomb.

Fragile: A description of a test case or suite which is easily broken by small modifications to the codebase or environment.

Functional requirement: A requirement that specifies exactly what a system should do under certain circumstances. For example, "the system shall display ERROR on the console if any parameter is negative." Contrast with **non-functional requirement**.

Fuzz testing: A form of **stochastic testing** whereby random but possible data is passed in to a system to see how it responds.

Greenfield development: Writing software from scratch, and thus being able to design the entire system without worrying about previous solutions.

Grey-box testing: Testing the code as a user would, but with knowledge of the codebase in order to understand where errors might be hiding. A mixture of **white-box testing** and **black-box testing**.

Hacker: According to the Jargon File, "[a] person who enjoys exploring the details of programmable systems and how to stretch their capabilities". Often used in modern times to mean the same as **cracker**.

Happy path: The easiest path a user will take through the system, when the system is operating properly, without attempting to perform anything that is an **edge case** or **corner case**.

IDE: Integrated Development Environment. A single tool which unifies much of the functionality allowing a developer to write, such as running tests, compiling, and configuring dependencies.

Idempotent: A quality of a function or request where the same result will be returned no matter how many times it is called. For example, multiplying a number by one is an idemepotent operation ($5 * 1 = 5, 5 * 1 * 1 = 5, 5 * 1 * 1 * 1 = 5$, etc.), but adding one two a number is a **non-idempotent** operation ($5 + 1 = 6, 5 + 1 + 1 = 7, 5 + 1 + 1 + 1 = 8$, etc.).

Identifier: A number or string which uniquely identifies a test case, defect, or anything else.

-ility requirement: Another term for **non-functional requirement**, so named because many of these requirements use words ending in "-ility" to describe them (e.g., usability, scalability, maintainability).

Impact: When reporting defects, how the defect will affect users of the system.

Implicit boundary value: A **boundary value** that is not explicitly called out by the system requirements, but may have an impact on the system's operation. For example, code written using 32-bit signed integers (such as `int` in Java) has an implicit boundary at 2,147,483,647, the maximum integer size. Adding one to this will cause the number to overflow.

Impure: The opposite of **pure**, a method or function which produces at least one **side effect**.

Information Security: The field of ensuring that computer systems successfully exhibit all three aspects of the **InfoSec Triad**.

InfoSec Triad: The three criteria that indicate a secure system—**confidentiality**, **integrity**, and **availability**.

Injection attack: A kind of attack where the malicious user tries to get the victim's computer to execute arbitrary code.

Injection error: An error where the system accidentally allows arbitrary code to be executed. Leaves the system vulnerable to an **injection attack**.

Input value: A particular value which will be passed in to a test case. The distinction between this and precondition can be hazy in manual or other black-box testing; in white-box testing, values that you are passing in to the method under test (e.g. as arguments or parameters) are input values.

Integration: Connecting multiple systems or subsystems to work together.

Integration error: A type of error resulting from incompatibilities or other problems at the boundary between different systems or subsystems.

Integrity: An attribute of a system, that only authorized users may write data. An element of the **InfoSec Triad**.

Interception: In **security testing**, an attack on **confidentiality**, such as eavesdropping on a network with a **packet analyzer** or on a computer with a **keylogger**.

Interface error: An error where the interface to another system is defined incorrectly, or the system accessing it does not do so correctly.

Interior value: A value which is not a boundary value in its equivalence class.

Intermittent failure: A test failure which does not occur all of the time, but only on certain runs. Often, the reason for the intermittent failure is unknown, or it would have been fixed already.

Internal quality: The quality of the codebase as seen from the developers' perspective - that is, is the code readable, understandable, maintainable, extensible, etc.

Internally consistent (requirements): The property of having no requirements contradict each other. For example, a requirements specification which has a requirement which states "The system shall always leave the red light on" and another requirement which states that "The system shall turn off the red light if `SWITCH1` is enabled" would not be internally consistent.

Interruption: In **security testing**, an attack on **availability**, such as a **DDoS attack** or pulling the plug from a network switch.

Invariant: In **property-based testing**, a property that should always hold for a function or method. For example, a sorting method which accepts an unsorted array should always return an array with the same number of elements as the unsorted original.

Keylogger: Software which stores all keys that were pressed by the user, usually to be transmitted to, or retrieved by, an attacker.

Key Performance Indicator: A **performance indicator** that is considered of primary importance in the development of the system.

KPI: Abbreviation for **Key Performance Indicator**.

Legacy code: Code which is running in production, and was written without using modern software engineering techniques and/or has substandard automated test coverage.

Linter: A static analysis tool which informs the user of potential issues with code.

Load testing: Running a full system with a specified amount of demand (e.g., a certain number of users or events) in order to determine how the system operates under realistic conditions.

Logic bomb: Code within a program which executes an unauthorized function, such as deleting all data on the first day of the month.

Logic error: An error in a program due to faulty logic being programmed.

Major: A defect of the third-highest level of severity, which indicates a severe problem but still allows the user to use the system.

Malware: Software which has pernicious and deliberate effects to the user of the software, such as a computer virus or key logger.

Mean time between failures: In **availability testing**, the mean (average) amount of time between failures on a system. Often abbreviated as **MTBF**.

Mean time to repair: In **availability testing**, the mean (average) amount of time it takes to repair a failure. Often abbreviated as **MTTR**.

Media testing: Ensuring that the media that the system is stored on (e.g., a CD-ROM or a server's hard drive) is operating correctly and has all of the data in the correct place.

Minor: A defect of a lower level of severity than **normal**, which causes only a very small problem for use of the system.

Missing data error: An error resulting from the system not receiving necessary data.

Mock: A particular kind of **test double** which keeps track of which methods on it have been called.

Modification: In **security testing**, an attack on **integrity**, which deliberately modifies data, such as an attack which allows a user to arbitrarily change the balance on their bank account.

Monkey testing: Another term for **stochastic testing**.

MTBF: An acronym for **mean time between failures**.

MTTR: An acronym for **mean time to repair**.

Mutation testing: A means of "testing the tests" of a system by **seeding** the system under test with defects by randomly modifying code.

n nines: A way of showing what percentage of the time the system is available, based on the number of nines in that number, and assuming nines are the only significant digit. For example, a system that is available 99.92% of the time has 3 nines' availability, while a system that is available 99.999% of the time has 5 nines' availability.

Negative test case: See **failure case**.

Network error: An error which results when network connectivity is suboptimal or missing altogether. For example, an application which freezes if Internet connectivity is lost in the middle of a transaction.

Nines: See **n nines**.

Non-deterministic: A test failure which does not occur all of the time, but only on certain runs, and for unknown reasons.

Non-functional requirement: A requirement that specifies how the system should operate, without specifying specific behavior. For example, "the system shall be extensible, allowing for the addition of plug-ins" or "the system shall be usable by personnel with less than one hour of training". Contrast with **functional requirement**.

Non-idempotent: A quality of a function or request where the same result may or may not be returned, depending on how many times that function is called. For example, multiplying a number by one is an **idempotent** operation ($5 * 1 = 5, 5 * 1 * 1 = 5, 5 * 1 * 1 * 1 = 5$, etc.), but adding one two a number is a non-idempotent operation ($5 + 1 = 6, 5 + 1 + 1 = 7, 5 + 1 + 1 + 1 = 8$, etc.)

Normal: A defect of a severity which is noticeable but does not strongly hamper the user's use of the system.

Null pointer error: An error resulting from the code trying to dereference a null pointer, or access a null object.

Observed behavior: What the system actually does under certain circumstances. For example, if I type in "2 + 2 =" on a calculator, the **expected behavior** may be that I see "4", but if I instead see "WALLA WALLA", then "WALLA WALLA" is the observed behavior.

Off-by-one error: A specific kind of **logic error** where a program does something wrong because a value is off by one unit.

Operational testing: Testing that a system works under real-world conditions.

Output value: A particular value which will be output by a test case. The distinction between these and postconditions in manual or other black-box testing can be hazy; in white-box testing, values that are directly returned from a method are output values.

Packet analyzer: A tool which allows you to view individual packets that are being transmitted over the network.

Packet sniffing: Using a **packet analyzer** or similar software to view data being transmitted over a network.

Pair programming: Two people working at the same time on a problem on a single computer. Can be a white-box tester and developer, looking at the code together.

Pairwise testing: A particular form of combinatorial testing where you are testing for all two-way interactions.

Partitioning: See **equivalence class partitioning**.

Passed: A status for a test case in a test run. It indicates that the test was executed without error, and that the system has met all postconditions and/or expected output values—the observed behavior was equal to the expected behavior.

Passive attack: In **security testing**, an attack on a system which causes no changes to the system, such as eavesdropping on network traffic.

Pathological case: Another term for **corner case**.

Paused: A status for a test case in a test run. It indicates that the tester has started to run the test, but it is temporarily on hold for external reasons (e.g., the tester went out to lunch).

Penetration testing: Testing the security of the system by attempting to compromise it as an unauthorized user would.

Performance indicator: A quantitative measure that indicates the level of performance of the system. For example, response time or memory usage.

Performance target: In **performance testing**, the target value for a **performance indicator**. If the indicator value meets or exceed the target, then the system has met the target. Contrast with **performance threshold**.

Performance testing: Testing that a system meets the **performance indicators** designated for it.

Performance threshold: In **performance testing**, an absolutely minimal value for a given performance indicator for the system to be considered releasable. Contrast with **performance target**.

Performant: A program which provides a high level of performance, which is usually measured by it meeting or exceeding its **KPIs**.

Permutation: An arrangement of a **set**, in which order matters. For example, the possible permutations of the set [1, 2] are [1, 2] and [2, 1]. The possible permutations of the set [1, 2, 3] are [1, 2, 3], [1, 3, 2], [2, 1, 3], [2, 3, 1], [3, 1, 2], and [3, 2, 1].

Phishing: A common **attack** which attempts to get personal or other sensitive information via email or other communications.

Phone phreak: A person who explores the telephone system, usually without the permission of relevant authorities. Famous phone phreaks include John Draper and Joe Engressia.

Phreaker: Another term for **phone phreak**.

Pinning test: An automated test (usually a unit test) which checks for the current response of a system, in order to modify code without modifying existing behavior. Note that pinning tests check for the current response, *not* the correct response. Often used when refactoring or adding to **legacy code**.

Positive test case: See **success case**.

Postcondition: All conditions which need to hold true after the execution steps in order for the test to pass. For example, a postcondition after editing your user name may be that the Account Information page shows the new user name.

Precondition: All conditions which need to hold true before the execution steps of a test case can begin. For example, when testing the Account Information of a website, a precondition may be that the user is already logged in.

Principle of Least Privilege: The principle that states that users should have the minimal amount of access to the system necessary to do their jobs. For example, a developer should not (in general) have access to payroll data, and HR personnel should not have access to source code.

Profiler: A tool which allows you to measure the resource utilization and internal events (such as method calls or instantiation of objects) of a running program.

Property-based testing: A method of testing, usually automated, where many values, often pseudorandomly generated, are given as inputs, and properties of the output are tested as opposed to checking for specific values or behavior.

Pure: A method or function which does not produce any **side effects**, but simply returns the result of a computation.

QA: See **quality assurance**.

Qualitative: Not able to be expressed numerically, such as "the system shall be *extremely* cool". Contrast with **quantitative**.

Quality assurance: Ensuring the quality of software, by a variety of methods. Software testing is an important, but not the only, part of quality assurance.

Quality attribute: Another (probably better) term for **non-functional requirement**.

Quantitative: Able to be expressed numerically, such as "the system shall respond within 500 milliseconds". Contrast with **qualitative**.

r-combination: A **subset** of r elements from a **set**, in which order does not matter. The value r can be replaced with a specific value, such as 2 or 3, to indicate the number of elements in the subset. For example, [2, 3, 1] is a 3-combination of the set [1, 2, 3, 4], and is equivalent to [1, 2, 3].

r-permutation: A **subset** of r elements from a **set**, in which order matters. The value r can be replaced with a specific value, such as 2 or 3, to indicate the number of elements in the subset. For example, [2, 3, 1] and [1, 2, 3] are two different 3-permutations of the set [1, 2, 3, 4].

Ransomware: A kind of **malware** which performs an unwanted action (e.g., encrypting your hard drive) and asks for money or other compensation in order to undo it.

Real time: The actual amount of time (the same kind of time as measured by a clock) taken for a process to perform some task. Also referred to as **wall clock time**. Not to be confused with "real-time system".

Refactoring: Modifying code without changing its functionality, so as to improve the program's internal quality (e.g., making the code easier to read, more understandable, or more maintainable).

Reflection: A way to determine class and method structure at run-time.

Regression failure: A failure of a previously-working piece of functionality that is caused by (seemingly) unrelated additional functionality or defect fixes.

Regulation acceptance testing: Testing that a system meets legal or other regulatory requirements.

Report: The act of filing a defect according to the agreed-upon system for the project.

Reproduction steps: The steps necessary for reproducing a defect. Often included in defect reports so that readers of the defect will understand what causes the defect and how to reproduce it.

Requirement: A statement of what the system under development needs to do in order to be considered complete and correct.

Requirements specification: A list of requirements for a given system. The system is expected to meet all of the requirements in the requirements specification.

Response time: In **performance testing**, how quickly a system responds after user input or other event.

Rounding error: An error in a program caused by the system rounding a number.

Running: A status for a test case in a test run. It indicates that the test is currently being executed, but has not yet completed.

Sanitization: "Cleaning up" user input so that it does not contain code that would be executed by the running program or other content that would cause harm to the system.

Scripted testing: Testing with a rigid script, such as a test plan, where steps are well-defined and ordered. Contrast with **unscripted testing**.

Seam: A place in the codebase where you can modify behavior without modifying the code itself.

"Seat of your pants" testing: Testing where the expected behavior is known to the tester through experience with the software or its domain, instead of being formally specified.

Security testing: Testing that the system meets the criteria of the InfoSec Triad, that the system is safe from unauthorized tampering and/or access.

Seeding: Deliberately adding defects to a program in order to determine if the testing strategy will find them.

Set: A group of unique elements. For example, [1, 2, 3] is a set, but [1, 1, 2, 3] is not because there are multiple instances of the element 1.

Service-oriented indicator: A performance metric related to how the user will interact with the system.

Service Level Agreement: An agreement by a service provider, which often includes a guarantee of **availability**.

Severity: The degree to which a particular **defect** is of concern to system designers, developers, and other stakeholders.

Side effect: Anything which is not strictly the returned result of a computation, such as displaying a message or setting a variable value.

SLA: An abbreviation for Service Level Agreement.

Smart monkey: A **stochastic testing** method whereby the data passed in mimics how an actual user would use the system. For example, a smart monkey test for a word processing system might type some letters, format them, and save the file (as an actual user might), as opposed to clicking buttons purely at random.

Smoke test: A small subset of tests which is used as a gateway for further testing.

Soak test: Another term for **stability test**.

Social engineering: Manipulating people to underhandedly cause them to perform actions that put security of a system at risk. For example, an attacker calling an administrative assistant falsely claiming that they are from the IT department and need to know the user's password.

Spear phishing: A specific kind of **phishing** which is aimed at highly targeted individuals and is customized for them. For example, a regular phishing email may be "Dear user, please to reset your email password for linked here" whereas a spear phishing email would be "Dear Mr. Jones, please reset your SuperDuperEmail password here. Sincerely, Jane Smith, SuperDuperCo. Vice President of Security".

Spyware: A kind of **malware** which surreptitiously monitors the actions of the user of the system.

SQL injection attack: A specific, common kind of **injection attack** where the malicious user attempts to have the system execute arbitrary SQL commands.

Stability test: A kind of **load test** where a small number of events are processed, but over a long period of time, in order to determine how stable the system is for non-trivial time periods.

Stakeholder: Any person who has a direct interest in the successful completion, execution, or release of the system, such as customers, developers, and project managers.

Statement coverage: What percentage of statements in the code are tested, usually by unit tests.

Static testing: Testing the system without executing any of its code. Examples would be code analysis or modeling tools.

Stochastic testing: Testing a system through the use of randomized inputs. These inputs do not have to be entirely random; for example, they can be a probability distribution of values or generated strings. Also called **monkey testing**.

Stress test: A kind of **load test** where a very high number of events are processed in a small amount of time, in order to determine how the system deals with periods of time where the system is "stressed".

Strict partitioning: Partitioning equivalence classes such that there is no overlap between the input values for any of them.

Stub: A "fake method" which can be used in unit testing to limit dependencies on other methods and focus testing on the method under test.

Success case: A kind of test case where the expected behavior of the system is to return the correct result or do the correct thing. Compare to **failure case**.

Summary (defect reporting): A brief description of the **defect** when filing a defect report.

System testing: Testing the system as a whole, as the user (as opposed to a developer) would interact with it. Usually done in a black-box or grey-box manner.

System time: The amount of time that kernel code executes while a system performs a task.

System under test: The system that is actually being tested.

Target: In **performance testing**, another term for **performance target**.

Tautological test case: A test case which was written so that it will always pass, for example `boolean foo = true; assertTrue(foo);`. This is usually done inadvertently.

Tcl: *Tool Command Language*, a programming language used to control the **expect** program which is used in the book for automating system tests.

Test artifact: A document or other byproduct of the testing process, such as test plans or results.

Test case: The smallest unit of a test plan, these are the individual tests which describe what is to be tested and a check for the expected behavior of a system.

Test coverage: A general term for which aspects or parts of the system are covered by tests.

Test double: A "fake object" which can be used in unit testing to limit dependencies on other classes, which may have problems of their own, not yet be developed, or simply be time- or resource-intensive to actually instantiate.

Test fixture: A procedure or program which puts a system into a state ready for testing.

Test hook: A "hidden" method which allows input to, or output from, the system in order to make it easier to test.

Test plan: A list of related test cases that are run together.

Test run: An actual iteration (run-through) of a test plan.

Test runner: A program which will automatically execute a suite of tests.

Test suite: A grouping of related test plans.

Testability: A quality of a system that specifies how easy it is to test—having well-designed and coherent methods, pure functions where possible, allowance for dependency injection, etc.

Testable code: Code which can be easily tested in an automated fashion at multiple levels of abstraction.

Test-Driven Development (TDD): A particular software development methodology which embraces **test-first development** along with several other tenets, such as continuous refactoring and expectation of change.

Test-First Development: Any software development methodology in which tests are written before the code that makes them pass.

Test-Unfriendly Construct: A part of the structure of the code which is difficult to test, such as a constructor, finalizer, or private method.

Test-Unfriendly Function: A functional aspect of a program which is difficult to test, such as communicating over a network or writing to disk.

Threshold: In **performance testing**, another term for **performance threshold**.

Throughput: In **performance testing**, the number of events or tasks the system can handle in a given time frame.

Total time: The total amount of time that code (user or kernel) executes, without taking into account other factors (such as time spent waiting for input). Compare to **real time**.

Traceability matrix: A two-dimensional matrix displaying test cases and requirements and indicating which test cases test which requirements.

Trapdoor: A program or piece of a program which provides secret access to a system or application.

Triage: A meeting or other way (e.g. email discussion) of prioritizing defects.

Trivial: A defect of a severity which is not noticeable, or hardly noticeable, and only causes the smallest of issues for a user of the system.

Trojan horse: A kind of **malware** which pretends to be another kind of program in order to trick users into installing and executing it.

Truth table: A table which shows all possible values of a group of Boolean (true/false) variables.

TUC: See **Test-Unfriendly Construct**.

TUF: See **Test-Unfriendly Function**.

Unambiguous (requirements): The property of having requirements which can be read and understood in one and only one way.

Undefined: In regards to a system specification, any area where the behavior is not specified. For example, if my entire system specification is "The first light shall turn on if the input value is less than 4", the behavior for how the system should behave if the input value is 7 is undefined.

Unit testing: Testing the smallest individual units of code, such as methods or functions, in a white-box manner.

Unscripted testing: Testing without a rigid script, where the tester has broad latitude to use their own volition and knowledge to determine the quality of the system or find defects. Contrast with **scripted testing**.

User acceptance testing: A particular kind of **acceptance testing** where the tester is the user of the software. It ensures that the system under test is acceptable to the user by meeting their needs.

User testing: Having an actual user of the system attempt to perform tasks, often without instruction, in order to determine how users interact with the system.

User time: The amount of time that user code executes while a system performs a task.

Utilization: In **performance testing**, the relative or absolute amount of a given computing resource (e.g., RAM, processor instructions, disk space) that is used under certain circumstances.

Validation: Ensuring that the system meets the needs of the customer. Checking that you built the right *system*.

Verification (category of testing): Ensuring that the system operates correctly, does not crash, provides correct answers, etc. Checking that you built the system *right*.

Verification (in unit testing): Checking that a particular method was called on a **mock** object.

Virus: A kind of **malware**, often small, that replicates itself with human intervention. This intervention could be something such as clicking on a link or running a program sent to you as an attachment.

Vulnerability: A potential defect that would allow a user to compromise or otherwise gain unauthorized access to a system.

Wall clock time: Another term for **real time**.

White-box testing: Testing the code directly and with full knowledge of the code under test. **Unit testing** is an example of white-box testing.

Workaround: A method for avoiding a known **defect** while still being able to use the system.

Worm: A kind of **malware**, often small, that replicates itself without human intervention.

YAGNI: You Ain't Gonna Need It. A tenet of **Test-Driven Development** which states that you should not do work or add features which are not immediately necessary.

Zombie: A computer with software installed which allows unauthorized users access to it to perform unauthorized functionality. For example, a system might have a mailer program built in which will allow other users to send spam from your machine, so that the original users cannot be tracked.

Chapter 27

Acknowledgments

Thanks to everybody who has helped make this book a reality or made it into a better reality, especially:

Ross Acheson, Nathaniel Blake, Will Engler, Jake Goulding, Brandon Hang, Joel McCracken, Robbie McKinstry, Ryan Rahuba, Steve Robbibaro, Nick Treu, Ed Wiancko, and Sheridan Zivanovich.

Special thanks go to:

Patrick Keane, who did an extremely thorough editing job and provided valuable perspective on the QA field as a whole.

Carol Nichols, who not only did an excellent job finding defects in my code, but also consistently amused me with her commit messages. She is also one of the people who has violated one of the principles of TDD with whom I have spent time, and definitely has not applied testing skills to test the integrity of this book by editing her own acknowledgment.

Tim Parenti, who found more typos and errors than I ever would have thought possible, and even better, did an excellent job fixing many of them.

98822216R00127

Made in the USA
Lexington, KY
09 September 2018